dun&bradstreet

Industry & Financial Consulting Services

INDUSTRY NORMS AND KEY BUSINESS RATIOS

**One Year
Desk-Top Edition
SIC #0100-8999**

Copyright © Dun & Bradstreet, Inc., 2021

ISBN 978-1-64972-113-6

All rights reserved. Except for use in a review, the reproduction or use of this work in any form or by any electronic, mechanical, or other means, now known or hereafter invented, including xerography, photocopying, and recording, and in any information storage and retrieval system is forbidden without the written permission of the publisher.

To obtain reprint permission, please send your correspondence to

Mergent Inc.
444 Madison Avenue Suite 1710
New York, NY 10022
Telephone: 800.342.5647
www.mergentbusinesspress.com

Manufactured in the United States of America.

CONTENTS

PREFACE   PAGE

Introduction i
Calculation of Industry Norms ii
Calculation of Key Business Ratios iii
Industry Norms for Financial Analysis vi
Applications by Functional Areas vii

INDUSTRY NORMS AND KEY BUSINESS RATIOS

Agriculture, Forestry and Fishing
(SIC 0100-0913) 1

Mining
(SIC 1000-1499) 1

Construction
(SIC 1500-1799) 3

Manufacturing
(SIC 2000-5199) 9

Transportation, Communications and Public Utilities
(SIC 4000-4971) 24

Wholesale Trade
(SIC 5000-5199) 29

Retail Trade
(SIC 5200-5999) 38

Finance and Real Estate
(SIC 6100-6799) 45

Services
(SIC 7000-8999) 48

APPENDIX - SIC Numbers Appearing in This Directory

INTRODUCTION

The Desk-Top Edition of The D&B Industry Norms and Key Business Ratios is made possible through over one million financial statements in the D&B Financial Information Base. This file consists of U.S. corporations, partnerships and proprietorships both public and privately owned, in all size ranges, and includes over 800 different lines of business as defined by the U.S. Standard Industrial Classification (SIC) code numbers. Our data is collected weekly, maintained daily, and constantly edited and updated. All of these factors combine to make this financial information unequaled anywhere for scope and timeliness*.

It should be noted that only general data is supplied in the Desk-Top Edition. However, for more detailed asset/geographical breakdowns of this data, an expanded set of Industry Norms and Key Business Ratios are also published by D&B for the Corporate Marketplace in the following five segments:

1. **Agriculture, Mining, Construction/ Transportation/Communication/Utilities**
2. **Manufacturing**
3. **Wholesaling**
4. **Retailing**
5. **Finance/Real Estate/Services**

All five segments are available in two other formats. The formats are as follows:

1. **Industry Norms and Key Business Ratios, Three Year Edition.**
   Directories and electronic file versions available.

2. **Industry Norms and Key Business Ratios, One Year Edition.**
   Directories and electronic file versions available.

Note that the Industry Norms contain "typical" balance sheets and income statements, and "common-size" financial figures, as well as Key Business Ratios. The Key Business Ratios books contain fourteen indicators of performance.

*To provide the most current information available, fiscal years January 1 - December 31 were utilized to calculate the Norms.

CALCULATIONS OF THE INDUSTRY NORMS

INDUSTRY NORM FORMAT

At the top of each industry norm will be identifying information: SIC code number and short title. Beside the year date, in parenthesis, is the number of companies in the sample. The "typical" balance-sheet figures are in the first column and the "common-size" balance-sheet figures are in the second. The respective income statements begin with the item "Net Sales", and the respective Key Business Ratios begin with the item "Ratios." The latter are further broken down, or refined, into the median, and the upper quartile and lower quartile.

THE COMMON - SIZE FINANCIAL STATEMENT

The common-size balance-sheet and income statement present each item of the financial statement as a percentage of its respective aggregate total. Common-size percentages are computed for all statement items of all the individual companies used in the industry sample. An average for each statement item is then determined and presented as the industry norm.

This enables the analyst to examine the current composition of assets, liabilities and sales of a particular industry.

THE TYPICAL FINANCIAL STATEMENT

The typical balance-sheet figures are the result of translating the common-size percentages into dollar figures. They permit, for example, a quick check of the relative size of assets and liabilities between one's own company and that company's own line of business.

After the common-size percentages have been computed for the particular sample, the actual financial statements are then sequenced by both *total assets* and *total sales*, with the median, or mid-point figure in both these groups serving as the "typical" amount. We then compute the typical balance-sheet and income statement dollar figures by multiplying the common-size percentages for each statement item by their respective total amounts.

(For example, if the median total assets for an SIC category are $669,599, and the common-size figure for cash is 9.2 percent, then by multiplying the two we derive a cash figure of $61,603 for the typical balance sheet.)

KEY BUSINESS RATIOS

The Fourteen Key Business Ratios are broken down into median figures, with upper and lower quartiles, giving the analyst an even more refined set of figures to work with. These ratios cover all those critical areas of business performance with indicators of solvency, efficiency and profitability.

They provide a profound and well-documented insight into all aspects for everyone interested in the financial workings of business—business executives and managers, credit executives, bankers, lenders, investors, academicians and students.

In the ratio tables appearing in this book, the figures are broken down into the median—which is the midpoint of all companies in the sample—and the upper quartile and lower quartile—which are mid-points of the upper and lower halves.

Upper quartile figures are not always the highest numerical value, nor are lower quartile figures always the lowest numerical value. The quartile listings reflect *judgmental ranking*, thus the upper quartile represents the best condition in any given ratio and is not necessarily the highest numerical value. (For example, see the items Total Liabilities-to-Net Worth or Collection Period, where a lower numerical value represents a better condition.)

Each of the fourteen ratios is calculated individually for every concern in the sample. These individual figures are then sequenced for each ratio according to condition (best to worst), and the figure that falls in the middle of this series becomes the median (or mid-point) for that ratio in that line of business. The figure halfway between the median and the best condition of the series becomes the upper quartile; and the number halfway between the median and the least favorable condition of the series is the lower quartile.

In a statistical sense, each median is considered the *typical* ratio figure for a concern in a given category.

CALCULATIONS OF THE 14 KEY BUSINESS RATIOS

SOLVENCY RATIOS

Quick Ratio

$$\frac{\text{Cash + Accounts Receivable}}{\text{Current Liabilities}}$$

The Quick Ratio is computed by dividing cash plus accounts receivable by total current liabilities. Current liabilities are all the liabilities that fall due within one year. This ratio reveals the protection afforded short-term creditors in cash or near-cash assets. It shows the number of dollars of liquid assets available to cover each dollar of current debt. Any time this ratio is as much as 1 to 1 (1.0) the business is said to be in a liquid condition. The larger the ratio the greater the liquidity.

Current Ratio

$$\frac{\text{Current Assets}}{\text{Current Liabilities}}$$

Total current assets are divided by total current liabilities. Current assets include cash, accounts and notes receivable (less reserves for bad debts), advances on inventories, merchandise inventories and marketable securities. This ratio measures the degree to which current assets cover current liabilities. The higher the ratio the more assurance exists that the retirement of current liabilities can be made. The current ratio measures the margin of safety available to cover any possible shrinkage in the value of current assets. Normally a ratio of 2 to 1 (2.0) or better is considered good.

Current Liabilities to Net Worth

$$\frac{\text{Current Liabilities}}{\text{Net Worth}}$$

Current Liabilities to Net Worth is derived by dividing current liabilities by net worth. This contrasts the funds that creditors temporarily are risking with the funds permanently invested by the owners. The smaller the net worth and the larger the liabilities, the less security for the creditors. Care should be exercised when selling any firm with current liabilities exceeding two-thirds (66.6 percent) of net worth.

Current Liabilities to Inventory

$$\frac{\text{Current Liabilities}}{\text{Inventory}}$$

Dividing current liabilities by inventory yields another indication of the extent to which the business relies on funds from disposal of unsold inventories to meet its debts. This ratio combines with Net Sales to Inventory to indicate how management controls inventory. It is possible to have decreasing liquidity while maintaining consistent sales-to-inventory ratios. Large increases in sales with corresponding increases in inventory levels can cause an inappropriate rise in current liabilities if growth isn't made wisely.

Total Liabilities to Net Worth

$$\frac{\text{Total Liabilities}}{\text{Net Worth}}$$

Obtained by dividing total current plus long-term and deferred liabilities by net worth. The effect of long-term (funded) debt on a business can be determined by comparing this ratio with Current Liabilities to Net Worth. The difference will pinpoint the relative size of long-term debt, which, if sizable, can burden a firm with substantial interest charges. In general, total liabilities shouldn't exceed net worth (100 percent) since in such cases creditors have more at stake than owners.

Fixed Assets to Net Worth

$$\frac{\text{Fixed Assets}}{\text{Net Worth}}$$

Fixed assets are divided by net worth. The proportion of net worth that consists of fixed assets will vary greatly from industry to industry but generally a smaller proportion is desirable. A high ratio is unfavorable because heavy investment in fixed assets indicates that either the concern has a low net working capital and is overtrading or has utilized large funded debt to supplement working capital. Also, the larger the fixed assets, the bigger the annual depreciation charge that must be deducted from the income statement. Normally, fixed assets above 75 percent of net worth indicate possible over-investment and should be examined with care.

CALCULATIONS OF THE 14 KEY BUSINESS RATIOS (continued)

EFFICIENCY RATIOS

Collection Period

$$\frac{\text{Accounts Receivable}}{\text{Sales}} \times 365$$

Accounts receivable are divided by sales and then multiplied by 365 days to obtain this figure. The quality of the receivables of a company can be determined by this relationship when compared with selling terms and industry norms. In some industries where credit sales are not the normal way of doing business, the percentage of cash sales should be taken into consideration. Generally, where most sales are for credit, any collection period more than one-third over normal selling terms (40.0 for 30-day terms) is indicative of some slow-turning receivables. When comparing the collection period of one concern with that of another, allowances should be made for possible variations in selling terms.

Sales to Inventory

$$\frac{\text{Annual Net Sales}}{\text{Inventory}}$$

Obtained by dividing annual net sales by inventory. Inventory control is a prime management objective since poor controls allow inventory to become costly to store, obsolete or insufficient to meet demands. The sales-to-inventory relationship is a guide to the rapidity at which merchandise is being moved and the effect on the flow of funds into the business. This ratio varies widely between lines of business and a company's figure is only meaningful when compared with industry norms. Individual figures that are outside either the upper or lower quartiles for a given industry should be examined with care. Although low figures are usually the biggest problem, as they indicate excessively high inventories, extremely high turnovers might reflect insufficient merchandise to meet customer demand and result in lost sales.

Asset to Sales

$$\frac{\text{Total Assets}}{\text{Net Sales}}$$

Assets to sales is calculated by dividing total assets by annual net sales. This ratio ties in sales and the total investment that is used to generate those sales. While figures vary greatly from industry to industry, by comparing a company's ratio with industry norms it can be determined whether a firm is overtrading (handling an excessive volume of sales in relation to investment) or undertrading (not generating sufficient sales to warrant the assets invested). Abnormally low percentages (above the upper quartile) can indicate overtrading which may lead to financial difficulties if not corrected. Extremely high percentages (below the lower quartile) can be the result of overly conservative or poor sales management, indicating a more aggressive sales policy may need to be followed.

Sales to Net Working Capital

$$\frac{\text{Sales}}{\text{Net Working Capital}}$$

Net sales are divided by net working capital (net working capital is current assets minus current liabilities.). This relationship indicates whether a company is overtrading or conversely carrying more liquid assets than needed for its volume. Each industry can vary substantially and it is necessary to compare a company with its peers to see if it is either overtrading on its available funds or being overly conservative. Companies with substantial sales gains often reach a level where their working capital becomes strained. Even if they maintain an adequate total investment for the volume being generated (Assets to Sales), that investment may be so centered in fixed assets or other noncurrent items that it will be difficult to continue meeting all current obligations without additional investment or reducing sales.

Accounts Payable to Sales

$$\frac{\text{Accounts Payable}}{\text{Annual Net Sales}}$$

Computed by dividing accounts payable by annual net sales. This ratio measures how the company is paying its suppliers in relation to the volume being transacted. An increasing percentage, or one larger than the industry norm, indicates the firm may be using suppliers to help finance operations. This ratio is especially important to short-term creditors since a high percentage could indicate potential problems in paying vendors.

CALCULATIONS OF THE 14 KEY BUSINESS RATIOS (continued)

PROFITABILITY RATIOS

Return on Sales (Profit Margin)

$$\frac{\text{Net Profit After Taxes}}{\text{Annual Net Sales}}$$

Obtained by dividing net profit after taxes by annual net sales. This reveals the profits earned per dollar of sales and therefore measures the efficiency of the operation. Return must be adequate for the firm to be able to achieve satisfactory profits for its owners. This ratio is an indicator of the firm's ability to withstand adverse conditions such as falling prices, rising costs and declining sales.

Return on Assets

$$\frac{\text{Net Profit After Taxes}}{\text{Total Assets}}$$

Net profit after taxes divided by total assets. This ratio is the key indicator of profitability for a firm. It matches operating profits with the assets available to earn a return. Companies efficiently using their assets will have a relatively high return while less well-run businesses will be relatively low.

Return on Net Worth (Return on Equity)

$$\frac{\text{Net Profit After Taxes}}{\text{Net Worth}}$$

Obtained by dividing net profit after tax by net worth. This ratio is used to analyze the ability of the firm's management to realize an adequate return on the capital invested by the owners of the firm. Tendency is to look increasingly to this ratio as a final criterion of profitability. Generally, a relationship of at least 10 percent is regarded as a desirable objective for providing dividends plus funds for future growth.

INDUSTRY NORMS FOR FINANCIAL ANALYSIS

Using Industry Norms for Financial Analysis

The principal purpose of financial analysis is to identify irregularities that require explanations to completely understand an industry's or company's current status and future potential. These irregularities can be identified by comparing the industry norms with the figures of specific companies (*comparative analysis*). D&B's Industry Norms are specifically formatted to accommodate this analysis.

Relative Position

Common-size and typical balance sheets provide an excellent picture of the makeup of the industry's assets and liabilities. Are assets concentrated in inventories or accounts receivable? Are payables to the trade or bank loans more important as a method for financing operations? The answers to these and other important questions are clearly shown by the Industry Norms, its common-size balance sheet approach and is then further crystallized by the typical balance sheets.

Financial Ratio Trends

Key Business Ratio changes indicate trends in the important *relationships* between key financial items, such as the relationship between Net Profits and Net Sales (a common indicator of profitability). Ratios that reflect short and long-term liquidity, efficiency in managing assets and controlling debt, and different measures of profitability are all included in the Key Business Ratios sections of the Industry Norms.

Comparative Analysis

Comparing a company with its peers is a reliable method for evaluating financial status. The key to this technique is the composition of the peer group and the timeliness of the data. The D&B Industry Norms are unique in scope of sample size and in level of detail.

Sample Size

The number of firms in the sample must be representative or they will be unduly influenced by irregular figures from relatively few companies. The more than one million companies used as a basis for the Industry Norms allow for more than adequate sample sizes in most cases.

Key Business Ratios Analysis

Valuable insights into an industry's performance can be obtained by equating two related statement items in the form of a financial ratio. For really effective ratio analysis, the items compared must be meaningful and the comparison should reflect the combined effort of two potentially diverse trends. While dozens of different ratios can be computed from financial statements, the fourteen included in the Industry Norms and Key Business Ratio books are those most commonly used and were rated as the most significant as shown in a survey of financial analysts. Many of the other ratios in existence are variations on these fourteen.

The fourteen Key Business Ratios are categorized into three major groups:

Solvency, or liquidity, measurements are significant in evaluating a company's ability to meet short and long-term obligations. These figures are of prime interest to credit managers of commercial companies and financial institutions.

Efficiency ratios indicate how effectively a company uses and controls its assets. This is critical information for evaluating how a company is managed. Studying these ratios is useful for credit, marketing and investment purposes.

Profitability ratios show how successfully a business is earning a return to its owners. Those interested in mergers and acquisitions consider this key data for selecting candidates.

APPLICATIONS BY FUNCTIONAL AREAS

Recent research efforts have revealed that the use of financial analysis (via Industry Norms) is very useful in several functional areas. To follow are only a few of the more widely used applications of this unique data.

Credit

Industry Norm data has proven to be an invaluable tool in determining minimum acceptable standards for risk. The credit worthiness of an existing or potential account is immediately visible by ranking its solvency status and comparing its solvency trends to that of the industry. Short term solvency gauges, such as the quick and current ratios, are ideal indicators when evaluating an account. Balance sheet comparisons supplement this qualification by allowing a comparison of the make-up of current assets and liability items. Moreover, leverage ratios such as current liability to net worth and total liability to net worth provide valuable benchmarks to spot potential problem accounts while profitability and collection period figures provide cash flow comparisons for an overall evaluation of accounts.

In addition to evaluating individual accounts against industry standards, internal credit polices also benefit from Industry Norm data. Are receivables growing at an excessive rate as compared to the industry? If so, how does your firm's collections stack up to the industry?

Finance

Here exists a unique opportunity for financial executives to rank their firm, or their firm's subsidiaries and divisions, against its peers. Determine the efficiency of management via ratio quartile breakdowns which provides you the opportunity to pinpoint your firm's profitability position versus the industry. For example, are returns on sales and gross profit margins comparatively low thereby indicating that pricing per unit may be too low or that the cost of goods is unnecessarily high?

In much the same way, matching the firm's growth and efficiency trends to that of the industry reveals conditions which prove to be vital in projecting budgets. If asset expansion exceeds the industry standard while asset utilization (as indicated by the asset to sales ratio) is sub par, should growth be slowed?

Investment executives have also utilized this diverse information when identifying optimal investment opportunities. By uncovering which industries exhibit the strongest sales growth while maintaining adequate returns, risk is minimized.

Corporate Planning

Corporate plans, competitive strategies and merger/acquisition decisions dictate a comprehensive analysis of the industry in question. Industry Norm data provides invaluable information in scrutinizing the performance of today's highly competitive, and sometimes unstable, markets. Does the liquidity of an industry provide a sufficient cushion to endure the recent record-high interest levels or is it too volatile to risk an entry? Are the profitability and equity statuses of an acquisition candidate among the best in the industry thereby qualifying it as an ideal acquisition target?

Industry Norm data provides these all-important benchmarks for setting strategic goals and measuring overall corporate performance.

Marketing and Sales

Attaining an in-depth knowledge of a potential or existing customer base is a key factor when developing successful marketing strategies and sales projections. Industry Norm data provides a competitive edge when determining market potential and market candidates. Identify those industries that meet or exceed your qualifications and take it one step further by focusing in on the specific region or size category that exhibits the greatest potential. For example, isolate the industries which have experienced the strongest growth trends in sales and inventory turnover and then fine tune marketing and sales strategies by identifying the particular *segment* which is the most attractive (such as firms with assets of $1 million or more).

You can also utilize this information from a different perspective by examining the industries of existing accounts. If an account's industry shows signs of faltering profitability and stagnating sales, should precautionary measures be taken? Will the next sale be profitable for your company or will it be written-off? Industry Norm data assist in answering these and many other important questions.

Page vii

FINAL NOTE

The SIC categories in this directory reflect those appearing in the 1987 edition of the Standard Industrial Classification Manual

The D&B Financial Information Base includes over one million U.S. companies and is the most extensive and complete source of financial information of its kind. This compilation of data should be regarded only as a source of financial information, to be used in conjunction with other sources of data, when performing financial analysis. When utilizing these figures, remember:

- Because of the size of this database, and in order to facilitate the many calculations and rankings, many of the very large group samples have been randomly reduced.

- On the other hand, some of the samples from our file are very small, and, therefore, may not present a true picture of an entire line of business. In these small groups there is a chance that a few extreme variations might have an undue influence on the overall figures in a particular category.

- The companies composing our database are organized by principal line of business without consideration for multiple-operation functions.

- Within the primary SIC numbers, no allowance has been made for differing accounting methods, terms of sale, or fiscal-year closing date, all of which might have had an effect on the composite data.

- Therefore, D&B advises users that the Industry Norms and Key Business Ratios be used as yardsticks and not as absolutes.

Page 1

	SIC 01 AGRICULTURL CROPS (NO BREAKDOWN) 2020 (16 Establishments)					SIC 07 AGRICULTURAL SERVICES (NO BREAKDOWN) 2020 (37 Establishments)					SIC 0782 LAWN GARDEN SVCS (NO BREAKDOWN) 2020 (11 Establishments)					SIC 10 METAL MINING (NO BREAKDOWN) 2020 (35 Establishments)	
	$	%				$	%				$	%				$	%
Cash	801,824	10.6				391,658	20.8				235,907	34.1				1,866,575	17.2
Accounts Receivable	1,346,460	17.8				259,850	13.8				114,840	16.6				227,896	2.1
Notes Receivable	196,674	2.6				0	0.0				0	0.0				0	0.0
Inventory	764,002	10.1				139,340	7.4				22,830	3.3				444,939	4.1
Other Current	983,370	13.0				111,095	5.9				22,830	3.3				1,085,218	10.0
Total Current	**4,092,330**	**54.1**				**901,943**	**47.9**				**396,407**	**57.3**				**3,624,628**	**33.4**
Fixed Assets	2,783,692	36.8				617,614	32.8				271,190	39.2				3,516,107	32.4
Other Non-current	688,359	9.1				363,413	19.3				24,213	3.5				3,711,446	34.2
Total Assets	**7,564,381**	**100.0**				**1,882,970**	**100.0**				**691,810**	**100.0**				**10,852,181**	**100.0**
Accounts Payable	1,406,975	18.6				197,712	10.5				15,220	2.2				49,985,146	460.6
Bank Loans	204,238	2.7				0	0.0				0	0.0				0	0.0
Notes Payable	151,288	2.0				143,106	7.6				4,151	0.6				13,858,235	127.7
Other Current	1,467,490	19.4				954,665	50.7				231,756	33.5				(629,427)	(5.8)
Total Current	**3,229,991**	**42.7**				**1,295,483**	**68.8**				**251,127**	**36.3**				**63,213,954**	**582.5**
Other Long Term	499,249	6.6				596,902	31.7				251,127	36.3				1,671,236	15.4
Deferred Credits	0	0.0				0	0.0				0	0.0				0	0.0
Net Worth	3,835,141	50.7				(9,415)	(0.5)				189,556	27.4				(54,033,009)	(497.9)
Total Liab & Net Worth	**7,564,381**	**100.0**				**1,882,970**	**100.0**				**691,810**	**100.0**				**10,852,181**	**100.0**
Net Sales	16,588,555	100.0				3,607,222	100.0				1,307,769	100.0				4,267,472	100.0
Gross Profit	5,640,109	34.0				1,442,889	40.0				653,885	50.0				529,167	12.4
Net Profit After Tax	812,839	4.9				126,253	3.5				137,316	10.5				(260,316)	(6.1)
Working Capital	862,339	---				(393,540)	---				145,280	---				(59,589,326)	---

RATIOS	UQ	MED	LQ	UQ	MED	LQ	UQ	MED	LQ	UQ	MED	LQ
SOLVENCY												
Quick Ratio (times)	1.6	0.8	0.4	3.1	1.2	0.5	6.0	2.2	1.1	1.2	0.4	0.1
Current Ratio (times)	3.4	1.6	1.1	3.4	1.7	1.0	6.8	2.4	1.6	3.0	1.0	0.1
Curr Liab To Nw (%)	17.2	33.9	445.2	21.4	52.1	141.5	21.9	29.3	55.1	6.7	16.8	28.6
Curr Liab To Inv (%)	72.1	112.2	568.5	162.1	814.5	999.9	93.1	506.0	773.9	138.2	288.2	999.9
Total Liab To Nw (%)	23.7	52.1	463.7	47.6	106.3	222.8	42.6	85.0	123.0	21.0	57.0	139.2
Fixed Assets To Nw (%)	20.6	59.4	128.4	40.2	76.9	143.7	48.0	65.7	112.7	9.5	63.8	113.0
EFFICIENCY												
Coll Period (days)	3.3	34.3	56.2	18.8	28.3	46.8	20.1	38.0	43.1	13.9	22.3	122.3
Sales To Inv (times)	30.1	19.8	2.8	67.7	20.4	13.7	201.9	21.4	7.1	20.0	9.9	5.8
Assets To Sales (%)	26.5	45.6	87.2	34.3	52.2	73.6	44.6	52.9	73.6	172.8	254.3	999.9
Sales To Nwc (times)	43.2	9.0	3.0	16.2	9.9	4.5	10.0	7.8	3.9	6.0	2.7	1.1
Acct Pay To Sales (%)	2.0	5.7	15.8	1.8	3.0	4.2	0.8	1.4	2.7	8.6	20.0	244.8
PROFITABILITY												
Return On Sales (%)	15.1	1.0	(2.0)	8.9	3.5	0.2	15.8	(23.7)	(1.0)	4.3	(23.7)	(999.9)
Return On Assets (%)	10.1	3.4	(6.4)	13.6	4.3	(2.6)	32.0	5.1	(2.1)	(0.5)	)(17.0	(122.3)
Return On Nw (%)	43.7	14.5	(9.6)	45.2	11.0	1.3	69.5	(12.1)	(7.8)	3.7	(12.1)	(61.9)

Page 2

	SIC 1041 GOLD ORES (NO BREAKDOWN) 2020 (20 Establishments)			SIC 13 OIL,GAS EXTRACTION (NO BREAKDOWN) 2020 (121 Establishments)		SIC 1381 DRILL OIL,GAS WELLS (NO BREAKDOWN) 2020 (10 Establishments)		SIC 1382 OIL GAS EXPLOR SVCS (NO BREAKDOWN) 2020 (17 Establishments)	
	$	%	$	%	$	%	$	%
Cash	2,304,649	23.5	65,373,538	9.7	39,665,157	9.8	8,736,510	12.2
Accounts Receivable	254,982	2.6	79,526,572	11.8	51,402,806	12.7	5,370,805	7.5
Notes Receivable	0	0.0	0	0.0	404,747	0.1	0	0.0
Inventory	137,298	1.4	18,196,758	2.7	9,309,170	2.3	358,054	0.5
Other Current	784,562	8.0	41,785,148	6.2	16,594,605	4.1	7,877,180	11.0
Total Current	**3,481,491**	**35.5**	**204,882,016**	**30.4**	**117,376,485**	**29.0**	**22,342,549**	**31.2**
Fixed Assets	3,471,684	35.4	395,610,998	58.7	238,395,689	58.9	44,183,823	61.7
Other Non-current	2,853,842	29.1	73,460,986	10.9	48,974,326	12.1	5,084,362	7.1
Total Assets	**9,807,017**	**100.0**	**673,954,000**	**100.0**	**404,746,500**	**100.0**	**71,610,734**	**100.0**
Accounts Payable	34,697,226	353.8	210,947,602	31.3	20,237,325	5.0	5,227,584	7.3
Bank Loans	0	0.0	0	0.0	0	0.0	0	0.0
Notes Payable	21,104,701	215.2	26,284,206	3.9	9,713,916	2.4	4,439,866	6.2
Other Current	(7,904,456)	(80.6)	321,476,058	47.7	37,236,678	9.2	32,368,051	45.2
Total Current	**47,897,471**	**488.4**	**558,707,866**	**82.9**	**67,187,919**	**16.6**	**42,035,501**	**58.7**
Other Long Term	813,982	8.3	307,996,978	45.7	110,900,541	27.4	34,731,206	48.5
Deferred Credits	0	0.0	0	0.0	0	0.0	0	0.0
Net Worth	(38,904,436)	(396.7)	(192,750,844)	(28.6)	226,658,040	56.0	(5,155,973)	(7.2)
Total Liab & Net Worth	**9,807,017**	**100.0**	**673,954,000**	**100.0**	**404,746,500**	**100.0**	**71,610,734**	**100.0**
Net Sales	5,016,377	100.0	329,079,102	100.0	250,772,305	100.0	30,615,962	100.0
Gross Profit	717,342	14.3	132,947,957	40.4	148,457,205	59.2	15,705,989	51.3
Net Profit After Tax	(546,785)	(10.9)	(12,505,006)	(3.8)	(16,801,744)	(6.7)	(4,929,170)	(16.1)
Working Capital	(44,415,980)	---	(353,825,850)	---	50,188,566	---	(19,692,952)	---

RATIOS	UQ	MED	LQ	UQ	MED	LQ	UQ	MED	LQ	UQ	MED	LQ
SOLVENCY												
Quick Ratio (times)	1.7	0.6	0.2	1.6	0.8	0.4	3.4	1.2	0.3	1.2	0.5	0.3
Current Ratio (times)	3.1	1.3	0.3	2.2	1.2	0.7	4.5	1.6	1.1	2.0	0.8	0.4
Curr Liab To Nw (%)	5.0	10.7	21.0	13.7	21.7	54.3	13.9	22.1	54.2	16.5	25.0	79.7
Curr Liab To Inv (%)	176.7	288.2	421.3	238.2	691.5	999.9	317.1	734.7	999.9	407.9	469.9	999.9
Total Liab To Nw (%)	14.7	23.3	106.7	54.8	101.9	203.9	59.7	92.0	106.6	99.9	129.9	241.1
Fixed Assets To Nw (%)	37.3	99.4	108.3	79.8	126.7	219.1	84.7	113.6	146.3	88.1	219.7	356.3
EFFICIENCY												
Coll Period (days)	9.5	18.1	122.3	36.5	50.0	71.9	14.6	24.2	59.1	45.3	50.9	63.2
Sales To Inv (times)	27.2	11.5	9.6	54.5	29.3	12.7	33.6	18.0	14.1	721.1	25.6	12.3
Assets To Sales (%)	161.4	195.5	705.2	102.2	204.8	414.2	143.4	161.4	179.7	143.6	233.9	534.4
Sales To Nwc (times)	6.0	2.5	1.1	10.7	5.8	2.8	12.1	6.4	4.3	5.2	2.6	2.4
Acct Pay To Sales (%)	8.6	10.8	38.3	4.5	8.2	14.8	1.0	5.2	6.9	5.6	14.7	23.3
PROFITABILITY												
Return On Sales (%)	17.0	(23.7)	(247.2)	8.6	(3.7)	(23.5)	10.0	1.4	(30.7)	(6.4)	(60.7)	(187.3)
Return On Assets (%)	1.2	(14.3)	(95.4)	3.8	(2.6)	(20.2)	6.8	1.0	(17.9)	(5.7)	(34.6)	(40.9)
Return On Nw (%)	3.7	(11.5)	(51.2)	12.2	(2.4)	(31.5)	14.1	1.8	(41.8)	(11.3)	(51.2)	(73.1)

Page 3

SIC 1389 OIL GAS FLD SVC,NEC
(NO BREAKDOWN)
2020 (35 Establishments)

	$	%
Cash	60,665,418	9.9
Accounts Receivable	155,646,628	25.4
Notes Receivable	0	0.0
Inventory	33,703,010	5.5
Other Current	23,285,716	3.8
Total Current	**273,300,772**	**44.6**
Fixed Assets	260,432,350	42.5
Other Non-current	79,048,878	12.9
Total Assets	**612,782,000**	**100.0**
Accounts Payable	48,409,778	7.9
Bank Loans	0	0.0
Notes Payable	0	0.0
Other Current	133,586,476	21.8
Total Current	**181,996,254**	**29.7**
Other Long Term	196,090,240	32.0
Deferred Credits	0	0.0
Net Worth	234,695,506	38.3
Total Liab & Net Worth	**612,782,000**	**100.0**
Net Sales	587,518,696	100.0
Gross Profit	196,818,763	33.5
Net Profit After Tax	(11,162,855)	(1.9)
Working Capital	91,304,518	---

RATIOS
	UQ	MED	LQ
SOLVENCY			
Quick Ratio (times)	3.0	1.6	1.0
Current Ratio (times)	4.2	2.1	1.4
Curr Liab To Nw (%)	12.8	23.5	60.8
Curr Liab To Inv (%)	181.4	301.0	738.6
Total Liab To Nw (%)	26.8	75.3	216.0
Fixed Assets To Nw (%)	34.7	79.8	210.3
EFFICIENCY			
Coll Period (days)	46.4	64.6	80.7
Sales To Inv (times)	34.1	17.1	10.4
Assets To Sales (%)	82.3	104.3	152.4
Sales To Nwc (times)	9.6	4.8	2.5
Acct Pay To Sales (%)	3.6	5.3	8.1
PROFITABILITY			
Return On Sales (%)	5.6	(0.1)	(12.6)
Return On Assets (%)	5.8	(0.7)	(12.7)
Return On Nw (%)	9.3	0.1	(32.0)

SIC 14 NONMETALLIC MINERALS
(NO BREAKDOWN)
2020 (22 Establishments)

	$	%
Cash	24,761,067	13.0
Accounts Receivable	18,285,095	9.6
Notes Receivable	0	0.0
Inventory	12,761,473	6.7
Other Current	14,856,640	7.8
Total Current	**70,664,275**	**37.1**
Fixed Assets	90,282,658	47.4
Other Non-current	29,522,810	15.5
Total Assets	**190,469,743**	**100.0**
Accounts Payable	675,215,239	354.5
Bank Loans	0	0.0
Notes Payable	7,047,380	3.7
Other Current	91,044,538	47.8
Total Current	**773,307,157**	**406.0**
Other Long Term	301,704,073	158.4
Deferred Credits	380,939	0.2
Net Worth	(884,922,426)	(464.6)
Total Liab & Net Worth	**190,469,743**	**100.0**
Net Sales	119,043,589	100.0
Gross Profit	28,451,418	23.9
Net Profit After Tax	(1,904,697)	(1.6)
Working Capital	(702,642,882)	---

	UQ	MED	LQ
Quick Ratio (times)	1.7	1.2	0.5
Current Ratio (times)	2.7	2.3	1.3
Curr Liab To Nw (%)	15.5	20.0	46.8
Curr Liab To Inv (%)	92.8	146.2	269.5
Total Liab To Nw (%)	33.1	74.7	181.5
Fixed Assets To Nw (%)	79.4	94.4	194.6
Coll Period (days)	41.3	45.3	58.8
Sales To Inv (times)	12.5	10.9	6.1
Assets To Sales (%)	117.1	160.0	213.8
Sales To Nwc (times)	7.0	4.6	4.1
Acct Pay To Sales (%)	3.2	5.3	8.5
Return On Sales (%)	12.9	9.3	(29.1)
Return On Assets (%)	10.5	2.6	(52.7)
Return On Nw (%)	19.8	11.4	3.1

SIC 15 GEN'L BLDG CONTRS
(NO BREAKDOWN)
2020 (394 Establishments)

	$	%
Cash	2,071,536	24.2
Accounts Receivable	3,150,104	36.8
Notes Receivable	34,240	0.4
Inventory	248,242	2.9
Other Current	1,686,333	19.7
Total Current	**7,190,455**	**84.0**
Fixed Assets	864,567	10.1
Other Non-current	505,043	5.9
Total Assets	**8,560,065**	**100.0**
Accounts Payable	2,508,099	29.3
Bank Loans	0	0.0
Notes Payable	68,481	0.8
Other Current	2,764,901	32.3
Total Current	**5,341,481**	**62.4**
Other Long Term	393,763	4.6
Deferred Credits	0	0.0
Net Worth	2,824,821	33.0
Total Liab & Net Worth	**8,560,065**	**100.0**
Net Sales	24,740,072	100.0
Gross Profit	4,032,632	16.3
Net Profit After Tax	1,039,083	4.2
Working Capital	1,848,974	---

	UQ	MED	LQ
Quick Ratio (times)	1.6	1.1	0.8
Current Ratio (times)	2.2	1.4	1.2
Curr Liab To Nw (%)	55.3	163.7	333.7
Curr Liab To Inv (%)	254.4	999.9	999.9
Total Liab To Nw (%)	73.2	183.1	363.2
Fixed Assets To Nw (%)	6.2	16.6	35.3
Coll Period (days)	35.0	55.5	73.8
Sales To Inv (times)	999.9	123.3	11.9
Assets To Sales (%)	26.4	34.6	46.9
Sales To Nwc (times)	18.5	10.6	5.5
Acct Pay To Sales (%)	5.1	9.6	15.2
Return On Sales (%)	5.9	3.1	1.1
Return On Assets (%)	16.4	8.6	2.8
Return On Nw (%)	52.2	25.1	9.7

SIC 1521 SNGL-FAM HSNG CNSTR
(NO BREAKDOWN)
2020 (59 Establishments)

	$	%
Cash	616,759	25.5
Accounts Receivable	599,828	24.8
Notes Receivable	0	0.0
Inventory	246,704	10.2
Other Current	437,778	18.1
Total Current	**1,901,069**	**78.6**
Fixed Assets	440,197	18.2
Other Non-current	77,397	3.2
Total Assets	**2,418,663**	**100.0**
Accounts Payable	384,567	15.9
Bank Loans	2,419	0.1
Notes Payable	33,861	1.4
Other Current	1,117,423	46.2
Total Current	**1,538,270**	**63.6**
Other Long Term	113,677	4.7
Deferred Credits	0	0.0
Net Worth	766,716	31.7
Total Liab & Net Worth	**2,418,663**	**100.0**
Net Sales	6,554,642	100.0
Gross Profit	1,710,762	26.1
Net Profit After Tax	465,380	7.1
Working Capital	362,799	---

	UQ	MED	LQ
Quick Ratio (times)	2.1	1.1	0.4
Current Ratio (times)	3.0	1.7	1.2
Curr Liab To Nw (%)	20.6	65.9	138.3
Curr Liab To Inv (%)	94.3	374.0	999.9
Total Liab To Nw (%)	31.9	87.1	175.5
Fixed Assets To Nw (%)	7.4	21.9	52.5
Coll Period (days)	23.7	40.2	60.2
Sales To Inv (times)	241.0	19.1	1.4
Assets To Sales (%)	23.6	36.9	51.6
Sales To Nwc (times)	17.3	7.1	4.6
Acct Pay To Sales (%)	3.1	5.8	9.5
Return On Sales (%)	8.8	5.5	3.4
Return On Assets (%)	29.4	15.1	4.7
Return On Nw (%)	61.2	28.8	10.6

Page 4

	SIC 1522 RSDNTL CNSTR, NEC (NO BREAKDOWN) 2020 (13 Establishments)				SIC 1541 INDL BLDNGS,WRHSES (NO BREAKDOWN) 2020 (58 Establishments)				SIC 1542 NONRESID CONSTR,NEC (NO BREAKDOWN) 2020 (256 Establishments)				SIC 16 HEAVY CONSTR CONTRS (NO BREAKDOWN) 2020 (213 Establishments)			
	$			%	$			%	$			%	$			%
Cash	1,722,921			21.6	1,811,110			25.7	2,563,390			24.0	1,925,572			17.5
Accounts Receivable	3,198,571			40.1	2,283,267			32.4	4,379,124			41.0	2,684,797			24.4
Notes Receivable	0			0.0	7,047			0.1	53,404			0.5	33,010			0.3
Inventory	135,600			1.7	35,236			0.5	170,893			1.6	187,056			1.7
Other Current	933,249			11.7	1,853,393			26.3	2,018,668			18.9	1,771,525			16.1
Total Current	**5,990,341**			**75.1**	**5,990,053**			**85.0**	**9,185,479**			**86.0**	**6,601,960**			**60.0**
Fixed Assets	1,387,909			17.4	627,194			8.9	875,825			8.2	3,411,013			31.0
Other Non-current	598,236			7.5	429,874			6.1	619,486			5.8	990,294			9.0
Total Assets	**7,976,486**			**100.0**	**7,047,121**			**100.0**	**10,680,790**			**100.0**	**11,003,267**			**100.0**
Accounts Payable	2,464,734			30.9	1,789,969			25.4	3,578,065			33.5	1,914,568			17.4
Bank Loans	0			0.0	0			0.0	0			0.0	0			0.0
Notes Payable	398,824			5.0	14,094			0.2	32,042			0.3	1,430,425			13.0
Other Current	2,839,629			35.6	2,001,382			28.4	3,193,556			29.9	4,951,470			45.0
Total Current	**5,703,187**			**71.5**	**3,805,445**			**54.0**	**6,803,663**			**63.7**	**8,296,463**			**75.4**
Other Long Term	518,472			6.5	204,367			2.9	480,636			4.5	2,156,641			19.6
Deferred Credits	0			0.0	0			0.0	0			0.0	11,003			0.1
Net Worth	1,754,827			22.0	3,037,309			43.1	3,396,491			31.8	539,160			4.9
Total Liab & Net Worth	**7,976,486**			**100.0**	**7,047,121**			**100.0**	**10,680,790**			**100.0**	**11,003,267**			**100.0**
Net Sales	23,391,455			100.0	17,977,349			100.0	32,268,248			100.0	19,861,493			100.0
Gross Profit	5,005,771			21.4	2,858,398			15.9	4,453,018			13.8	4,329,805			21.8
Net Profit After Tax	1,754,359			7.5	665,162			3.7	1,097,120			3.4	1,549,196			7.8
Working Capital	287,154			---	2,184,608			---	2,381,816			---	(1,694,503)			---
RATIOS	UQ	MED	LQ		UQ	MED	LQ		UQ	MED	LQ		UQ	MED	LQ	
SOLVENCY																
Quick Ratio (times)	1.3	1.1	1.0		2.1	1.1	0.8		1.6	1.1	0.8		2.2	1.2	0.7	
Current Ratio (times)	1.7	1.3	1.2		3.5	1.6	1.3		2.0	1.4	1.2		3.1	1.8	1.3	
Curr Liab To Nw (%)	115.7	161.5	393.4		33.9	144.0	341.2		84.1	194.9	390.7		24.4	57.5	110.6	
Curr Liab To Inv (%)	568.4	954.7	999.9		999.9	999.9	999.9		299.4	999.9	999.9		406.2	999.9	999.9	
Total Liab To Nw (%)	142.8	224.9	443.5		38.5	147.4	356.3		86.9	209.7	414.7		45.1	97.4	190.8	
Fixed Assets To Nw (%)	6.2	13.5	42.6		6.2	21.1	33.4		6.1	15.0	32.8		29.6	54.1	95.8	
EFFICIENCY																
Coll Period (days)	32.1	52.6	62.1		29.2	53.7	79.8		39.4	58.8	75.6		33.6	49.5	73.0	
Sales To Inv (times)	999.9	83.0	52.2		993.9	386.1	242.2		999.9	114.8	12.5		198.8	56.9	23.7	
Assets To Sales (%)	26.7	34.1	43.1		26.7	39.2	49.7		26.3	33.1	43.9		38.7	55.4	78.3	
Sales To Nwc (times)	20.5	11.9	7.4		16.4	9.5	3.9		20.3	11.6	6.0		10.8	6.7	3.6	
Acct Pay To Sales (%)	5.3	8.4	15.8		5.1	8.1	12.4		6.2	10.6	15.9		3.5	6.9	10.4	
PROFITABILITY																
Return On Sales (%)	7.0	3.9	2.3		5.8	2.6	0.7		5.2	2.7	1.0		9.8	5.1	2.2	
Return On Assets (%)	19.0	9.7	6.3		16.2	6.4	2.2		14.0	7.2	2.5		17.3	8.1	2.9	
Return On Nw (%)	68.4	35.6	22.0		38.9	22.0	7.5		54.6	25.1	8.6		32.5	17.0	6.3	

	SIC 1611 HIGHWAY,ST CONSTR (NO BREAKDOWN) 2020 (69 Establishments)					SIC 1622 BRDGE,TNNEL,ELV HGY (NO BREAKDOWN) 2020 (10 Establishments)					SIC 1623 WTER,SWER,UTIL LNES (NO BREAKDOWN) 2020 (83 Establishments)					SIC 1629 HEAVY CONSTR,NEC (NO BREAKDOWN) 2020 (51 Establishments)		
		$			%		$			%		$			%		$	%
Cash		1,800,492			20.6		4,551,856			15.3		1,504,784			16.2		2,628,912	15.9
Accounts Receivable		2,115,141			24.2		7,645,928			25.7		2,136,421			23.0		4,431,122	26.8
Notes Receivable		26,221			0.3		0			0.0		37,155			0.4		0	0.0
Inventory		201,026			2.3		892,521			3.0		83,599			0.9		314,147	1.9
Other Current		1,083,791			12.4		6,009,639			20.2		1,783,448			19.2		2,562,776	15.5
Total Current		**5,226,671**			**59.8**		**19,099,944**			**64.2**		**5,545,407**			**59.7**		**9,936,957**	**60.1**
Fixed Assets		2,569,634			29.4		7,467,423			25.1		3,121,033			33.6		4,976,745	30.1
Other Non-current		943,947			10.8		3,183,324			10.7		622,349			6.7		1,620,336	9.8
Total Assets		**8,740,252**			**100.0**		**29,750,691**			**100.0**		**9,288,789**			**100.0**		**16,534,038**	**100.0**
Accounts Payable		1,214,895			13.9		4,968,365			16.7		2,052,822			22.1		2,430,504	14.7
Bank Loans		0			0.0		0			0.0		0			0.0		0	0.0
Notes Payable		69,922			0.8		89,252			0.3		3,018,856			32.5		66,136	0.4
Other Current		1,363,479			15.6		6,307,147			21.2		8,174,135			88.0		3,191,069	19.3
Total Current		**2,648,296**			**30.3**		**11,364,764**			**38.2**		**13,245,813**			**142.6**		**5,687,709**	**34.4**
Other Long Term		2,115,141			24.2		3,183,324			10.7		1,709,137			18.4		2,827,321	17.1
Deferred Credits		0			0.0		0			0.0		9,289			0.1		33,068	0.2
Net Worth		3,976,815			45.5		15,202,603			51.1		(5,675,450)			(61.1)		7,985,940	48.3
Total Liab & Net Worth		**8,740,252**			**100.0**		**29,750,691**			**100.0**		**9,288,789**			**100.0**		**16,534,038**	**100.0**
Net Sales		15,524,426			100.0		44,805,258			100.0		18,652,187			100.0		29,684,090	100.0
Gross Profit		3,368,800			21.7		5,735,073			12.8		4,588,438			24.6		5,758,713	19.4
Net Profit After Tax		1,304,052			8.4		1,926,626			4.3		1,548,132			8.3		2,077,886	7.0
Working Capital		2,578,375			---		7,735,180			---		(7,700,406)			---		4,249,248	---
RATIOS	UQ	MED		LQ		UQ	MED		LQ		UQ	MED		LQ		UQ	MED	LQ
SOLVENCY																		
Quick Ratio (times)	2.2	1.3		0.8		1.7	1.1		1.0		2.1	1.2		0.6		2.2	1.2	0.7
Current Ratio (times)	3.1	1.8		1.3		2.8	1.7		1.2		3.0	1.8		1.4		3.0	1.7	1.3
Curr Liab To Nw (%)	16.9	51.0		98.7		31.9	67.3		214.1		27.6	53.8		108.9		20.3	75.8	129.2
Curr Liab To Inv (%)	194.0	632.4		999.9		238.0	660.6		973.7		584.0	999.9		999.9		604.4	999.9	999.9
Total Liab To Nw (%)	22.6	86.8		171.2		54.8	102.5		280.1		56.6	107.2		190.8		47.3	90.6	216.2
Fixed Assets To Nw (%)	23.8	55.0		85.6		24.3	52.6		85.1		35.1	59.7		105.4		29.1	46.0	91.7
EFFICIENCY																		
Coll Period (days)	27.0	46.0		68.6		43.3	53.3		84.0		36.1	48.0		72.6		32.9	53.9	83.6
Sales To Inv (times)	140.3	56.9		26.5		67.0	30.8		15.3		281.7	65.3		37.2		215.5	61.9	16.9
Assets To Sales (%)	35.7	56.3		88.0		55.4	66.4		72.6		36.7	49.8		67.7		43.6	55.7	75.2
Sales To Nwc (times)	13.6	7.3		2.7		6.4	4.9		4.1		10.4	6.5		4.0		11.1	7.6	3.7
Acct Pay To Sales (%)	3.5	7.4		10.8		4.1	5.9		11.6		3.0	6.4		9.3		3.7	7.6	11.0
PROFITABILITY																		
Return On Sales (%)	11.4	7.0		2.7		5.9	4.3		1.6		9.2	4.7		2.3		9.6	3.8	2.0
Return On Assets (%)	19.3	9.7		2.4		11.3	7.5		2.7		17.8	8.7		2.7		13.9	6.7	3.6
Return On Nw (%)	44.0	18.8		4.2		28.9	12.6		4.1		31.1	17.1		7.8		25.6	13.9	8.2

Page 6

SIC 17 — SPECIAL TRADE CONTRS
(NO BREAKDOWN)
2020 (666 Establishments)

	$	%
Cash	754,562	19.8
Accounts Receivable	1,432,906	37.6
Notes Receivable	11,433	0.3
Inventory	137,193	3.6
Other Current	567,828	14.9
Total Current	**2,903,922**	**76.2**
Fixed Assets	689,777	18.1
Other Non-current	217,222	5.7
Total Assets	**3,810,921**	**100.0**
Accounts Payable	358,227	9.4
Bank Loans	3,811	0.1
Notes Payable	53,353	1.4
Other Current	1,093,734	28.7
Total Current	**1,509,125**	**39.6**
Other Long Term	666,911	17.5
Deferred Credits	3,811	0.1
Net Worth	1,631,074	42.8
Total Liab & Net Worth	**3,810,921**	**100.0**
Net Sales	9,950,185	100.0
Gross Profit	2,825,853	28.4
Net Profit After Tax	547,260	5.5
Working Capital	1,394,797	---

RATIOS

	UQ	MED	LQ
SOLVENCY			
Quick Ratio (times)	2.5	1.5	1.0
Current Ratio (times)	3.5	2.0	1.4
Curr Liab To Nw (%)	30.3	71.5	145.0
Curr Liab To Inv (%)	323.1	999.9	999.9
Total Liab To Nw (%)	39.5	92.5	189.5
Fixed Assets To Nw (%)	11.5	25.3	53.8
EFFICIENCY			
Coll Period (days)	39.4	59.1	79.8
Sales To Inv (times)	321.7	94.1	31.8
Assets To Sales (%)	28.1	38.3	52.6
Sales To Nwc (times)	11.7	6.9	4.1
Acct Pay To Sales (%)	2.3	4.3	7.7
PROFITABILITY			
Return On Sales (%)	8.6	4.5	1.6
Return On Assets (%)	23.7	10.8	4.0
Return On Nw (%)	54.8	24.0	8.8

SIC 1711 — PLBNG,HTNG,AIR-COND
(NO BREAKDOWN)
2020 (152 Establishments)

	$	%
Cash	661,004	20.6
Accounts Receivable	1,097,395	34.2
Notes Receivable	9,626	0.3
Inventory	160,438	5.0
Other Current	600,038	18.7
Total Current	**2,528,501**	**78.8**
Fixed Assets	500,566	15.6
Other Non-current	179,690	5.6
Total Assets	**3,208,757**	**100.0**
Accounts Payable	539,071	16.8
Bank Loans	0	0.0
Notes Payable	38,505	1.2
Other Current	965,836	30.1
Total Current	**1,543,412**	**48.1**
Other Long Term	985,089	30.7
Deferred Credits	0	0.0
Net Worth	680,256	21.2
Total Liab & Net Worth	**3,208,757**	**100.0**
Net Sales	9,578,379	100.0
Gross Profit	2,854,357	29.8
Net Profit After Tax	421,449	4.4
Working Capital	985,089	---

RATIOS

	UQ	MED	LQ
SOLVENCY			
Quick Ratio (times)	2.2	1.4	0.9
Current Ratio (times)	2.8	1.8	1.4
Curr Liab To Nw (%)	45.0	80.6	160.5
Curr Liab To Inv (%)	317.8	836.7	999.9
Total Liab To Nw (%)	57.9	108.3	202.4
Fixed Assets To Nw (%)	10.4	23.4	53.5
EFFICIENCY			
Coll Period (days)	27.0	48.8	69.0
Sales To Inv (times)	242.7	56.2	25.9
Assets To Sales (%)	24.3	33.5	44.3
Sales To Nwc (times)	11.8	8.1	5.0
Acct Pay To Sales (%)	2.4	4.9	8.9
PROFITABILITY			
Return On Sales (%)	7.1	3.2	1.4
Return On Assets (%)	20.9	9.6	3.8
Return On Nw (%)	54.4	19.4	8.5

SIC 1721 — PNTNG,PAPER HANGING
(NO BREAKDOWN)
2020 (24 Establishments)

	$	%
Cash	627,345	23.8
Accounts Receivable	1,120,260	42.5
Notes Receivable	2,636	0.1
Inventory	44,810	1.7
Other Current	384,842	14.6
Total Current	**2,179,893**	**82.7**
Fixed Assets	495,550	18.8
Other Non-current	(39,538)	(1.5)
Total Assets	**2,635,905**	**100.0**
Accounts Payable	456,012	17.3
Bank Loans	0	0.0
Notes Payable	44,810	1.7
Other Current	1,621,082	61.5
Total Current	**2,121,904**	**80.5**
Other Long Term	108,072	4.1
Deferred Credits	0	0.0
Net Worth	405,929	15.4
Total Liab & Net Worth	**2,635,905**	**100.0**
Net Sales	7,939,473	100.0
Gross Profit	2,373,902	29.9
Net Profit After Tax	603,400	7.6
Working Capital	57,989	---

RATIOS

	UQ	MED	LQ
SOLVENCY			
Quick Ratio (times)	4.7	2.1	0.9
Current Ratio (times)	6.1	2.6	1.5
Curr Liab To Nw (%)	16.4	52.5	117.5
Curr Liab To Inv (%)	231.5	543.6	999.9
Total Liab To Nw (%)	27.4	68.1	127.8
Fixed Assets To Nw (%)	11.9	25.2	50.4
EFFICIENCY			
Coll Period (days)	39.8	56.9	67.0
Sales To Inv (times)	357.9	126.7	68.8
Assets To Sales (%)	28.1	33.2	50.7
Sales To Nwc (times)	10.8	5.9	4.6
Acct Pay To Sales (%)	1.0	2.7	7.2
PROFITABILITY			
Return On Sales (%)	11.0	7.4	2.6
Return On Assets (%)	37.8	24.1	7.4
Return On Nw (%)	58.7	37.5	13.0

SIC 1731 — ELECTRICAL WORK
(NO BREAKDOWN)
2020 (215 Establishments)

	$	%
Cash	894,884	20.6
Accounts Receivable	1,798,456	41.4
Notes Receivable	13,032	0.3
Inventory	82,538	1.9
Other Current	668,991	15.4
Total Current	**3,457,901**	**79.6**
Fixed Assets	629,894	14.5
Other Non-current	256,302	5.9
Total Assets	**4,344,097**	**100.0**
Accounts Payable	629,894	14.5
Bank Loans	4,344	0.1
Notes Payable	43,441	1.0
Other Current	1,142,498	26.3
Total Current	**1,820,177**	**41.9**
Other Long Term	425,721	9.8
Deferred Credits	8,688	0.2
Net Worth	2,089,511	48.1
Total Liab & Net Worth	**4,344,097**	**100.0**
Net Sales	11,401,829	100.0
Gross Profit	3,169,708	27.8
Net Profit After Tax	684,110	6.0
Working Capital	1,637,724	---

RATIOS

	UQ	MED	LQ
SOLVENCY			
Quick Ratio (times)	2.4	1.5	1.1
Current Ratio (times)	3.5	1.9	1.4
Curr Liab To Nw (%)	32.3	76.1	155.3
Curr Liab To Inv (%)	510.5	999.9	999.9
Total Liab To Nw (%)	40.1	90.9	204.5
Fixed Assets To Nw (%)	11.2	22.1	43.6
EFFICIENCY			
Coll Period (days)	45.6	66.1	81.8
Sales To Inv (times)	478.9	176.6	55.7
Assets To Sales (%)	28.6	38.1	52.8
Sales To Nwc (times)	11.6	7.2	3.9
Acct Pay To Sales (%)	2.4	4.4	7.5
PROFITABILITY			
Return On Sales (%)	8.7	4.8	1.6
Return On Assets (%)	22.7	10.6	4.4
Return On Nw (%)	52.2	26.4	8.9

SIC 1741 MSNRY,OTHER STNWRK
(NO BREAKDOWN)
2020 (19 Establishments)

	$	%
Cash	575,793	20.5
Accounts Receivable	1,303,257	46.4
Notes Receivable	0	0.0
Inventory	36,514	1.3
Other Current	455,016	16.2
Total Current	**2,370,580**	**84.4**
Fixed Assets	393,224	14.0
Other Non-current	44,940	1.6
Total Assets	**2,808,744**	**100.0**
Accounts Payable	258,404	9.2
Bank Loans	0	0.0
Notes Payable	106,732	3.8
Other Current	690,952	24.6
Total Current	**1,056,088**	**37.6**
Other Long Term	244,360	8.7
Deferred Credits	0	0.0
Net Worth	1,508,296	53.7
Total Liab & Net Worth	**2,808,744**	**100.0**
Net Sales	7,430,540	100.0
Gross Profit	1,924,510	25.9
Net Profit After Tax	378,958	5.1
Working Capital	1,314,492	—

RATIOS	UQ	MED	LQ
SOLVENCY			
Quick Ratio (times)	3.0	1.7	1.3
Current Ratio (times)	3.5	2.2	1.8
Curr Liab To Nw (%)	38.7	78.2	139.4
Curr Liab To Inv (%)	855.5	892.3	999.9
Total Liab To Nw (%)	47.4	85.5	163.0
Fixed Assets To Nw (%)	12.0	19.4	36.8
EFFICIENCY			
Coll Period (days)	54.8	70.5	93.1
Sales To Inv (times)	258.7	159.1	68.9
Assets To Sales (%)	30.5	37.8	50.8
Sales To Nwc (times)	7.9	5.3	4.3
Acct Pay To Sales (%)	1.6	3.2	4.6
PROFITABILITY			
Return On Sales (%)	10.7	1.4	0.6
Return On Assets (%)	20.1	4.4	1.6
Return On Nw (%)	35.5	9.9	2.3

SIC 1742 PLSTRNG,DWALL,INSUL
(NO BREAKDOWN)
2020 (16 Establishments)

	$	%
Cash	1,966,948	24.1
Accounts Receivable	3,085,088	37.8
Notes Receivable	0	0.0
Inventory	146,909	1.8
Other Current	995,716	12.2
Total Current	**6,194,661**	**75.9**
Fixed Assets	636,606	7.8
Other Non-current	1,330,342	16.3
Total Assets	**8,161,609**	**100.0**
Accounts Payable	759,030	9.3
Bank Loans	0	0.0
Notes Payable	8,162	0.1
Other Current	1,673,129	20.5
Total Current	**2,440,321**	**29.9**
Other Long Term	693,737	8.5
Deferred Credits	0	0.0
Net Worth	5,027,551	61.6
Total Liab & Net Worth	**8,161,609**	**100.0**
Net Sales	20,714,744	100.0
Gross Profit	4,640,103	22.4
Net Profit After Tax	1,926,471	9.3
Working Capital	3,754,340	—

RATIOS	UQ	MED	LQ
SOLVENCY			
Quick Ratio (times)	3.5	2.2	1.2
Current Ratio (times)	4.2	2.6	1.8
Curr Liab To Nw (%)	27.2	52.1	66.5
Curr Liab To Inv (%)	507.4	999.9	999.9
Total Liab To Nw (%)	28.9	71.9	103.3
Fixed Assets To Nw (%)	3.3	13.4	18.0
EFFICIENCY			
Coll Period (days)	44.0	50.7	66.3
Sales To Inv (times)	556.9	362.4	60.3
Assets To Sales (%)	22.4	39.4	44.3
Sales To Nwc (times)	11.7	7.4	3.6
Acct Pay To Sales (%)	1.8	3.5	6.1
PROFITABILITY			
Return On Sales (%)	10.7	8.6	7.3
Return On Assets (%)	38.5	23.7	14.5
Return On Nw (%)	80.3	38.0	20.8

SIC 1751 CARPENTRY WORK
(NO BREAKDOWN)
2020 (13 Establishments)

	$	%
Cash	357,879	15.5
Accounts Receivable	914,323	39.6
Notes Receivable	0	0.0
Inventory	150,078	6.5
Other Current	473,324	20.5
Total Current	**1,895,604**	**82.1**
Fixed Assets	223,963	9.7
Other Non-current	189,330	8.2
Total Assets	**2,308,897**	**100.0**
Accounts Payable	293,230	12.7
Bank Loans	0	0.0
Notes Payable	20,780	0.9
Other Current	595,695	25.8
Total Current	**909,705**	**39.4**
Other Long Term	413,293	17.9
Deferred Credits	0	0.0
Net Worth	985,899	42.7
Total Liab & Net Worth	**2,308,897**	**100.0**
Net Sales	8,365,569	100.0
Gross Profit	2,618,423	31.3
Net Profit After Tax	301,160	3.6
Working Capital	985,899	—

RATIOS	UQ	MED	LQ
SOLVENCY			
Quick Ratio (times)	2.6	1.6	0.9
Current Ratio (times)	3.6	2.6	1.7
Curr Liab To Nw (%)	37.6	68.7	106.7
Curr Liab To Inv (%)	197.0	284.7	552.3
Total Liab To Nw (%)	38.8	90.2	163.1
Fixed Assets To Nw (%)	11.9	16.6	22.8
EFFICIENCY			
Coll Period (days)	33.3	52.9	69.6
Sales To Inv (times)	65.8	27.9	20.3
Assets To Sales (%)	23.3	27.6	40.9
Sales To Nwc (times)	12.7	7.6	6.6
Acct Pay To Sales (%)	2.4	3.0	6.1
PROFITABILITY			
Return On Sales (%)	7.3	3.3	0.8
Return On Assets (%)	32.3	10.1	2.9
Return On Nw (%)	87.5	29.3	4.0

SIC 1752 FLR LAYING WORK,NEC
(NO BREAKDOWN)
2020 (12 Establishments)

	$	%
Cash	1,112,940	19.1
Accounts Receivable	2,721,167	46.7
Notes Receivable	0	0.0
Inventory	530,249	9.1
Other Current	536,076	9.2
Total Current	**4,900,432**	**84.1**
Fixed Assets	425,365	7.3
Other Non-current	501,114	8.6
Total Assets	**5,826,911**	**100.0**
Accounts Payable	617,653	10.6
Bank Loans	0	0.0
Notes Payable	64,096	1.1
Other Current	2,051,072	35.2
Total Current	**2,732,821**	**46.9**
Other Long Term	903,171	15.5
Deferred Credits	0	0.0
Net Worth	2,190,919	37.6
Total Liab & Net Worth	**5,826,911**	**100.0**
Net Sales	18,918,542	100.0
Gross Profit	5,240,436	27.7
Net Profit After Tax	1,172,950	6.2
Working Capital	2,167,611	—

RATIOS	UQ	MED	LQ
SOLVENCY			
Quick Ratio (times)	2.7	1.6	0.9
Current Ratio (times)	2.9	1.7	1.5
Curr Liab To Nw (%)	35.7	130.1	181.1
Curr Liab To Inv (%)	264.1	347.2	999.9
Total Liab To Nw (%)	48.8	130.1	182.7
Fixed Assets To Nw (%)	5.6	10.6	14.4
EFFICIENCY			
Coll Period (days)	37.3	56.9	104.6
Sales To Inv (times)	377.2	33.6	12.0
Assets To Sales (%)	23.5	30.8	46.3
Sales To Nwc (times)	7.6	5.8	3.5
Acct Pay To Sales (%)	2.5	3.6	5.9
PROFITABILITY			
Return On Sales (%)	8.3	5.3	3.7
Return On Assets (%)	25.6	21.8	11.1
Return On Nw (%)	64.1	34.8	19.2

Page 8

	SIC 1761 RRNF.SDNG.SHT MTLWK (NO BREAKDOWN) 2020 (52 Establishments)		SIC 1771 CONCRETE WORK (NO BREAKDOWN) 2020 (26 Establishments)		SIC 1791 STRUCT STEEL ERCTN (NO BREAKDOWN) 2020 (13 Establishments)		SIC 1793 GLASS,GLAZING WORK (NO BREAKDOWN) 2020 (12 Establishments)	
	$	%	$	%	$	%	$	%
Cash	554,864	21.0	399,027	11.3	1,766,666	15.0	626,686	21.8
Accounts Receivable	906,278	34.3	1,313,612	37.2	5,288,220	44.9	1,135,509	39.5
Notes Receivable	5,284	0.2	3,531	0.1	0	0.0	0	0.0
Inventory	140,037	5.3	56,499	1.6	318,000	2.7	252,974	8.8
Other Current	449,177	17.0	(98,874)	(2.8)	1,354,443	11.5	370,838	12.9
Total Current	**2,055,640**	**77.8**	**1,673,795**	**47.4**	**8,727,329**	**74.1**	**2,386,007**	**83.0**
Fixed Assets	459,745	17.4	1,634,952	46.3	2,826,665	24.0	408,208	14.2
Other Non-current	126,826	4.8	222,467	6.3	223,778	1.9	80,492	2.8
Total Assets	**2,642,211**	**100.0**	**3,531,214**	**100.0**	**11,777,772**	**100.0**	**2,874,707**	**100.0**
Accounts Payable	324,992	12.3	(3,778,399)	(107.0)	2,214,221	18.8	474,327	16.5
Bank Loans	0	0.0	38,843	1.1	0	0.0	0	0.0
Notes Payable	71,340	2.7	109,468	3.1	141,333	1.2	34,496	1.2
Other Current	716,039	27.1	1,945,699	55.1	3,156,443	26.8	520,322	18.1
Total Current	**1,112,371**	**42.1**	**(1,684,389)**	**(47.7)**	**5,511,997**	**46.8**	**1,029,145**	**35.8**
Other Long Term	306,496	11.6	1,917,449	54.3	1,460,444	12.4	181,107	6.3
Deferred Credits	0	0.0	0	0.0	0	0.0	0	0.0
Net Worth	1,223,344	46.3	3,298,154	93.4	4,805,331	40.8	1,664,455	57.9
Total Liab & Net Worth	**2,642,211**	**100.0**	**3,531,214**	**100.0**	**11,777,772**	**100.0**	**2,874,707**	**100.0**
Net Sales	7,319,144	100.0	9,543,822	100.0	35,157,528	100.0	6,812,102	100.0
Gross Profit	2,107,913	28.8	2,605,463	27.3	7,629,184	21.7	1,927,825	28.3
Net Profit After Tax	358,638	4.9	601,261	6.3	1,968,822	5.6	395,102	5.8
Working Capital	943,269	---	3,358,184	---	3,215,332	---	1,356,862	---

RATIOS	UQ	MED	LQ	UQ	MED	LQ	UQ	MED	LQ	UQ	MED	LQ
SOLVENCY												
Quick Ratio (times)	2.9	1.6	0.9	1.7	1.0	0.6	1.5	1.4	1.1	2.9	2.2	1.3
Current Ratio (times)	3.7	2.2	1.3	1.9	1.4	0.7	1.8	1.6	1.4	4.2	3.1	1.8
Curr Liab To Nw (%)	27.7	67.7	101.2	35.2	123.1	202.3	81.7	105.3	170.5	24.1	37.4	58.6
Curr Liab To Inv (%)	321.7	802.9	999.9	999.9	999.9	999.9	683.7	999.9	999.9	239.1	674.0	999.9
Total Liab To Nw (%)	34.3	73.6	120.4	83.3	170.0	288.4	105.3	155.1	265.0	24.1	43.5	63.9
Fixed Assets To Nw (%)	13.2	20.2	39.9	27.2	54.4	140.4	33.4	51.4	111.0	7.3	10.0	29.0
EFFICIENCY												
Coll Period (days)	36.9	58.6	67.4	26.9	67.9	90.4	35.4	53.0	82.5	52.2	61.0	79.2
Sales To Inv (times)	161.3	60.1	27.3	247.7	148.7	53.5	277.0	166.7	58.5	724.2	146.5	10.3
Assets To Sales (%)	27.0	36.1	50.6	30.7	37.0	54.2	25.5	33.5	44.7	38.8	42.2	53.4
Sales To Nwc (times)	10.0	7.2	4.1	12.0	9.1	6.2	16.5	9.2	7.4	34.5	4.3	3.4
Acct Pay To Sales (%)	2.6	4.3	7.5	2.0	5.4	10.4	4.1	6.3	8.9	4.3	5.4	11.0
PROFITABILITY												
Return On Sales (%)	8.8	4.0	1.5	9.5	4.8	0.8	7.6	3.2	2.0	8.5	5.1	4.0
Return On Assets (%)	20.5	9.7	3.4	26.6	13.0	1.9	20.2	11.3	5.8	31.1	14.0	5.7
Return On Nw (%)	47.2	16.3	7.7	75.1	30.1	5.9	60.8	21.8	17.3	37.2	24.0	13.0

	SIC 1794 EXCAVATION WORK (NO BREAKDOWN) 2020 (34 Establishments)			SIC 1799 SPCL TRD CNTRS.NEC (NO BREAKDOWN) 2020 (56 Establishments)			SIC 20 FOOD,KINDRED PRODUCT (NO BREAKDOWN) 2020 (133 Establishments)			SIC 2086 BOTL.CND SFT DRNKS (NO BREAKDOWN) 2020 (13 Establishments)		
		$	%		$	%		$	%		$	%
Cash		1,189,104	19.8		826,828	16.4		11,659,308	12.9		3,982,008	24.9
Accounts Receivable		1,627,512	27.1		1,835,155	36.4		11,026,633	12.2		1,343,328	8.4
Notes Receivable		108,100	1.8		10,083	0.2		0	0.0		15,992	0.1
Inventory		72,067	1.2		317,623	6.3		16,359,185	18.1		2,302,848	14.4
Other Current		756,703	12.6		554,580	11.0		5,965,228	6.6		2,126,936	13.3
Total Current		**3,753,486**	**62.5**		**3,544,269**	**70.3**		**45,010,354**	**49.8**		**9,771,112**	**61.1**
Fixed Assets		2,156,003	35.9		1,048,660	20.8		23,499,381	26.0		1,423,288	8.9
Other Non-current		96,089	1.6		448,706	8.9		21,872,501	24.2		4,797,600	30.0
Total Assets		**6,005,578**	**100.0**		**5,041,635**	**100.0**		**90,382,236**	**100.0**		**15,992,000**	**100.0**
Accounts Payable		534,496	8.9		720,954	14.3		25,758,937	28.5		24,019,984	150.2
Bank Loans		0	0.0		0	0.0		90,382	0.1		0	0.0
Notes Payable		132,123	2.2		30,250	0.6		36,152,894	40.0		57,251,360	358.0
Other Current		1,621,506	27.0		1,038,576	20.6		17,805,301	19.7		(6,412,792)	(40.1)
Total Current		**2,288,125**	**38.1**		**1,789,780**	**35.5**		**79,807,514**	**88.3**		**74,858,552**	**468.1**
Other Long Term		984,915	16.4		872,203	17.3		32,718,370	36.2		15,528,232	97.1
Deferred Credits		18,017	0.3		0	0.0		90,382	0.1		63,968	0.4
Net Worth		2,714,521	45.2		2,379,652	47.2		(22,234,030)	(24.6)		(74,458,752)	(465.6)
Total Liab & Net Worth		**6,005,578**	**100.0**		**5,041,635**	**100.0**		**90,382,236**	**100.0**		**15,992,000**	**100.0**
Net Sales		10,999,227	100.0		12,417,820	100.0		101,896,546	100.0		13,293,433	100.0
Gross Profit		2,496,825	22.7		4,023,374	32.4		33,829,653	33.2		5,157,852	38.8
Net Profit After Tax		417,971	3.8		732,651	5.9		3,158,793	3.1		(451,977)	(3.4)
Working Capital		1,465,361	---		1,754,489	---		(34,797,160)	---		(65,087,440)	---
RATIOS	UQ	MED	LQ	UQ	MED	LQ	UQ	MED	LQ	UQ	MED	LQ
SOLVENCY												
Quick Ratio (times)	2.5	1.4	0.9	3.3	1.5	1.0	1.5	0.8	0.4	1.6	0.5	0.2
Current Ratio (times)	3.1	1.8	1.3	3.9	1.9	1.4	2.8	1.8	1.2	1.9	1.2	0.2
Curr Liab To Nw (%)	27.3	46.2	120.5	15.7	82.2	151.9	20.4	37.4	94.0	27.8	42.0	153.9
Curr Liab To Inv (%)	503.2	773.8	999.9	178.2	652.7	999.9	89.4	140.1	286.0	137.2	229.4	989.9
Total Liab To Nw (%)	47.8	86.5	169.8	36.1	121.8	210.5	38.5	97.2	212.0	38.2	112.9	576.8
Fixed Assets To Nw (%)	44.8	61.6	107.0	12.8	38.0	97.6	22.8	51.4	87.2	5.4	8.7	91.8
EFFICIENCY												
Coll Period (days)	37.6	44.4	64.2	43.8	65.3	85.8	22.3	31.0	42.2	31.4	37.1	49.6
Sales To Inv (times)	227.6	105.7	44.3	156.5	79.3	17.3	14.7	8.9	4.9	14.3	6.4	4.6
Assets To Sales (%)	43.7	54.6	71.4	30.5	40.6	57.7	47.9	88.7	156.8	56.1	120.3	317.2
Sales To Nwc (times)	11.9	6.4	4.3	13.0	7.0	3.8	14.3	7.2	3.1	14.6	4.5	2.8
Acct Pay To Sales (%)	1.4	4.6	6.9	2.2	4.9	10.4	3.8	7.1	12.2	6.5	16.4	38.5
PROFITABILITY												
Return On Sales (%)	8.1	5.4	2.2	8.5	3.8	1.2	9.5	(4.1)	(3.9)	12.3	(4.1)	(35.9)
Return On Assets (%)	18.6	7.4	3.6	24.0	12.4	3.6	10.1	(28.2)	(2.8)	2.5	(28.2)	(372.2)
Return On Nw (%)	52.4	14.4	9.6	54.7	29.3	10.8	22.5	9.4	1.2	15.7	4.1	(39.0)

SIC 2099 FOOD PRPRTNS,NEC
(NO BREAKDOWN)
2020 (15 Establishments)

	$	%
Cash	12,347,468	9.9
Accounts Receivable	14,343,019	11.5
Notes Receivable	0	0.0
Inventory	24,570,214	19.7
Other Current	4,739,433	3.8
Total Current	**56,000,134**	**44.9**
Fixed Assets	26,690,487	21.4
Other Non-current	42,031,280	33.7
Total Assets	**124,721,901**	**100.0**
Accounts Payable	11,723,859	9.4
Bank Loans	0	0.0
Notes Payable	997,775	0.8
Other Current	11,100,249	8.9
Total Current	**23,821,883**	**19.1**
Other Long Term	38,289,623	30.7
Deferred Credits	249,444	0.2
Net Worth	62,360,951	50.0
Total Liab & Net Worth	**124,721,901**	**100.0**
Net Sales	289,377,961	100.0
Gross Profit	109,384,869	37.8
Net Profit After Tax	21,992,725	7.6
Working Capital	32,178,251	—

RATIOS	UQ	MED	LQ
SOLVENCY			
Quick Ratio (times)	2.1	1.2	0.8
Current Ratio (times)	5.5	2.4	1.7
Curr Liab To Nw (%)	14.9	38.6	62.3
Curr Liab To Inv (%)	63.7	120.2	194.0
Total Liab To Nw (%)	36.6	79.4	199.8
Fixed Assets To Nw (%)	11.8	27.6	51.4
EFFICIENCY			
Coll Period (days)	23.0	30.7	37.2
Sales To Inv (times)	16.4	9.6	6.6
Assets To Sales (%)	27.3	43.1	131.5
Sales To Nwc (times)	10.8	7.3	4.3
Acct Pay To Sales (%)	2.1	6.3	13.3
PROFITABILITY			
Return On Sales (%)	10.8	8.6	3.2
Return On Assets (%)	18.9	6.8	4.2
Return On Nw (%)	44.9	18.7	9.7

SIC 22 TEXTILE MILL PDTS
(NO BREAKDOWN)
2020 (16 Establishments)

	$	%
Cash	19,812,679	10.0
Accounts Receivable	24,171,469	12.2
Notes Receivable	594,380	0.3
Inventory	45,172,909	22.8
Other Current	10,500,720	5.3
Total Current	**100,252,157**	**50.6**
Fixed Assets	39,625,358	20.0
Other Non-current	58,249,277	29.4
Total Assets	**198,126,792**	**100.0**
Accounts Payable	11,491,354	5.8
Bank Loans	0	0.0
Notes Payable	0	0.0
Other Current	40,417,866	20.4
Total Current	**51,909,220**	**26.2**
Other Long Term	58,249,276	29.4
Deferred Credits	0	0.0
Net Worth	87,968,296	44.4
Total Liab & Net Worth	**198,126,792**	**100.0**
Net Sales	209,436,355	100.0
Gross Profit	52,359,089	25.0
Net Profit After Tax	1,466,054	0.7
Working Capital	48,342,937	—

RATIOS	UQ	MED	LQ
SOLVENCY			
Quick Ratio (times)	2.2	1.7	0.7
Current Ratio (times)	3.9	3.2	1.6
Curr Liab To Nw (%)	10.7	25.1	143.3
Curr Liab To Inv (%)	52.5	81.1	170.8
Total Liab To Nw (%)	11.5	80.3	286.5
Fixed Assets To Nw (%)	19.7	41.6	88.2
EFFICIENCY			
Coll Period (days)	29.2	39.4	48.9
Sales To Inv (times)	5.8	5.2	3.9
Assets To Sales (%)	66.1	94.6	114.6
Sales To Nwc (times)	4.5	3.6	2.7
Acct Pay To Sales (%)	3.8	5.5	6.8
PROFITABILITY			
Return On Sales (%)	8.6	2.2	0.0
Return On Assets (%)	8.2	2.8	0.0
Return On Nw (%)	22.7	15.3	1.0

SIC 23 APPAREL,RELATED PDTS
(NO BREAKDOWN)
2020 (33 Establishments)

	$	%
Cash	37,739,800	17.5
Accounts Receivable	31,054,464	14.4
Notes Receivable	215,656	0.1
Inventory	65,775,080	30.5
Other Current	10,567,144	4.9
Total Current	**145,352,144**	**67.4**
Fixed Assets	28,466,592	13.2
Other Non-current	41,837,264	19.4
Total Assets	**215,656,000**	**100.0**
Accounts Payable	123,786,544	57.4
Bank Loans	0	0.0
Notes Payable	646,968	0.3
Other Current	335,992,048	155.8
Total Current	**460,425,560**	**213.5**
Other Long Term	40,327,672	18.7
Deferred Credits	0	0.0
Net Worth	(285,097,232)	(132.2)
Total Liab & Net Worth	**215,656,000**	**100.0**
Net Sales	300,775,453	100.0
Gross Profit	115,196,998	38.3
Net Profit After Tax	14,737,997	4.9
Working Capital	(315,073,416)	—

RATIOS	UQ	MED	LQ
SOLVENCY			
Quick Ratio (times)	1.8	0.9	0.5
Current Ratio (times)	3.1	2.3	1.7
Curr Liab To Nw (%)	26.9	48.8	78.3
Curr Liab To Inv (%)	64.9	97.0	134.5
Total Liab To Nw (%)	44.3	103.6	157.6
Fixed Assets To Nw (%)	15.5	28.7	39.9
EFFICIENCY			
Coll Period (days)	22.8	32.5	49.1
Sales To Inv (times)	7.1	5.6	4.0
Assets To Sales (%)	51.9	71.7	93.1
Sales To Nwc (times)	7.0	4.8	2.6
Acct Pay To Sales (%)	5.0	6.8	9.9
PROFITABILITY			
Return On Sales (%)	7.8	6.0	1.2
Return On Assets (%)	10.5	6.9	1.5
Return On Nw (%)	28.0	13.2	7.7

SIC 24 LUMBER,WOOD PRODUCTS
(NO BREAKDOWN)
2020 (33 Establishments)

	$	%
Cash	1,205,982	12.2
Accounts Receivable	1,532,191	15.5
Notes Receivable	108,736	1.1
Inventory	2,313,114	23.4
Other Current	563,451	5.7
Total Current	**5,723,474**	**57.9**
Fixed Assets	2,392,195	24.2
Other Non-current	1,769,433	17.9
Total Assets	**9,885,102**	**100.0**
Accounts Payable	731,498	7.4
Bank Loans	0	0.0
Notes Payable	138,391	1.4
Other Current	1,393,799	14.1
Total Current	**2,263,688**	**22.9**
Other Long Term	2,135,182	21.6
Deferred Credits	0	0.0
Net Worth	5,486,232	55.5
Total Liab & Net Worth	**9,885,102**	**100.0**
Net Sales	19,269,205	100.0
Gross Profit	4,836,570	25.1
Net Profit After Tax	924,922	4.8
Working Capital	3,459,786	—

RATIOS	UQ	MED	LQ
SOLVENCY			
Quick Ratio (times)	1.9	0.9	0.8
Current Ratio (times)	3.9	2.2	1.6
Curr Liab To Nw (%)	12.7	42.0	83.9
Curr Liab To Inv (%)	57.4	103.4	160.2
Total Liab To Nw (%)	31.9	76.6	204.1
Fixed Assets To Nw (%)	22.1	38.1	84.7
EFFICIENCY			
Coll Period (days)	15.3	26.8	39.8
Sales To Inv (times)	14.7	11.1	6.5
Assets To Sales (%)	38.5	51.3	105.6
Sales To Nwc (times)	12.1	6.8	3.3
Acct Pay To Sales (%)	2.3	3.2	6.1
PROFITABILITY			
Return On Sales (%)	5.3	2.9	0.3
Return On Assets (%)	12.8	5.6	0.2
Return On Nw (%)	27.3	13.5	(0.1)

	SIC 25 FURNITURE,FIXTURES (NO BREAKDOWN) 2020 (33 Establishments)			SIC 26 PAPER,ALLIED PDTS (NO BREAKDOWN) 2020 (36 Establishments)			SIC 27 PRINTING,PUBLISHING (NO BREAKDOWN) 2020 (50 Establishments)			SIC 2752 COMMRCL PRTNG,LITH (NO BREAKDOWN) 2020 (14 Establishments)	
		$	%		$	%		$	%		$	%
Cash		32,407,056	14.4		2,823,013	4.8		1,630,222	19.8		524,531	22.0
Accounts Receivable		29,706,468	13.2		11,762,553	20.0		1,531,421	18.6		638,974	26.8
Notes Receivable		0	0.0		0	0.0		0	0.0		0	0.0
Inventory		60,088,083	26.7		12,585,932	21.4		839,811	10.2		200,276	8.4
Other Current		25,430,537	11.3		2,881,825	4.9		757,478	9.2		140,670	5.9
Total Current		**147,632,144**	**65.6**		**30,053,323**	**51.1**		**4,758,932**	**57.8**		**1,504,451**	**63.1**
Fixed Assets		40,058,722	17.8		16,526,387	28.1		1,506,721	18.3		584,137	24.5
Other Non-current		37,358,134	16.6		12,233,056	20.8		1,967,793	23.9		295,645	12.4
Total Assets		**225,049,000**	**100.0**		**58,812,766**	**100.0**		**8,233,446**	**100.0**		**2,384,233**	**100.0**
Accounts Payable		34,657,546	15.4		8,469,038	14.4		773,944	9.4		216,965	9.1
Bank Loans		0	0.0		0	0.0		0	0.0		0	0.0
Notes Payable		0	0.0		58,813	0.1		57,634	0.7		0	0.0
Other Current		60,763,230	27.0		10,586,298	18.0		2,091,295	25.4		979,920	41.1
Total Current		**95,420,776**	**42.4**		**19,114,149**	**32.5**		**2,922,873**	**35.5**		**1,196,885**	**50.2**
Other Long Term		42,534,261	18.9		18,643,647	31.7		1,934,860	23.5		393,398	16.5
Deferred Credits		0	0.0		0	0.0		0	0.0		0	0.0
Net Worth		87,093,963	38.7		21,054,970	35.8		3,375,713	41.0		793,950	33.3
Total Liab & Net Worth		**225,049,000**	**100.0**		**58,812,766**	**100.0**		**8,233,446**	**100.0**		**2,384,233**	**100.0**
Net Sales		404,764,388	100.0		83,540,861	100.0		12,072,501	100.0		4,047,934	100.0
Gross Profit		139,238,949	34.4		18,880,235	22.6		5,855,163	48.5		2,193,980	54.2
Net Profit After Tax		10,523,874	2.6		2,255,603	2.7		205,233	1.7		425,033	10.5
Working Capital		52,211,368	---		10,939,174	---		1,836,059	---		307,566	---

RATIOS	UQ	MED	LQ	UQ	MED	LQ	UQ	MED	LQ	UQ	MED	LQ
SOLVENCY												
Quick Ratio (times)	1.1	0.7	0.4	1.5	0.8	0.6	2.2	1.1	0.7	2.8	1.7	1.1
Current Ratio (times)	2.3	1.8	1.2	3.0	1.8	1.1	3.0	1.8	1.2	4.9	2.3	1.3
Curr Liab To Nw (%)	30.4	58.9	74.3	25.6	61.6	143.5	17.8	50.8	74.9	13.7	49.8	171.9
Curr Liab To Inv (%)	80.9	146.9	274.6	97.6	139.2	254.2	161.5	386.4	936.4	206.2	451.1	558.1
Total Liab To Nw (%)	52.1	79.3	152.1	71.2	140.9	290.2	33.8	77.8	203.0	14.0	66.8	237.8
Fixed Assets To Nw (%)	21.1	45.2	63.3	32.2	75.6	117.5	11.4	36.9	65.8	9.2	52.9	83.0
EFFICIENCY												
Coll Period (days)	17.4	29.9	43.3	32.7	42.3	47.5	27.9	40.9	61.5	23.4	42.3	70.1
Sales To Inv (times)	11.6	7.4	4.6	11.3	9.5	6.3	50.6	20.1	6.9	53.7	27.1	6.7
Assets To Sales (%)	45.2	55.6	66.5	39.1	70.4	118.9	45.0	68.2	115.3	26.4	58.9	91.9
Sales To Nwc (times)	11.9	6.4	3.8	17.2	8.3	3.9	13.0	7.4	3.9	12.2	6.9	3.1
Acct Pay To Sales (%)	4.0	7.0	12.2	5.1	8.6	13.1	3.1	5.0	7.8	1.4	5.0	6.7
PROFITABILITY												
Return On Sales (%)	6.3	4.0	(0.4)	5.7	3.4	0.7	6.4	2.2	0.3	19.3	6.4	1.5
Return On Assets (%)	10.2	5.9	(0.7)	7.3	4.7	1.8	10.5	3.8	0.2	27.7	13.2	8.8
Return On Nw (%)	24.9	15.0	4.5	19.4	9.6	1.6	15.1	7.3	0.7	43.5	20.8	7.5

Page 11

Page 12

	SIC 28 CHEMICALS,ALLIED PDT (NO BREAKDOWN) 2020 (615 Establishments)		SIC 2819 IND INORG CHEM,NEC (NO BREAKDOWN) 2020 (18 Establishments)		SIC 2833 MEDCNLS,BOTANICALS (NO BREAKDOWN) 2020 (26 Establishments)		SIC 2834 PHRMCTCL PREPRTNS (NO BREAKDOWN) 2020 (372 Establishments)	
	$	%	$	%	$	%	$	%
Cash	32,107,373	34.3	80,774,244	11.4	1,683,858	13.5	35,884,134	42.9
Accounts Receivable	5,897,273	6.3	95,653,710	13.5	636,124	5.1	3,596,778	4.3
Notes Receivable	93,608	0.1	0	0.0	62,365	0.5	0	0.0
Inventory	5,710,058	6.1	87,151,158	12.3	1,758,696	14.1	2,425,734	2.9
Other Current	19,002,321	20.3	29,758,932	4.2	1,908,374	15.3	21,078,792	25.2
Total Current	**62,810,633**	**67.1**	**293,338,044**	**41.4**	**6,049,417**	**48.5**	**62,985,438**	**75.3**
Fixed Assets	10,952,078	11.7	193,433,058	27.3	2,394,821	19.2	4,684,176	5.6
Other Non-current	19,844,789	21.2	221,774,898	31.3	4,028,786	32.3	15,976,386	19.1
Total Assets	**93,607,500**	**100.0**	**708,546,000**	**100.0**	**12,473,024**	**100.0**	**83,646,000**	**100.0**
Accounts Payable	66,835,755	71.4	70,854,600	10.0	3,380,190	27.1	77,037,966	92.1
Bank Loans	0	0.0	0	0.0	0	0.0	0	0.0
Notes Payable	16,287,705	17.4	7,085,460	1.0	661,070	5.3	23,253,588	27.8
Other Current	50,267,228	53.7	102,739,170	14.5	11,013,680	88.3	22,668,066	27.1
Total Current	**133,390,688**	**142.5**	**180,679,230**	**25.5**	**15,054,940**	**120.7**	**122,959,620**	**147.0**
Other Long Term	42,497,805	45.4	312,468,786	44.1	2,631,808	21.1	32,287,356	38.6
Deferred Credits	936,075	1.0	708,546	0.1	49,892	0.4	920,106	1.1
Net Worth	(83,217,068)	(88.9)	214,689,438	30.3	(5,263,616)	(42.2)	(72,521,082)	(86.7)
Total Liab & Net Worth	**93,607,500**	**100.0**	**708,546,000**	**100.0**	**12,473,024**	**100.0**	**83,646,000**	**100.0**
Net Sales	39,748,408	100.0	407,678,941	100.0	6,396,423	100.0	23,803,643	100.0
Gross Profit	18,204,771	45.8	117,003,856	28.7	2,053,252	32.1	14,782,062	62.1
Net Profit After Tax	(1,947,672)	(4.9)	16,714,837	4.1	(908,292)	(14.2)	(2,380,364)	(10.0)
Working Capital	(70,580,055)	—	112,658,814	—	(9,005,523)	—	(59,974,182)	—

RATIOS	UQ	MED	LQ	UQ	MED	LQ	UQ	MED	LQ	UQ	MED	LQ
SOLVENCY												
Quick Ratio (times)	3.5	1.6	0.8	1.6	0.9	0.7	1.4	0.5	0.1	4.3	1.9	1.0
Current Ratio (times)	6.8	3.1	1.5	2.3	2.1	1.6	2.4	1.1	0.2	7.9	3.9	1.8
Curr Liab To Nw (%)	13.0	29.1	66.6	18.8	42.7	150.6	19.9	60.8	105.0	12.4	25.1	61.8
Curr Liab To Inv (%)	134.0	257.5	643.8	108.0	155.6	169.0	130.6	418.4	927.2	208.7	476.3	999.9
Total Liab To Nw (%)	22.0	62.8	166.0	76.0	184.5	492.4	44.6	98.0	165.1	17.7	46.0	154.9
Fixed Assets To Nw (%)	1.7	8.8	34.8	37.4	71.4	132.8	10.3	24.4	69.0	1.0	3.8	12.1
EFFICIENCY												
Coll Period (days)	34.7	55.7	86.1	38.3	48.4	64.1	21.9	26.7	36.9	40.0	63.7	106.1
Sales To Inv (times)	12.9	7.5	4.4	8.9	6.6	5.9	11.3	5.4	1.9	15.5	7.6	4.0
Assets To Sales (%)	114.0	235.5	753.4	128.5	173.8	233.5	67.6	195.0	549.7	181.5	351.4	999.9
Sales To Nwc (times)	4.4	1.3	0.2	6.2	5.0	1.8	5.7	2.5	1.3	1.7	0.6	0.1
Acct Pay To Sales (%)	6.3	12.7	36.7	8.2	10.7	18.4	9.9	19.4	157.2	7.1	17.9	57.1
PROFITABILITY												
Return On Sales (%)	4.2	(41.5)	(428.6)	7.6	4.6	(15.5)	(11.9)	)(152.9	(551.3)	(18.8)	)(188.5	(922.4)
Return On Assets (%)	(1.9)	)(38.0	(79.4)	5.0	1.9	(8.0)	(12.1)	)(70.2	(167.7)	(22.2)	)(50.0	(92.8)
Return On Nw (%)	1.9	(43.4)	(112.2)	26.5	8.6	(5.9)	10.4	(100.9)	(209.3)	(25.7)	)(68.0	(148.1)

Page 13

SIC 2835 DGNOSTIC SUBSTANCES
(NO BREAKDOWN)
2020 (14 Establishments)

	$	%
Cash	120,109,594	35.6
Accounts Receivable	28,340,466	8.4
Notes Receivable	0	0.0
Inventory	22,604,896	6.7
Other Current	16,869,325	5.0
Total Current	**187,924,281**	**55.7**
Fixed Assets	47,908,883	14.2
Other Non-current	101,553,336	30.1
Total Assets	**337,386,500**	**100.0**
Accounts Payable	15,519,779	4.6
Bank Loans	0	0.0
Notes Payable	0	0.0
Other Current	25,303,988	7.5
Total Current	**40,823,767**	**12.1**
Other Long Term	73,887,642	21.9
Deferred Credits	2,361,706	0.7
Net Worth	220,313,385	65.3
Total Liab & Net Worth	**337,386,500**	**100.0**
Net Sales	147,717,382	100.0
Gross Profit	83,017,169	56.2
Net Profit After Tax	3,840,652	2.6
Working Capital	147,100,514	--

RATIOS	UQ	MED	LQ
SOLVENCY			
Quick Ratio (times)	5.0	3.2	1.9
Current Ratio (times)	6.9	4.6	3.0
Curr Liab To Nw (%)	10.7	16.2	31.8
Curr Liab To Inv (%)	105.6	216.7	313.5
Total Liab To Nw (%)	31.8	50.9	70.4
Fixed Assets To Nw (%)	8.8	12.8	25.7
EFFICIENCY			
Coll Period (days)	60.8	72.1	102.4
Sales To Inv (times)	19.5	7.8	5.3
Assets To Sales (%)	166.1	228.4	293.4
Sales To Nwc (times)	2.8	1.5	0.5
Acct Pay To Sales (%)	3.8	5.8	22.8
PROFITABILITY			
Return On Sales (%)	11.9	9.7	(27.7)
Return On Assets (%)	5.1	0.3	(45.6)
Return On Nw (%)	8.2	0.4	(60.1)

SIC 2836 BIOL PRD,EXC DGNSTC
(NO BREAKDOWN)
2020 (60 Establishments)

	$	%
Cash	56,357,492	41.7
Accounts Receivable	4,865,395	3.6
Notes Receivable	0	0.0
Inventory	5,270,845	3.9
Other Current	37,166,212	27.5
Total Current	**103,659,944**	**76.7**
Fixed Assets	9,865,940	7.3
Other Non-current	21,623,978	16.0
Total Assets	**135,149,862**	**100.0**
Accounts Payable	17,164,032	12.7
Bank Loans	0	0.0
Notes Payable	2,702,997	2.0
Other Current	115,417,983	85.4
Total Current	**135,285,012**	**100.1**
Other Long Term	29,462,669	21.8
Deferred Credits	3,378,747	2.5
Net Worth	(32,976,566)	(24.4)
Total Liab & Net Worth	**135,149,862**	**100.0**
Net Sales	19,457,222	100.0
Gross Profit	12,141,307	62.4
Net Profit After Tax	(2,529,439)	(13.0)
Working Capital	(31,625,068)	--

RATIOS	UQ	MED	LQ
SOLVENCY			
Quick Ratio (times)	5.2	2.5	1.1
Current Ratio (times)	10.0	6.0	2.8
Curr Liab To Nw (%)	9.1	17.3	42.5
Curr Liab To Inv (%)	73.2	291.1	999.9
Total Liab To Nw (%)	17.6	37.3	77.9
Fixed Assets To Nw (%)	1.5	6.6	16.1
EFFICIENCY			
Coll Period (days)	56.9	75.4	110.6
Sales To Inv (times)	10.0	5.7	3.4
Assets To Sales (%)	240.6	694.6	999.9
Sales To Nwc (times)	1.0	0.3	0.1
Acct Pay To Sales (%)	5.4	18.2	111.7
PROFITABILITY			
Return On Sales (%)	(17.3)	(285.3)	(999.9)
Return On Assets (%)	(18.0)	(35.5)	(75.3)
Return On Nw (%)	(22.4)	(47.1)	(133.5)

SIC 2842 POLISHES,SANT GOODS
(NO BREAKDOWN)
2020 (11 Establishments)

	$	%
Cash	4,409,379	16.9
Accounts Receivable	3,783,195	14.5
Notes Receivable	0	0.0
Inventory	3,287,466	12.6
Other Current	1,904,643	7.3
Total Current	**13,384,683**	**51.3**
Fixed Assets	6,079,203	23.3
Other Non-current	6,627,114	25.4
Total Assets	**26,091,000**	**100.0**
Accounts Payable	3,731,013	14.3
Bank Loans	0	0.0
Notes Payable	861,003	3.3
Other Current	2,739,555	10.5
Total Current	**7,331,571**	**28.1**
Other Long Term	5,583,474	21.4
Deferred Credits	0	0.0
Net Worth	13,175,955	50.5
Total Liab & Net Worth	**26,091,000**	**100.0**
Net Sales	33,364,450	100.0
Gross Profit	13,679,425	41.0
Net Profit After Tax	2,735,885	8.2
Working Capital	6,053,112	--

RATIOS	UQ	MED	LQ
SOLVENCY			
Quick Ratio (times)	2.5	1.6	1.0
Current Ratio (times)	5.9	2.5	1.3
Curr Liab To Nw (%)	10.3	28.6	78.9
Curr Liab To Inv (%)	134.9	319.1	468.9
Total Liab To Nw (%)	24.6	64.4	169.1
Fixed Assets To Nw (%)	30.4	67.0	87.6
EFFICIENCY			
Coll Period (days)	36.9	51.5	61.6
Sales To Inv (times)	23.0	11.2	5.8
Assets To Sales (%)	54.2	78.2	91.7
Sales To Nwc (times)	5.8	4.1	2.9
Acct Pay To Sales (%)	6.4	7.6	18.3
PROFITABILITY			
Return On Sales (%)	20.3	(4.6)	(2.3)
Return On Assets (%)	16.0	(5.3)	(2.5)
Return On Nw (%)	83.0	13.5	9.3

SIC 2844 TOILET PREPARATIONS
(NO BREAKDOWN)
2020 (17 Establishments)

	$	%
Cash	2,118,203	20.6
Accounts Receivable	1,017,971	9.9
Notes Receivable	0	0.0
Inventory	2,169,615	21.1
Other Current	431,867	4.2
Total Current	**5,737,656**	**55.8**
Fixed Assets	1,028,254	10.0
Other Non-current	3,516,627	34.2
Total Assets	**10,282,537**	**100.0**
Accounts Payable	4,565,446	44.4
Bank Loans	0	0.0
Notes Payable	0	0.0
Other Current	11,598,702	112.8
Total Current	**16,164,148**	**157.2**
Other Long Term	2,992,218	29.1
Deferred Credits	0	0.0
Net Worth	(8,873,829)	(86.3)
Total Liab & Net Worth	**10,282,537**	**100.0**
Net Sales	12,601,148	100.0
Gross Profit	6,426,585	51.0
Net Profit After Tax	(1,234,913)	(9.8)
Working Capital	(10,426,492)	--

RATIOS	UQ	MED	LQ
SOLVENCY			
Quick Ratio (times)	1.5	0.8	0.4
Current Ratio (times)	2.2	1.6	0.9
Curr Liab To Nw (%)	23.8	63.1	87.0
Curr Liab To Inv (%)	90.1	212.2	301.5
Total Liab To Nw (%)	82.5	141.9	243.2
Fixed Assets To Nw (%)	5.4	30.4	45.8
EFFICIENCY			
Coll Period (days)	21.0	33.2	51.7
Sales To Inv (times)	11.5	7.5	5.4
Assets To Sales (%)	29.9	81.6	141.5
Sales To Nwc (times)	12.7	5.7	5.6
Acct Pay To Sales (%)	8.4	10.4	16.6
PROFITABILITY			
Return On Sales (%)	9.8	(4.6)	(30.5)
Return On Assets (%)	9.2	(5.3)	(21.3)
Return On Nw (%)	40.7	12.5	(28.6)

Page 14

SIC 2869 IND ORG CHEM, NEC
(NO BREAKDOWN)
2020 (31 Establishments)

	$	%
Cash	12,986,480	13.0
Accounts Receivable	10,489,080	10.5
Notes Receivable	0	0.0
Inventory	10,189,392	10.2
Other Current	13,386,064	13.4
Total Current	**47,051,016**	**47.1**
Fixed Assets	39,758,608	39.8
Other Non-current	13,086,376	13.1
Total Assets	**99,896,000**	**100.0**
Accounts Payable	64,532,816	64.6
Bank Loans	0	0.0
Notes Payable	499,480	0.5
Other Current	275,812,856	276.1
Total Current	**340,845,152**	**341.2**
Other Long Term	26,971,920	27.0
Deferred Credits	0	0.0
Net Worth	(267,921,072)	(268.2)
Total Liab & Net Worth	**99,896,000**	**100.0**
Net Sales	147,775,148	100.0
Gross Profit	25,712,876	17.4
Net Profit After Tax	(295,550)	(0.2)
Working Capital	(293,794,136)	—

RATIOS	UQ	MED	LQ
SOLVENCY			
Quick Ratio (times)	1.9	1.0	0.5
Current Ratio (times)	3.1	1.9	1.2
Curr Liab To Nw (%)	14.9	24.9	45.2
Curr Liab To Inv (%)	90.6	149.8	407.1
Total Liab To Nw (%)	17.9	35.9	129.4
Fixed Assets To Nw (%)	60.8	82.2	96.8
EFFICIENCY			
Coll Period (days)	9.1	16.1	38.3
Sales To Inv (times)	19.3	13.2	7.3
Assets To Sales (%)	50.8	67.6	127.6
Sales To Nwc (times)	9.6	6.2	3.0
Acct Pay To Sales (%)	2.4	5.0	9.4
PROFITABILITY			
Return On Sales (%)	5.9	(2.5)	(13.6)
Return On Assets (%)	6.6	(5.7)	(26.8)
Return On Nw (%)	14.4	2.8	(17.1)

SIC 30 RUBBER & PLASTICS
(NO BREAKDOWN)
2020 (54 Establishments)

	$	%
Cash	4,149,255	13.3
Accounts Receivable	6,333,073	20.3
Notes Receivable	0	0.0
Inventory	5,740,323	18.4
Other Current	1,466,278	4.7
Total Current	**17,688,929**	**56.7**
Fixed Assets	7,674,562	24.6
Other Non-current	5,833,915	18.7
Total Assets	**31,197,406**	**100.0**
Accounts Payable	3,712,491	11.9
Bank Loans	0	0.0
Notes Payable	436,764	1.4
Other Current	49,666,270	159.2
Total Current	**53,815,525**	**172.5**
Other Long Term	15,879,480	50.9
Deferred Credits	31,197	0.1
Net Worth	(38,528,796)	(123.5)
Total Liab & Net Worth	**31,197,406**	**100.0**
Net Sales	44,440,749	100.0
Gross Profit	13,154,462	29.6
Net Profit After Tax	1,333,222	3.0
Working Capital	(36,126,596)	—

RATIOS	UQ	MED	LQ
SOLVENCY			
Quick Ratio (times)	1.7	1.1	0.7
Current Ratio (times)	2.9	2.1	1.2
Curr Liab To Nw (%)	31.9	51.8	116.3
Curr Liab To Inv (%)	90.5	151.8	239.7
Total Liab To Nw (%)	43.4	115.8	257.9
Fixed Assets To Nw (%)	22.6	49.1	75.2
EFFICIENCY			
Coll Period (days)	32.1	47.8	63.2
Sales To Inv (times)	13.0	7.7	5.7
Assets To Sales (%)	56.9	70.2	101.8
Sales To Nwc (times)	8.6	5.4	3.4
Acct Pay To Sales (%)	4.1	7.0	9.9
PROFITABILITY			
Return On Sales (%)	8.9	4.6	1.2
Return On Assets (%)	14.4	6.8	2.5
Return On Nw (%)	42.7	15.4	4.0

SIC 3089 PLSTCS PRODUCTS,NEC
(NO BREAKDOWN)
2020 (33 Establishments)

	$	%
Cash	2,491,710	13.5
Accounts Receivable	4,079,021	22.1
Notes Receivable	0	0.0
Inventory	3,562,222	19.3
Other Current	572,170	3.1
Total Current	**10,705,123**	**58.0**
Fixed Assets	4,798,848	26.0
Other Non-current	2,953,137	16.0
Total Assets	**18,457,108**	**100.0**
Accounts Payable	2,436,338	13.2
Bank Loans	0	0.0
Notes Payable	387,599	2.1
Other Current	3,377,651	18.3
Total Current	**6,201,588**	**33.6**
Other Long Term	3,063,880	16.6
Deferred Credits	18,457	0.1
Net Worth	9,173,183	49.7
Total Liab & Net Worth	**18,457,108**	**100.0**
Net Sales	27,713,375	100.0
Gross Profit	7,870,599	28.4
Net Profit After Tax	304,847	1.1
Working Capital	4,503,535	—

RATIOS	UQ	MED	LQ
SOLVENCY			
Quick Ratio (times)	1.7	1.1	0.6
Current Ratio (times)	3.5	1.8	1.0
Curr Liab To Nw (%)	22.7	49.6	126.0
Curr Liab To Inv (%)	51.7	185.1	281.0
Total Liab To Nw (%)	36.5	112.4	213.1
Fixed Assets To Nw (%)	18.5	41.1	92.7
EFFICIENCY			
Coll Period (days)	29.9	45.1	63.5
Sales To Inv (times)	14.2	7.6	6.0
Assets To Sales (%)	43.0	66.6	106.9
Sales To Nwc (times)	9.1	5.2	3.4
Acct Pay To Sales (%)	3.7	7.0	9.7
PROFITABILITY			
Return On Sales (%)	8.1	4.0	0.9
Return On Assets (%)	12.9	5.2	1.8
Return On Nw (%)	36.2	15.1	4.0

SIC 32 STONE CLAY,GLASS PDT
(NO BREAKDOWN)
2020 (31 Establishments)

	$	%
Cash	5,180,145	12.3
Accounts Receivable	6,738,400	16.0
Notes Receivable	0	0.0
Inventory	6,401,480	15.2
Other Current	3,958,810	9.4
Total Current	**22,278,835**	**52.9**
Fixed Assets	13,561,030	32.2
Other Non-current	6,275,135	14.9
Total Assets	**42,115,000**	**100.0**
Accounts Payable	3,706,120	8.8
Bank Loans	0	0.0
Notes Payable	6,485,710	15.4
Other Current	20,215,200	48.0
Total Current	**30,407,030**	**72.2**
Other Long Term	9,812,795	23.3
Deferred Credits	42,115	0.1
Net Worth	1,853,060	4.4
Total Liab & Net Worth	**42,115,000**	**100.0**
Net Sales	55,269,029	100.0
Gross Profit	12,932,953	23.4
Net Profit After Tax	2,100,223	3.8
Working Capital	(8,128,195)	—

RATIOS	UQ	MED	LQ
SOLVENCY			
Quick Ratio (times)	1.7	1.1	0.7
Current Ratio (times)	5.0	1.7	1.6
Curr Liab To Nw (%)	17.2	30.9	80.4
Curr Liab To Inv (%)	69.0	148.7	319.2
Total Liab To Nw (%)	20.7	87.4	135.4
Fixed Assets To Nw (%)	21.2	63.6	128.6
EFFICIENCY			
Coll Period (days)	36.1	46.0	57.3
Sales To Inv (times)	16.3	6.7	4.5
Assets To Sales (%)	59.0	76.2	116.7
Sales To Nwc (times)	9.8	5.6	2.5
Acct Pay To Sales (%)	3.7	5.8	9.2
PROFITABILITY			
Return On Sales (%)	6.6	3.0	(0.2)
Return On Assets (%)	8.3	3.7	(2.2)
Return On Nw (%)	11.4	7.4	2.9

Page 15

SIC 33 PRIMARY METAL INDS
(NO BREAKDOWN)
2020 (59 Establishments)

	$	%
Cash	19,559,283	11.3
Accounts Receivable	29,079,288	16.8
Notes Receivable	0	0.0
Inventory	36,695,292	21.2
Other Current	11,770,188	6.8
Total Current	**97,104,051**	**56.1**
Fixed Assets	55,389,120	32.0
Other Non-current	20,597,829	11.9
Total Assets	**173,091,000**	**100.0**
Accounts Payable	14,366,553	8.3
Bank Loans	0	0.0
Notes Payable	692,364	0.4
Other Current	23,021,103	13.3
Total Current	**38,080,020**	**22.0**
Other Long Term	43,099,659	24.9
Deferred Credits	173,091	0.1
Net Worth	91,738,230	53.0
Total Liab & Net Worth	**173,091,000**	**100.0**
Net Sales	228,051,383	100.0
Gross Profit	51,767,664	22.7
Net Profit After Tax	5,929,336	2.6
Working Capital	59,024,031	---

RATIOS | UQ | MED | LQ

SOLVENCY
Quick Ratio (times)	2.3	1.0	0.7
Current Ratio (times)	4.6	2.7	1.9
Curr Liab To Nw (%)	19.8	38.7	73.6
Curr Liab To Inv (%)	58.6	96.9	122.6
Total Liab To Nw (%)	36.6	98.7	153.7
Fixed Assets To Nw (%)	35.0	64.4	125.3

EFFICIENCY
Coll Period (days)	28.8	43.4	58.8
Sales To Inv (times)	9.2	6.3	4.3
Assets To Sales (%)	61.6	75.9	116.6
Sales To Nwc (times)	6.9	4.3	2.8
Acct Pay To Sales (%)	3.7	6.2	11.1

PROFITABILITY
Return On Sales (%)	7.4	3.4	(3.1)
Return On Assets (%)	11.5	4.3	(2.6)
Return On Nw (%)	19.8	7.5	(12.0)

SIC 34 FABRICATED METAL PDT
(NO BREAKDOWN)
2020 (148 Establishments)

	$	%
Cash	1,982,255	15.8
Accounts Receivable	2,885,560	23.0
Notes Receivable	37,638	0.3
Inventory	1,969,709	15.7
Other Current	1,053,856	8.4
Total Current	**7,929,018**	**63.2**
Fixed Assets	2,546,821	20.3
Other Non-current	2,070,076	16.5
Total Assets	**12,545,915**	**100.0**
Accounts Payable	1,292,229	10.3
Bank Loans	25,092	0.2
Notes Payable	37,638	0.3
Other Current	2,408,816	19.2
Total Current	**3,763,775**	**30.0**
Other Long Term	2,433,907	19.4
Deferred Credits	50,184	0.4
Net Worth	6,298,049	50.2
Total Liab & Net Worth	**12,545,915**	**100.0**
Net Sales	19,154,069	100.0
Gross Profit	5,841,991	30.5
Net Profit After Tax	919,395	4.8
Working Capital	4,165,243	---

RATIOS | UQ | MED | LQ

SOLVENCY
Quick Ratio (times)	2.6	1.4	0.9
Current Ratio (times)	4.4	2.5	1.5
Curr Liab To Nw (%)	15.9	39.5	76.8
Curr Liab To Inv (%)	60.5	155.3	388.2
Total Liab To Nw (%)	32.2	75.8	147.8
Fixed Assets To Nw (%)	16.0	32.8	56.7

EFFICIENCY
Coll Period (days)	37.4	50.0	62.8
Sales To Inv (times)	22.3	9.0	5.7
Assets To Sales (%)	43.2	65.5	109.1
Sales To Nwc (times)	8.7	4.4	2.7
Acct Pay To Sales (%)	2.7	5.0	8.2

PROFITABILITY
Return On Sales (%)	9.6	4.3	1.6
Return On Assets (%)	13.0	5.9	1.9
Return On Nw (%)	27.9	11.2	4.2

SIC 3441 FBRCTED STRCTRL MTL
(NO BREAKDOWN)
2020 (28 Establishments)

	$	%
Cash	1,420,535	20.8
Accounts Receivable	1,768,839	25.9
Notes Receivable	0	0.0
Inventory	464,406	6.8
Other Current	819,540	12.0
Total Current	**4,473,320**	**65.5**
Fixed Assets	1,741,521	25.5
Other Non-current	614,655	9.0
Total Assets	**6,829,496**	**100.0**
Accounts Payable	785,392	11.5
Bank Loans	0	0.0
Notes Payable	13,659	0.2
Other Current	1,782,498	26.1
Total Current	**2,581,549**	**37.8**
Other Long Term	969,789	14.2
Deferred Credits	13,659	0.2
Net Worth	3,264,499	47.8
Total Liab & Net Worth	**6,829,496**	**100.0**
Net Sales	12,152,128	100.0
Gross Profit	3,281,075	27.0
Net Profit After Tax	619,759	5.1
Working Capital	1,891,771	---

RATIOS | UQ | MED | LQ

SOLVENCY
Quick Ratio (times)	2.6	1.5	0.9
Current Ratio (times)	3.5	2.1	1.6
Curr Liab To Nw (%)	29.9	53.8	79.5
Curr Liab To Inv (%)	155.3	383.4	753.9
Total Liab To Nw (%)	38.3	77.7	104.7
Fixed Assets To Nw (%)	14.9	34.0	77.9

EFFICIENCY
Coll Period (days)	32.1	48.9	65.3
Sales To Inv (times)	89.0	30.0	11.7
Assets To Sales (%)	44.7	56.2	81.4
Sales To Nwc (times)	7.5	5.1	3.8
Acct Pay To Sales (%)	2.8	5.0	7.2

PROFITABILITY
Return On Sales (%)	12.2	3.6	1.7
Return On Assets (%)	15.1	6.9	3.9
Return On Nw (%)	31.6	13.3	6.0

SIC 3443 FBRCT PLT WK BLR SH
(NO BREAKDOWN)
2020 (12 Establishments)

	$	%
Cash	29,334,429	17.2
Accounts Receivable	22,683,018	13.3
Notes Receivable	0	0.0
Inventory	33,768,704	19.8
Other Current	11,938,431	7.0
Total Current	**97,724,582**	**57.3**
Fixed Assets	33,768,704	19.8
Other Non-current	39,055,722	22.9
Total Assets	**170,549,008**	**100.0**
Accounts Payable	11,426,784	6.7
Bank Loans	0	0.0
Notes Payable	0	0.0
Other Current	35,303,644	20.7
Total Current	**46,730,428**	**27.4**
Other Long Term	35,474,194	20.8
Deferred Credits	0	0.0
Net Worth	88,344,386	51.8
Total Liab & Net Worth	**170,549,008**	**100.0**
Net Sales	173,146,201	100.0
Gross Profit	48,480,936	28.0
Net Profit After Tax	7,098,994	4.1
Working Capital	50,994,154	---

RATIOS | UQ | MED | LQ

SOLVENCY
Quick Ratio (times)	4.0	1.5	0.6
Current Ratio (times)	6.0	2.7	1.3
Curr Liab To Nw (%)	16.3	31.8	87.5
Curr Liab To Inv (%)	85.4	154.0	265.5
Total Liab To Nw (%)	20.5	101.3	152.4
Fixed Assets To Nw (%)	30.1	37.9	63.7

EFFICIENCY
Coll Period (days)	36.0	52.8	62.3
Sales To Inv (times)	23.5	9.5	2.9
Assets To Sales (%)	67.5	98.5	121.2
Sales To Nwc (times)	8.3	4.4	2.3
Acct Pay To Sales (%)	2.8	5.3	9.5

PROFITABILITY
Return On Sales (%)	8.6	5.7	3.8
Return On Assets (%)	10.0	5.6	2.5
Return On Nw (%)	15.9	12.6	9.3

	SIC 3444 SHEET METALWORK (NO BREAKDOWN) 2020 (11 Establishments)		SIC 3469 METAL STAMPINGS,NEC (NO BREAKDOWN) 2020 (10 Establishments)		SIC 35 MACHINERY EX ELECTRL (NO BREAKDOWN) 2020 (247 Establishments)		SIC 3559 SPEC IND MCHNRY,NEC (NO BREAKDOWN) 2020 (14 Establishments)	
	$	%	$	%	$	%	$	%
Cash	698,794	9.0	929,634	14.6	4,078,920	18.3	6,071,260	21.2
Accounts Receivable	2,764,120	35.6	1,547,268	24.3	4,145,788	18.6	5,212,119	18.2
Notes Receivable	0	0.0	0	0.0	0	0.0	0	0.0
Inventory	1,164,657	15.0	993,308	15.6	3,700,004	16.6	4,839,825	16.9
Other Current	970,549	12.5	267,429	4.2	1,939,159	8.7	3,236,095	11.3
Total Current	**5,598,120**	**72.1**	**3,737,639**	**58.7**	**13,863,871**	**62.2**	**19,359,299**	**67.6**
Fixed Assets	1,560,641	20.1	1,814,697	28.5	3,989,764	17.9	5,212,119	18.2
Other Non-current	605,622	7.8	815,021	12.8	4,435,547	19.9	4,066,599	14.2
Total Assets	**7,764,383**	**100.0**	**6,367,357**	**100.0**	**22,289,182**	**100.0**	**28,638,017**	**100.0**
Accounts Payable	854,082	11.0	923,267	14.5	6,508,441	29.2	2,548,784	8.9
Bank Loans	0	0.0	0	0.0	0	0.0	0	0.0
Notes Payable	62,115	0.8	108,245	1.7	846,989	3.8	0	0.0
Other Current	1,708,164	22.0	1,572,737	24.7	13,418,088	60.2	5,412,585	18.9
Total Current	**2,624,361**	**33.8**	**2,604,249**	**40.9**	**20,773,518**	**93.2**	**7,961,369**	**27.8**
Other Long Term	621,151	8.0	636,736	10.0	5,416,271	24.3	3,952,046	13.8
Deferred Credits	54,351	0.7	0	0.0	156,024	0.7	28,638	0.1
Net Worth	4,464,520	57.5	3,126,372	49.1	(4,056,631)	(18.2)	16,695,964	58.3
Total Liab & Net Worth	**7,764,383**	**100.0**	**6,367,357**	**100.0**	**22,289,182**	**100.0**	**28,638,017**	**100.0**
Net Sales	18,486,626	100.0	10,171,497	100.0	26,377,730	100.0	24,687,946	100.0
Gross Profit	6,063,613	32.8	2,380,130	23.4	9,284,961	35.2	10,319,561	41.8
Net Profit After Tax	1,552,877	8.4	264,459	2.6	1,055,109	4.0	1,086,270	4.4
Working Capital	2,973,759	---	1,133,390	---	(6,909,647)	---	11,397,930	---

RATIOS	UQ	MED	LQ	UQ	MED	LQ	UQ	MED	LQ	UQ	MED	LQ
SOLVENCY												
Quick Ratio (times)	1.6	1.5	1.3	3.2	0.9	0.6	2.5	1.4	0.8	2.8	1.5	1.4
Current Ratio (times)	3.8	2.5	1.6	6.0	1.7	1.0	3.8	2.4	1.5	4.4	3.5	2.3
Curr Liab To Nw (%)	40.6	54.7	58.1	13.3	28.7	51.4	20.6	38.5	74.0	20.5	31.6	54.1
Curr Liab To Inv (%)	88.8	418.6	869.8	111.5	196.2	948.5	83.2	144.5	264.3	86.1	102.2	302.4
Total Liab To Nw (%)	52.3	59.0	90.0	26.3	57.9	79.9	33.7	73.5	155.7	31.9	46.9	116.2
Fixed Assets To Nw (%)	14.3	38.7	68.0	11.7	33.0	59.5	12.2	27.8	50.4	6.1	13.9	23.1
EFFICIENCY												
Coll Period (days)	40.2	55.0	67.5	24.8	47.9	59.9	41.8	55.5	69.7	40.5	62.8	69.9
Sales To Inv (times)	58.4	28.6	18.0	11.4	10.2	6.3	12.0	7.2	4.4	12.4	6.4	4.3
Assets To Sales (%)	37.9	42.0	55.5	34.5	62.6	83.8	57.0	84.5	132.8	59.3	116.0	159.8
Sales To Nwc (times)	11.6	6.1	2.6	12.3	7.9	5.1	5.7	3.7	2.5	4.1	2.5	1.3
Acct Pay To Sales (%)	3.4	5.4	6.7	3.4	5.7	6.4	3.2	6.9	11.1	4.5	6.8	15.5
PROFITABILITY												
Return On Sales (%)	11.1	9.6	2.0	8.0	3.5	0.5	9.8	5.2	(0.1)	15.0	5.0	1.2
Return On Assets (%)	24.6	18.5	5.9	13.1	5.9	1.7	12.5	5.3	(0.1)	14.2	5.0	3.1
Return On Nw (%)	41.5	31.1	8.7	39.4	19.0	2.2	26.3	11.4	0.8	42.1	8.2	5.0

SIC 3577
CMPTR PRPRL EQP,NEC
(NO BREAKDOWN)
2020 (22 Establishments)

	$	%
Cash	26,192,286	27.1
Accounts Receivable	15,077,478	15.6
Notes Receivable	193,301	0.2
Inventory	11,211,458	11.6
Other Current	10,148,302	10.5
Total Current	**62,822,825**	**65.0**
Fixed Assets	5,219,127	5.4
Other Non-current	28,608,548	29.6
Total Assets	**96,650,500**	**100.0**
Accounts Payable	49,195,105	50.9
Bank Loans	0	0.0
Notes Payable	193,301	0.2
Other Current	143,525,992	148.5
Total Current	**192,914,398**	**199.6**
Other Long Term	36,533,889	37.8
Deferred Credits	6,572,234	6.8
Net Worth	(139,370,021)	(144.2)
Total Liab & Net Worth	**96,650,500**	**100.0**
Net Sales	92,311,843	100.0
Gross Profit	47,171,352	51.1
Net Profit After Tax	5,446,399	5.9
Working Capital	(130,091,573)	—

RATIOS	UQ	MED	LQ
SOLVENCY			
Quick Ratio (times)	2.2	1.5	1.0
Current Ratio (times)	3.3	2.4	1.8
Curr Liab To Nw (%)	29.5	38.6	76.3
Curr Liab To Inv (%)	105.0	158.0	276.2
Total Liab To Nw (%)	39.1	91.7	132.8
Fixed Assets To Nw (%)	4.1	9.1	16.8
EFFICIENCY			
Coll Period (days)	41.6	58.2	72.6
Sales To Inv (times)	11.6	9.4	4.9
Assets To Sales (%)	75.1	104.7	180.5
Sales To Nwc (times)	3.5	2.9	1.8
Acct Pay To Sales (%)	3.8	5.7	10.5
PROFITABILITY			
Return On Sales (%)	15.0	0.6	(1.5)
Return On Assets (%)	11.5	0.7	(1.5)
Return On Nw (%)	24.7	2.0	(3.1)

SIC 3589
SVC IND MCHNRY,NEC
(NO BREAKDOWN)
2020 (12 Establishments)

	$	%
Cash	1,235,275	19.5
Accounts Receivable	1,659,703	26.2
Notes Receivable	0	0.0
Inventory	804,513	12.7
Other Current	842,521	13.3
Total Current	**4,542,012**	**71.7**
Fixed Assets	893,199	14.1
Other Non-current	899,534	14.2
Total Assets	**6,334,745**	**100.0**
Accounts Payable	829,852	13.1
Bank Loans	0	0.0
Notes Payable	0	0.0
Other Current	16,875,760	266.4
Total Current	**17,705,612**	**279.5**
Other Long Term	2,546,568	40.2
Deferred Credits	0	0.0
Net Worth	(13,917,435)	(219.7)
Total Liab & Net Worth	**6,334,745**	**100.0**
Net Sales	9,049,636	100.0
Gross Profit	3,004,479	33.2
Net Profit After Tax	552,028	6.1
Working Capital	(13,163,600)	—

RATIOS	UQ	MED	LQ
SOLVENCY			
Quick Ratio (times)	2.6	1.7	0.9
Current Ratio (times)	4.0	2.6	1.1
Curr Liab To Nw (%)	20.6	44.3	76.1
Curr Liab To Inv (%)	74.9	116.1	163.8
Total Liab To Nw (%)	29.0	123.6	156.9
Fixed Assets To Nw (%)	15.9	26.8	48.0
EFFICIENCY			
Coll Period (days)	54.0	65.0	68.9
Sales To Inv (times)	10.8	6.4	3.4
Assets To Sales (%)	41.1	70.0	119.6
Sales To Nwc (times)	5.2	3.3	1.7
Acct Pay To Sales (%)	2.7	8.3	9.4
PROFITABILITY			
Return On Sales (%)	12.2	3.7	(1.6)
Return On Assets (%)	8.6	7.0	(3.1)
Return On Nw (%)	19.7	12.7	(2.3)

SIC 3599
IND MACHINERY,NEC
(NO BREAKDOWN)
2020 (54 Establishments)

	$	%
Cash	610,180	19.6
Accounts Receivable	744,046	23.9
Notes Receivable	0	0.0
Inventory	470,087	15.1
Other Current	152,545	4.9
Total Current	**1,976,858**	**63.5**
Fixed Assets	806,309	25.9
Other Non-current	329,995	10.6
Total Assets	**3,113,162**	**100.0**
Accounts Payable	252,166	8.1
Bank Loans	0	0.0
Notes Payable	21,792	0.7
Other Current	1,354,226	43.5
Total Current	**1,628,184**	**52.3**
Other Long Term	725,367	23.3
Deferred Credits	3,113	0.1
Net Worth	756,498	24.3
Total Liab & Net Worth	**3,113,162**	**100.0**
Net Sales	5,021,229	100.0
Gross Profit	2,028,577	40.4
Net Profit After Tax	411,741	8.2
Working Capital	348,674	—

RATIOS	UQ	MED	LQ
SOLVENCY			
Quick Ratio (times)	6.1	2.5	0.9
Current Ratio (times)	8.2	3.3	2.0
Curr Liab To Nw (%)	10.3	25.8	58.8
Curr Liab To Inv (%)	54.4	158.9	295.4
Total Liab To Nw (%)	16.1	55.7	132.9
Fixed Assets To Nw (%)	14.2	41.1	84.2
EFFICIENCY			
Coll Period (days)	39.3	50.4	65.5
Sales To Inv (times)	37.4	12.1	7.6
Assets To Sales (%)	48.4	62.0	76.6
Sales To Nwc (times)	6.5	3.9	2.6
Acct Pay To Sales (%)	1.9	3.3	7.9
PROFITABILITY			
Return On Sales (%)	15.2	8.6	4.0
Return On Assets (%)	25.2	14.8	5.4
Return On Nw (%)	37.5	21.9	9.6

SIC 36
ELECTRICAL EQUIPMENT
(NO BREAKDOWN)
2020 (304 Establishments)

	$	%
Cash	21,254,823	19.7
Accounts Receivable	17,802,263	16.5
Notes Receivable	107,893	0.1
Inventory	17,262,800	16.0
Other Current	11,220,819	10.4
Total Current	**67,648,598**	**62.7**
Fixed Assets	15,320,735	14.2
Other Non-current	24,923,167	23.1
Total Assets	**107,892,500**	**100.0**
Accounts Payable	19,960,113	18.5
Bank Loans	0	0.0
Notes Payable	4,963,055	4.6
Other Current	65,922,317	61.1
Total Current	**90,845,485**	**84.2**
Other Long Term	48,335,840	44.8
Deferred Credits	323,678	0.3
Net Worth	(31,612,503)	(29.3)
Total Liab & Net Worth	**107,892,500**	**100.0**
Net Sales	97,288,097	100.0
Gross Profit	35,412,867	36.4
Net Profit After Tax	(97,288)	(0.1)
Working Capital	(23,196,887)	—

RATIOS	UQ	MED	LQ
SOLVENCY			
Quick Ratio (times)	2.2	1.3	0.8
Current Ratio (times)	4.2	2.2	1.5
Curr Liab To Nw (%)	17.8	37.5	84.5
Curr Liab To Inv (%)	95.2	164.0	336.4
Total Liab To Nw (%)	33.0	81.5	157.2
Fixed Assets To Nw (%)	8.5	19.9	43.6
EFFICIENCY			
Coll Period (days)	42.0	55.5	74.1
Sales To Inv (times)	10.4	6.7	4.4
Assets To Sales (%)	73.3	110.9	168.4
Sales To Nwc (times)	5.1	3.0	1.5
Acct Pay To Sales (%)	4.8	8.0	13.6
PROFITABILITY			
Return On Sales (%)	9.1	1.9	(10.0)
Return On Assets (%)	8.7	1.9	(7.5)
Return On Nw (%)	15.2	6.1	(9.1)

SIC 3621 MOTORS,GENERATORS
(NO BREAKDOWN)
2020 (12 Establishments)

	$	%
Cash	93,998,007	24.4
Accounts Receivable	56,629,947	14.7
Notes Receivable	0	0.0
Inventory	60,867,562	15.8
Other Current	34,286,158	8.9
Total Current	**245,781,674**	**63.8**
Fixed Assets	59,326,611	15.4
Other Non-current	80,129,448	20.8
Total Assets	**385,237,733**	**100.0**
Accounts Payable	147,931,289	38.4
Bank Loans	0	0.0
Notes Payable	0	0.0
Other Current	130,980,830	34.0
Total Current	**278,912,119**	**72.4**
Other Long Term	344,402,533	89.4
Deferred Credits	0	0.0
Net Worth	(238,076,919)	(61.8)
Total Liab & Net Worth	**385,237,733**	**100.0**
Net Sales	402,127,070	100.0
Gross Profit	119,431,740	29.7
Net Profit After Tax	20,106,354	5.0
Working Capital	(33,130,445)	---

RATIOS
	UQ	MED	LQ
SOLVENCY			
Quick Ratio (times)	2.6	1.3	0.4
Current Ratio (times)	4.1	2.5	1.2
Curr Liab To Nw (%)	22.4	23.5	48.1
Curr Liab To Inv (%)	72.3	91.3	98.4
Total Liab To Nw (%)	22.4	86.1	156.6
Fixed Assets To Nw (%)	8.1	25.2	30.7
EFFICIENCY			
Coll Period (days)	46.4	51.8	59.1
Sales To Inv (times)	9.2	4.8	4.3
Assets To Sales (%)	72.9	95.8	136.8
Sales To Nwc (times)	5.0	3.4	3.2
Acct Pay To Sales (%)	6.3	9.7	12.8
PROFITABILITY			
Return On Sales (%)	7.5	5.6	(15.0)
Return On Assets (%)	8.8	5.6	(28.8)
Return On Nw (%)	20.7	13.9	11.1

SIC 3651 HSHLD AUDIO,VDEO EQ
(NO BREAKDOWN)
2020 (11 Establishments)

	$	%
Cash	11,779,996	25.0
Accounts Receivable	8,811,437	18.7
Notes Receivable	0	0.0
Inventory	6,361,198	13.5
Other Current	6,172,717	13.1
Total Current	**33,125,348**	**70.3**
Fixed Assets	3,769,599	8.0
Other Non-current	10,225,036	21.7
Total Assets	**47,119,983**	**100.0**
Accounts Payable	41,889,665	88.9
Bank Loans	0	0.0
Notes Payable	282,720	0.6
Other Current	100,506,924	213.3
Total Current	**142,679,309**	**302.8**
Other Long Term	177,500,975	376.7
Deferred Credits	376,960	0.8
Net Worth	(273,437,261)	(580.3)
Total Liab & Net Worth	**47,119,983**	**100.0**
Net Sales	43,791,806	100.0
Gross Profit	17,954,640	41.0
Net Profit After Tax	(218,959)	(0.5)
Working Capital	(109,553,961)	---

RATIOS
	UQ	MED	LQ
SOLVENCY			
Quick Ratio (times)	2.4	1.6	1.2
Current Ratio (times)	4.0	2.6	1.6
Curr Liab To Nw (%)	13.3	36.9	143.3
Curr Liab To Inv (%)	100.1	183.1	688.7
Total Liab To Nw (%)	28.4	79.9	171.1
Fixed Assets To Nw (%)	6.4	17.1	27.8
EFFICIENCY			
Coll Period (days)	32.7	61.0	70.1
Sales To Inv (times)	22.4	5.7	5.3
Assets To Sales (%)	67.7	107.6	170.2
Sales To Nwc (times)	4.6	2.3	1.5
Acct Pay To Sales (%)	5.5	6.6	16.8
PROFITABILITY			
Return On Sales (%)	6.6	0.5	(11.8)
Return On Assets (%)	4.5	0.6	(3.2)
Return On Nw (%)	7.9	2.1	(1.7)

SIC 3661 TLPHNE,TLGPH APPTUS
(NO BREAKDOWN)
2020 (18 Establishments)

	$	%
Cash	87,039,150	22.0
Accounts Receivable	68,048,790	17.2
Notes Receivable	0	0.0
Inventory	58,157,978	14.7
Other Current	42,728,310	10.8
Total Current	**255,974,228**	**64.7**
Fixed Assets	38,771,985	9.8
Other Non-current	100,886,287	25.5
Total Assets	**395,632,500**	**100.0**
Accounts Payable	51,432,225	13.0
Bank Loans	0	0.0
Notes Payable	0	0.0
Other Current	60,927,405	15.4
Total Current	**112,359,630**	**28.4**
Other Long Term	79,126,500	20.0
Deferred Credits	5,538,855	1.4
Net Worth	198,607,515	50.2
Total Liab & Net Worth	**395,632,500**	**100.0**
Net Sales	352,613,636	100.0
Gross Profit	138,929,773	39.4
Net Profit After Tax	(20,451,591)	(5.8)
Working Capital	143,614,598	---

RATIOS
	UQ	MED	LQ
SOLVENCY			
Quick Ratio (times)	2.1	1.6	1.0
Current Ratio (times)	4.4	2.3	1.4
Curr Liab To Nw (%)	23.9	49.0	87.2
Curr Liab To Inv (%)	89.0	158.2	429.1
Total Liab To Nw (%)	43.3	103.4	331.8
Fixed Assets To Nw (%)	5.0	15.3	31.8
EFFICIENCY			
Coll Period (days)	39.4	63.9	74.8
Sales To Inv (times)	12.8	6.5	4.4
Assets To Sales (%)	95.7	112.2	183.7
Sales To Nwc (times)	6.6	2.5	1.3
Acct Pay To Sales (%)	7.2	8.5	11.2
PROFITABILITY			
Return On Sales (%)	2.6	(3.2)	(10.0)
Return On Assets (%)	2.7	(0.7)	(10.0)
Return On Nw (%)	6.1	(11.7)	(27.6)

SIC 3663 RDIO,TV CMMNCTNS EQ
(NO BREAKDOWN)
2020 (33 Establishments)

	$	%
Cash	28,285,544	19.6
Accounts Receivable	19,193,762	13.3
Notes Receivable	0	0.0
Inventory	17,606,308	12.2
Other Current	15,441,598	10.7
Total Current	**80,527,212**	**55.8**
Fixed Assets	22,945,926	15.9
Other Non-current	40,840,862	28.3
Total Assets	**144,314,000**	**100.0**
Accounts Payable	17,029,052	11.8
Bank Loans	0	0.0
Notes Payable	4,329,420	3.0
Other Current	76,053,478	52.7
Total Current	**97,411,950**	**67.5**
Other Long Term	80,382,898	55.7
Deferred Credits	1,010,198	0.7
Net Worth	(34,491,046)	(23.9)
Total Liab & Net Worth	**144,314,000**	**100.0**
Net Sales	109,246,026	100.0
Gross Profit	50,362,418	46.1
Net Profit After Tax	(8,739,682)	(8.0)
Working Capital	(16,884,738)	---

RATIOS
	UQ	MED	LQ
SOLVENCY			
Quick Ratio (times)	2.2	1.2	0.7
Current Ratio (times)	3.3	1.9	1.3
Curr Liab To Nw (%)	17.7	38.0	99.1
Curr Liab To Inv (%)	144.5	209.2	999.9
Total Liab To Nw (%)	45.0	99.8	174.7
Fixed Assets To Nw (%)	7.8	21.4	77.0
EFFICIENCY			
Coll Period (days)	37.4	66.8	78.3
Sales To Inv (times)	17.6	9.0	4.4
Assets To Sales (%)	92.5	132.1	220.1
Sales To Nwc (times)	6.3	3.4	1.6
Acct Pay To Sales (%)	5.8	9.2	13.5
PROFITABILITY			
Return On Sales (%)	6.5	(3.2)	(28.9)
Return On Assets (%)	4.2	0.7	(15.3)
Return On Nw (%)	18.3	1.9	(11.2)

Page 19

SIC 3669 CMMNCTNS EQPMNT,NEC
(NO BREAKDOWN)
2020 (12 Establishments)

	$	%
Cash	4,199,781	12.3
Accounts Receivable	9,458,043	27.7
Notes Receivable	0	0.0
Inventory	6,009,442	17.6
Other Current	5,121,683	15.0
Total Current	**24,788,949**	**72.6**
Fixed Assets	2,390,119	7.0
Other Non-current	6,965,490	20.4
Total Assets	**34,144,558**	**100.0**
Accounts Payable	5,463,129	16.0
Bank Loans	0	0.0
Notes Payable	1,399,927	4.1
Other Current	23,252,444	68.1
Total Current	**30,115,500**	**88.2**
Other Long Term	3,107,155	9.1
Deferred Credits	0	0.0
Net Worth	921,903	2.7
Total Liab & Net Worth	**34,144,558**	**100.0**
Net Sales	35,753,464	100.0
Gross Profit	13,085,768	36.6
Net Profit After Tax	0	0.0
Working Capital	(5,326,551)	--

RATIOS
	UQ	MED	LQ
SOLVENCY			
Quick Ratio (times)	2.0	1.1	0.5
Current Ratio (times)	3.9	2.3	1.4
Curr Liab To Nw (%)	30.3	44.7	73.9
Curr Liab To Inv (%)	103.8	314.9	999.9
Total Liab To Nw (%)	46.2	75.7	92.7
Fixed Assets To Nw (%)	5.3	13.3	20.0
EFFICIENCY			
Coll Period (days)	49.9	70.1	86.9
Sales To Inv (times)	55.0	8.6	4.9
Assets To Sales (%)	38.2	95.5	159.4
Sales To Nwc (times)	6.0	3.3	1.5
Acct Pay To Sales (%)	6.2	8.3	11.4
PROFITABILITY			
Return On Sales (%)	6.3	1.0	(7.6)
Return On Assets (%)	5.2	2.2	(5.1)
Return On Nw (%)	12.1	6.5	(2.4)

SIC 3674 SMCNDCTRS,RLTD DVCS
(NO BREAKDOWN)
2020 (86 Establishments)

	$	%
Cash	85,760,928	21.4
Accounts Receivable	48,490,992	12.1
Notes Receivable	400,752	0.1
Inventory	49,292,496	12.3
Other Current	48,891,744	12.2
Total Current	**232,836,912**	**58.1**
Fixed Assets	64,120,320	16.0
Other Non-current	103,794,768	25.9
Total Assets	**400,752,000**	**100.0**
Accounts Payable	60,513,552	15.1
Bank Loans	0	0.0
Notes Payable	1,603,008	0.4
Other Current	308,579,040	77.0
Total Current	**370,695,600**	**92.5**
Other Long Term	168,716,592	42.1
Deferred Credits	1,202,256	0.3
Net Worth	(139,862,448)	(34.9)
Total Liab & Net Worth	**400,752,000**	**100.0**
Net Sales	271,144,790	100.0
Gross Profit	109,000,206	40.2
Net Profit After Tax	(5,422,896)	(2.0)
Working Capital	(137,858,688)	--

RATIOS
	UQ	MED	LQ
SOLVENCY			
Quick Ratio (times)	2.2	1.6	1.0
Current Ratio (times)	5.1	2.7	1.7
Curr Liab To Nw (%)	16.5	25.5	54.7
Curr Liab To Inv (%)	109.0	188.5	324.5
Total Liab To Nw (%)	33.5	68.2	125.3
Fixed Assets To Nw (%)	9.7	17.4	40.7
EFFICIENCY			
Coll Period (days)	44.2	54.4	66.1
Sales To Inv (times)	10.2	7.1	4.7
Assets To Sales (%)	97.5	147.8	219.6
Sales To Nwc (times)	3.1	1.9	1.3
Acct Pay To Sales (%)	4.2	7.0	13.0
PROFITABILITY			
Return On Sales (%)	7.6	0.9	(18.0)
Return On Assets (%)	6.8	0.7	(13.5)
Return On Nw (%)	11.7	1.6	(19.1)

SIC 3679 ELEC COMPONENTS,NEC
(NO BREAKDOWN)
2020 (23 Establishments)

	$	%
Cash	8,957,566	25.1
Accounts Receivable	6,423,752	18.0
Notes Receivable	0	0.0
Inventory	5,888,440	16.5
Other Current	4,924,877	13.8
Total Current	**26,194,635**	**73.4**
Fixed Assets	3,889,939	10.9
Other Non-current	5,602,939	15.7
Total Assets	**35,687,513**	**100.0**
Accounts Payable	5,638,627	15.8
Bank Loans	0	0.0
Notes Payable	214,125	0.6
Other Current	14,025,193	39.3
Total Current	**19,877,945**	**55.7**
Other Long Term	4,460,939	12.5
Deferred Credits	0	0.0
Net Worth	11,348,629	31.8
Total Liab & Net Worth	**35,687,513**	**100.0**
Net Sales	29,037,846	100.0
Gross Profit	10,482,662	36.1
Net Profit After Tax	1,422,854	4.9
Working Capital	6,316,690	--

RATIOS
	UQ	MED	LQ
SOLVENCY			
Quick Ratio (times)	3.6	1.6	0.8
Current Ratio (times)	5.2	2.7	1.4
Curr Liab To Nw (%)	14.5	47.3	196.4
Curr Liab To Inv (%)	79.1	139.8	364.3
Total Liab To Nw (%)	16.9	107.2	321.4
Fixed Assets To Nw (%)	8.1	18.0	30.4
EFFICIENCY			
Coll Period (days)	36.1	52.9	99.7
Sales To Inv (times)	8.6	5.3	3.9
Assets To Sales (%)	80.6	122.9	153.1
Sales To Nwc (times)	3.5	1.7	1.2
Acct Pay To Sales (%)	5.9	9.0	21.0
PROFITABILITY			
Return On Sales (%)	12.7	2.2	(14.4)
Return On Assets (%)	6.6	(0.1)	(4.9)
Return On Nw (%)	17.5	3.4	(5.4)

SIC 3699 ELEC EQPT,SPPLS,NEC
(NO BREAKDOWN)
2020 (24 Establishments)

	$	%
Cash	1,923,697	20.5
Accounts Receivable	1,492,038	15.9
Notes Receivable	0	0.0
Inventory	1,435,735	15.3
Other Current	581,802	6.2
Total Current	**5,433,272**	**57.9**
Fixed Assets	1,370,048	14.6
Other Non-current	2,580,569	27.5
Total Assets	**9,383,889**	**100.0**
Accounts Payable	1,398,199	14.9
Bank Loans	0	0.0
Notes Payable	3,237,442	34.5
Other Current	12,405,501	132.2
Total Current	**17,041,142**	**181.6**
Other Long Term	1,961,233	20.9
Deferred Credits	28,152	0.3
Net Worth	(9,646,638)	(102.8)
Total Liab & Net Worth	**9,383,889**	**100.0**
Net Sales	8,786,413	100.0
Gross Profit	3,207,041	36.5
Net Profit After Tax	386,602	4.4
Working Capital	(11,607,870)	--

RATIOS
	UQ	MED	LQ
SOLVENCY			
Quick Ratio (times)	2.6	1.0	0.4
Current Ratio (times)	3.8	1.8	0.7
Curr Liab To Nw (%)	8.1	32.3	100.9
Curr Liab To Inv (%)	71.5	120.7	274.2
Total Liab To Nw (%)	15.8	108.5	253.7
Fixed Assets To Nw (%)	8.9	25.4	42.2
EFFICIENCY			
Coll Period (days)	44.9	61.2	102.2
Sales To Inv (times)	7.7	5.4	3.5
Assets To Sales (%)	74.7	106.8	216.2
Sales To Nwc (times)	6.3	3.6	1.5
Acct Pay To Sales (%)	2.7	8.2	37.1
PROFITABILITY			
Return On Sales (%)	13.3	6.1	(43.0)
Return On Assets (%)	9.4	2.8	(82.2)
Return On Nw (%)	29.3	11.8	2.4

Page 20

	SIC 37 TRANSPORTATION EQPT (NO BREAKDOWN) 2020 (126 Establishments)					SIC 3711 MTR VHCL,CAR BODIES (NO BREAKDOWN) 2020 (18 Establishments)					SIC 3714 MTR VHCLE PRTS,ACCS (NO BREAKDOWN) 2020 (46 Establishments)					SIC 3728 AIRCRFT PRT.EQP.NEC (NO BREAKDOWN) 2020 (17 Establishments)	
	$	%				$	%				$	%				$	%
Cash	43,549,350	11.5				56,601,532	11.8				33,151,048	9.2				5,517,720	10.8
Accounts Receivable	58,696,950	15.5				44,130,008	9.2				60,897,033	16.9				9,911,460	19.4
Notes Receivable	757,380	0.2				0	0.0				1,081,012	0.3				0	0.0
Inventory	72,329,790	19.1				100,251,866	20.9				68,464,120	19.0				10,269,090	20.1
Other Current	29,159,130	7.7				47,008,052	9.8				22,340,924	6.2				4,138,290	8.1
Total Current	**204,492,600**	**54.0**				**247,991,458**	**51.7**				**185,934,137**	**51.6**				**29,836,560**	**58.4**
Fixed Assets	62,862,540	16.6				46,048,704	9.6				66,302,095	18.4				11,393,070	22.3
Other Non-current	111,334,860	29.4				185,633,838	38.7				108,101,243	30.0				9,860,370	19.3
Total Assets	**378,690,000**	**100.0**				**479,674,000**	**100.0**				**360,337,475**	**100.0**				**51,090,000**	**100.0**
Accounts Payable	51,123,150	13.5				62,837,294	13.1				40,718,135	11.3				4,598,100	9.0
Bank Loans	1,136,070	0.3				1,439,022	0.3				0	0.0				0	0.0
Notes Payable	5,301,660	1.4				2,398,370	0.5				4,324,050	1.2				153,270	0.3
Other Current	103,003,680	27.2				94,495,778	19.7				74,950,194	20.8				6,999,330	13.7
Total Current	**160,564,560**	**42.4**				**161,170,464**	**33.6**				**119,992,379**	**33.3**				**11,750,700**	**23.0**
Other Long Term	127,618,530	33.7				170,284,270	35.5				157,107,139	43.6				14,100,840	27.6
Deferred Credits	757,380	0.2				959,348	0.2				720,675	0.2				0	0.0
Net Worth	89,749,530	23.7				147,259,918	30.7				82,517,282	22.9				25,238,460	49.4
Total Liab & Net Worth	**378,690,000**	**100.0**				**479,674,000**	**100.0**				**360,337,475**	**100.0**				**51,090,000**	**100.0**
Net Sales	473,954,944	100.0				779,957,724	100.0				456,701,489	100.0				54,583,333	100.0
Gross Profit	107,113,817	22.6				131,812,855	16.9				91,340,298	20.0				16,047,500	29.4
Net Profit After Tax	15,166,558	3.2				22,618,774	2.9				(2,283,507)	(0.5)				3,875,417	7.1
Working Capital	43,928,040	---				86,820,994	---				65,941,758	---				18,085,860	---

RATIOS	UQ	MED	LQ			UQ	MED	LQ			UQ	MED	LQ			UQ	MED	LQ
SOLVENCY																		
Quick Ratio (times)	1.5	1.0	0.5			1.3	0.6	0.4			1.4	1.1	0.7			2.1	1.5	0.7
Current Ratio (times)	2.7	1.9	1.2			2.0	1.5	1.1			2.4	1.8	1.3			3.7	2.8	1.9
Curr Liab To Nw (%)	27.8	48.2	109.2			24.1	83.3	179.1			33.5	48.0	104.7			23.2	31.0	46.9
Curr Liab To Inv (%)	94.9	150.7	293.8			93.0	158.2	346.1			111.1	153.2	281.7			56.4	119.4	196.1
Total Liab To Nw (%)	67.7	128.9	290.8			114.1	179.1	464.5			81.0	181.4	469.8			32.2	77.5	143.2
Fixed Assets To Nw (%)	19.7	39.9	73.8			15.3	22.7	49.6			26.7	58.3	101.8			26.4	37.0	73.4
EFFICIENCY																		
Coll Period (days)	21.9	40.7	58.8			17.9	21.7	38.3			34.2	46.4	59.0			35.0	52.2	67.9
Sales To Inv (times)	11.7	7.2	4.6			13.2	6.8	4.4			11.7	9.4	5.8			18.6	5.1	3.5
Assets To Sales (%)	56.7	79.9	119.0			51.7	61.5	115.8			64.1	78.9	103.4			57.5	93.6	123.2
Sales To Nwc (times)	8.8	5.6	3.4			9.8	7.9	5.6			8.1	6.0	4.6			7.1	3.6	2.7
Acct Pay To Sales (%)	5.2	8.5	13.1			6.3	9.5	13.3			5.6	8.9	13.9			4.1	7.4	11.8
PROFITABILITY																		
Return On Sales (%)	8.4	4.4	(1.2)			6.5	2.2	(0.2)			6.7	2.8	(2.6)			14.4	6.7	(1.1)
Return On Assets (%)	10.0	4.3	(1.7)			9.1	1.7	(0.9)			7.9	3.4	(1.9)			18.0	5.5	(1.9)
Return On Nw (%)	25.7	14.9	0.3			28.3	14.5	(2.4)			21.8	13.0	(2.8)			26.9	13.4	(1.3)

Page 21

SIC 38 INSTRUMENTS RLTD PDTS
(NO BREAKDOWN)
2020 (294 Establishments)

	$	%
Cash	11,457,344	25.9
Accounts Receivable	6,060,448	13.7
Notes Receivable	44,237	0.1
Inventory	6,414,343	14.5
Other Current	4,290,974	9.7
Total Current	**28,267,346**	**63.9**
Fixed Assets	4,954,527	11.2
Other Non-current	11,014,975	24.9
Total Assets	**44,236,848**	**100.0**
Accounts Payable	12,165,133	27.5
Bank Loans	0	0.0
Notes Payable	4,512,158	10.2
Other Current	43,352,112	98.0
Total Current	**60,029,403**	**135.7**
Other Long Term	23,489,766	53.1
Deferred Credits	575,079	1.3
Net Worth	(39,857,400)	(90.1)
Total Liab & Net Worth	**44,236,848**	**100.0**
Net Sales	34,372,065	100.0
Gross Profit	17,289,149	50.3
Net Profit After Tax	(1,581,115)	(4.6)
Working Capital	(31,762,057)	---

RATIOS	UQ	MED	LQ
SOLVENCY			
Quick Ratio (times)	2.3	1.3	0.8
Current Ratio (times)	4.5	2.5	1.4
Curr Liab To Nw (%)	18.3	31.0	79.6
Curr Liab To Inv (%)	102.2	170.5	311.5
Total Liab To Nw (%)	31.2	76.3	148.6
Fixed Assets To Nw (%)	6.6	15.5	32.4
EFFICIENCY			
Coll Period (days)	44.9	60.3	72.8
Sales To Inv (times)	9.6	6.0	4.0
Assets To Sales (%)	80.1	128.7	210.8
Sales To Nwc (times)	4.5	2.2	1.3
Acct Pay To Sales (%)	4.1	6.9	11.9
PROFITABILITY			
Return On Sales (%)	8.0	(0.2)	(46.4)
Return On Assets (%)	7.1	(2.6)	(46.4)
Return On Nw (%)	13.6	0.7	(43.5)

SIC 3812 SEARCH,NVGTN EQPMNT
(NO BREAKDOWN)
2020 (15 Establishments)

	$	%
Cash	3,054,790	18.5
Accounts Receivable	3,038,278	18.4
Notes Receivable	0	0.0
Inventory	3,236,426	19.6
Other Current	1,238,428	7.5
Total Current	**10,567,922**	**64.0**
Fixed Assets	1,799,849	10.9
Other Non-current	4,144,607	25.1
Total Assets	**16,512,378**	**100.0**
Accounts Payable	1,420,065	8.6
Bank Loans	0	0.0
Notes Payable	264,198	1.6
Other Current	11,063,293	67.0
Total Current	**12,747,556**	**77.2**
Other Long Term	3,797,847	23.0
Deferred Credits	412,809	2.5
Net Worth	(445,834)	(2.7)
Total Liab & Net Worth	**16,512,378**	**100.0**
Net Sales	16,015,886	100.0
Gross Profit	6,486,434	40.5
Net Profit After Tax	464,461	2.9
Working Capital	(2,179,634)	---

RATIOS	UQ	MED	LQ
SOLVENCY			
Quick Ratio (times)	1.3	0.9	0.4
Current Ratio (times)	2.1	1.6	1.0
Curr Liab To Nw (%)	32.4	92.1	108.9
Curr Liab To Inv (%)	65.1	156.8	519.7
Total Liab To Nw (%)	77.9	168.2	296.8
Fixed Assets To Nw (%)	20.8	27.6	57.8
EFFICIENCY			
Coll Period (days)	24.8	45.6	74.5
Sales To Inv (times)	13.6	5.4	4.1
Assets To Sales (%)	64.5	103.1	136.7
Sales To Nwc (times)	6.1	3.6	2.1
Acct Pay To Sales (%)	5.1	6.6	8.9
PROFITABILITY			
Return On Sales (%)	14.0	7.8	0.5
Return On Assets (%)	14.2	5.8	(5.2)
Return On Nw (%)	30.8	24.0	15.4

SIC 3823 PROC CNTL INSTRMNTS
(NO BREAKDOWN)
2020 (18 Establishments)

	$	%
Cash	2,039,086	19.6
Accounts Receivable	1,342,052	12.9
Notes Receivable	20,807	0.2
Inventory	2,226,349	21.4
Other Current	592,999	5.7
Total Current	**6,221,293**	**59.8**
Fixed Assets	1,113,175	10.7
Other Non-current	3,069,032	29.5
Total Assets	**10,403,500**	**100.0**
Accounts Payable	3,266,699	31.4
Bank Loans	0	0.0
Notes Payable	20,807	0.2
Other Current	7,480,117	71.9
Total Current	**10,767,623**	**103.5**
Other Long Term	1,310,840	12.6
Deferred Credits	31,211	0.3
Net Worth	(1,706,174)	(16.4)
Total Liab & Net Worth	**10,403,500**	**100.0**
Net Sales	10,882,322	100.0
Gross Profit	4,929,692	45.3
Net Profit After Tax	467,940	4.3
Working Capital	(4,546,330)	---

RATIOS	UQ	MED	LQ
SOLVENCY			
Quick Ratio (times)	2.9	2.3	0.8
Current Ratio (times)	6.9	3.9	1.2
Curr Liab To Nw (%)	14.1	22.7	71.2
Curr Liab To Inv (%)	30.3	142.3	220.2
Total Liab To Nw (%)	16.4	39.1	114.0
Fixed Assets To Nw (%)	6.6	9.1	19.2
EFFICIENCY			
Coll Period (days)	48.2	53.2	59.9
Sales To Inv (times)	11.2	6.6	4.0
Assets To Sales (%)	70.6	95.6	158.6
Sales To Nwc (times)	8.5	1.9	1.6
Acct Pay To Sales (%)	2.5	4.4	7.3
PROFITABILITY			
Return On Sales (%)	11.1	6.3	1.3
Return On Assets (%)	9.4	4.4	(12.3)
Return On Nw (%)	18.4	6.9	(1.0)

SIC 3825 INSTRMNTS MEAS ELEC
(NO BREAKDOWN)
2020 (14 Establishments)

	$	%
Cash	8,419,860	14.7
Accounts Receivable	10,310,033	18.0
Notes Receivable	0	0.0
Inventory	12,085,650	21.1
Other Current	4,467,681	7.8
Total Current	**35,283,224**	**61.6**
Fixed Assets	5,956,908	10.4
Other Non-current	16,037,829	28.0
Total Assets	**57,277,961**	**100.0**
Accounts Payable	4,066,735	7.1
Bank Loans	0	0.0
Notes Payable	400,946	0.7
Other Current	10,424,589	18.2
Total Current	**14,892,270**	**26.0**
Other Long Term	10,882,812	19.0
Deferred Credits	57,278	0.1
Net Worth	31,445,601	54.9
Total Liab & Net Worth	**57,277,961**	**100.0**
Net Sales	47,181,187	100.0
Gross Profit	19,344,287	41.0
Net Profit After Tax	566,174	1.2
Working Capital	20,390,954	---

RATIOS	UQ	MED	LQ
SOLVENCY			
Quick Ratio (times)	2.1	1.8	1.1
Current Ratio (times)	4.5	3.1	1.5
Curr Liab To Nw (%)	23.4	30.8	37.1
Curr Liab To Inv (%)	64.1	129.8	239.2
Total Liab To Nw (%)	33.2	76.5	123.1
Fixed Assets To Nw (%)	6.8	17.9	31.3
EFFICIENCY			
Coll Period (days)	35.4	55.9	65.7
Sales To Inv (times)	8.2	6.7	2.6
Assets To Sales (%)	65.4	121.4	183.1
Sales To Nwc (times)	5.5	2.6	1.4
Acct Pay To Sales (%)	2.9	6.1	8.3
PROFITABILITY			
Return On Sales (%)	4.4	1.9	(11.9)
Return On Assets (%)	7.7	3.0	(7.9)
Return On Nw (%)	12.9	7.1	(24.2)

Page 22

SIC 3829 MEAS.CTLNG DVCS,NEC
(NO BREAKDOWN)
2020 (20 Establishments)

	$	%
Cash	2,261,033	27.6
Accounts Receivable	1,613,854	19.7
Notes Receivable	0	0.0
Inventory	1,056,787	12.9
Other Current	548,874	6.7
Total Current	**5,480,548**	**66.9**
Fixed Assets	745,486	9.1
Other Non-current	1,966,116	24.0
Total Assets	**8,192,150**	**100.0**
Accounts Payable	483,337	5.9
Bank Loans	0	0.0
Notes Payable	0	0.0
Other Current	2,261,033	27.6
Total Current	**2,744,370**	**33.5**
Other Long Term	507,914	6.2
Deferred Credits	0	0.0
Net Worth	4,939,866	60.3
Total Liab & Net Worth	**8,192,150**	**100.0**
Net Sales	6,425,216	100.0
Gross Profit	3,084,104	48.0
Net Profit After Tax	(250,583)	(3.9)
Working Capital	2,736,178	—

RATIOS

	UQ	MED	LQ
SOLVENCY			
Quick Ratio (times)	3.3	2.2	1.1
Current Ratio (times)	5.5	3.7	1.8
Curr Liab To Nw (%)	8.6	29.4	74.5
Curr Liab To Inv (%)	95.7	137.1	294.6
Total Liab To Nw (%)	14.9	47.9	106.7
Fixed Assets To Nw (%)	2.1	6.7	19.0
EFFICIENCY			
Coll Period (days)	56.6	67.9	80.3
Sales To Inv (times)	11.0	7.5	4.7
Assets To Sales (%)	61.9	127.5	210.8
Sales To Nwc (times)	4.3	2.3	1.7
Acct Pay To Sales (%)	2.4	4.2	9.1
PROFITABILITY			
Return On Sales (%)	5.7	2.1	(16.3)
Return On Assets (%)	9.2	1.9	(11.2)
Return On Nw (%)	13.8	5.4	(12.0)

SIC 3841 SRGL,MDCL INSTRMNTS
(NO BREAKDOWN)
2020 (109 Establishments)

	$	%
Cash	13,234,116	31.7
Accounts Receivable	3,924,312	9.4
Notes Receivable	83,496	0.2
Inventory	4,634,028	11.1
Other Current	5,009,760	12.0
Total Current	**26,885,712**	**64.4**
Fixed Assets	4,550,532	10.9
Other Non-current	10,311,756	24.7
Total Assets	**41,748,000**	**100.0**
Accounts Payable	14,653,548	35.1
Bank Loans	0	0.0
Notes Payable	4,968,012	11.9
Other Current	40,161,576	96.2
Total Current	**59,783,136**	**143.2**
Other Long Term	17,993,388	43.1
Deferred Credits	1,043,700	2.5
Net Worth	(37,072,224)	(88.8)
Total Liab & Net Worth	**41,748,000**	**100.0**
Net Sales	27,215,124	100.0
Gross Profit	15,485,406	56.9
Net Profit After Tax	(2,775,943)	(10.2)
Working Capital	(32,897,424)	—

RATIOS

	UQ	MED	LQ
SOLVENCY			
Quick Ratio (times)	2.5	1.6	0.8
Current Ratio (times)	4.8	2.7	1.4
Curr Liab To Nw (%)	17.4	27.3	63.6
Curr Liab To Inv (%)	109.5	166.4	308.2
Total Liab To Nw (%)	29.4	62.4	127.2
Fixed Assets To Nw (%)	5.7	15.1	28.1
EFFICIENCY			
Coll Period (days)	40.5	56.9	69.6
Sales To Inv (times)	7.8	5.4	3.8
Assets To Sales (%)	103.3	153.4	284.7
Sales To Nwc (times)	2.9	1.8	1.0
Acct Pay To Sales (%)	4.3	6.9	17.0
PROFITABILITY			
Return On Sales (%)	6.5	(19.7)	(119.1)
Return On Assets (%)	4.2	(23.3)	(94.5)
Return On Nw (%)	9.4	(16.0)	(128.2)

SIC 3842 SRGCL APPL,SUPPLS
(NO BREAKDOWN)
2020 (20 Establishments)

	$	%
Cash	13,675,661	19.8
Accounts Receivable	8,840,831	12.8
Notes Receivable	0	0.0
Inventory	14,711,696	21.3
Other Current	7,666,657	11.1
Total Current	**44,894,845**	**65.0**
Fixed Assets	10,981,970	15.9
Other Non-current	13,192,178	19.1
Total Assets	**69,068,993**	**100.0**
Accounts Payable	23,897,872	34.6
Bank Loans	0	0.0
Notes Payable	345,345	0.5
Other Current	133,095,949	192.7
Total Current	**157,339,166**	**227.8**
Other Long Term	14,228,213	20.6
Deferred Credits	483,483	0.7
Net Worth	(102,981,869)	(149.1)
Total Liab & Net Worth	**69,068,993**	**100.0**
Net Sales	40,179,752	100.0
Gross Profit	24,348,930	60.6
Net Profit After Tax	(3,174,200)	(7.9)
Working Capital	(112,444,321)	—

RATIOS

	UQ	MED	LQ
SOLVENCY			
Quick Ratio (times)	2.0	1.5	0.9
Current Ratio (times)	4.5	2.9	1.6
Curr Liab To Nw (%)	14.6	27.8	86.1
Curr Liab To Inv (%)	51.9	175.5	326.4
Total Liab To Nw (%)	25.2	56.4	176.2
Fixed Assets To Nw (%)	13.0	15.1	25.6
EFFICIENCY			
Coll Period (days)	45.6	62.1	76.3
Sales To Inv (times)	7.5	4.8	2.4
Assets To Sales (%)	120.2	171.9	263.1
Sales To Nwc (times)	5.5	1.6	1.0
Acct Pay To Sales (%)	4.2	9.2	11.9
PROFITABILITY			
Return On Sales (%)	11.7	(6.1)	(107.4)
Return On Assets (%)	7.8	(5.1)	(58.4)
Return On Nw (%)	13.8	(11.6)	(154.5)

SIC 3845 ELECTROMDCL EQPT
(NO BREAKDOWN)
2020 (27 Establishments)

	$	%
Cash	23,389,632	25.2
Accounts Receivable	12,994,240	14.0
Notes Receivable	0	0.0
Inventory	10,302,576	11.1
Other Current	11,787,632	12.7
Total Current	**58,474,080**	**63.0**
Fixed Assets	7,703,728	8.3
Other Non-current	26,638,192	28.7
Total Assets	**92,816,000**	**100.0**
Accounts Payable	16,799,696	18.1
Bank Loans	0	0.0
Notes Payable	2,506,032	2.7
Other Current	45,387,024	48.9
Total Current	**64,692,752**	**69.7**
Other Long Term	33,413,760	36.0
Deferred Credits	649,712	0.7
Net Worth	(5,940,224)	(6.4)
Total Liab & Net Worth	**92,816,000**	**100.0**
Net Sales	61,918,612	100.0
Gross Profit	26,501,166	42.8
Net Profit After Tax	(1,547,965)	(2.5)
Working Capital	(6,218,672)	—

RATIOS

	UQ	MED	LQ
SOLVENCY			
Quick Ratio (times)	2.2	1.3	0.8
Current Ratio (times)	3.4	1.9	1.2
Curr Liab To Nw (%)	26.5	38.2	106.0
Curr Liab To Inv (%)	146.2	245.6	786.2
Total Liab To Nw (%)	50.7	92.7	149.8
Fixed Assets To Nw (%)	6.1	12.8	18.4
EFFICIENCY			
Coll Period (days)	56.6	68.5	85.4
Sales To Inv (times)	11.5	7.4	5.1
Assets To Sales (%)	79.3	149.9	262.8
Sales To Nwc (times)	4.7	2.8	1.0
Acct Pay To Sales (%)	5.5	7.8	17.9
PROFITABILITY			
Return On Sales (%)	3.0	(6.1)	(54.1)
Return On Assets (%)	2.6	(5.1)	(35.6)
Return On Nw (%)	8.1	(11.6)	(61.4)

Page 23

SIC 3861 PHT.GRPH EQPT.SUPPLS
(NO BREAKDOWN)
2020 (12 Establishments)

	$	%
Cash	6,789,151	28.8
Accounts Receivable	3,323,855	14.1
Notes Receivable	0	0.0
Inventory	1,791,582	7.6
Other Current	2,640,226	11.2
Total Current	**14,544,814**	**61.7**
Fixed Assets	4,313,940	18.3
Other Non-current	4,714,688	20.0
Total Assets	**23,573,442**	**100.0**
Accounts Payable	24,351,366	103.3
Bank Loans	0	0.0
Notes Payable	30,834,062	130.8
Other Current	56,646,981	240.3
Total Current	**111,832,409**	**474.4**
Other Long Term	5,893,361	25.0
Deferred Credits	330,028	1.4
Net Worth	(94,482,356)	(400.8)
Total Liab & Net Worth	**23,573,442**	**100.0**
Net Sales	34,769,088	100.0
Gross Profit	13,073,177	37.6
Net Profit After Tax	(695,382)	(2.0)
Working Capital	(97,287,595)	—

RATIOS
	UQ	MED	LQ
SOLVENCY			
Quick Ratio (times)	1.2	1.0	0.5
Current Ratio (times)	1.9	1.5	0.8
Curr Liab To Nw (%)	49.6	94.8	141.8
Curr Liab To Inv (%)	199.0	449.9	664.5
Total Liab To Nw (%)	92.3	122.8	269.3
Fixed Assets To Nw (%)	28.4	64.2	119.8
EFFICIENCY			
Coll Period (days)	55.7	61.6	65.2
Sales To Inv (times)	17.9	10.5	8.2
Assets To Sales (%)	60.3	67.8	94.0
Sales To Nwc (times)	6.6	5.6	3.7
Acct Pay To Sales (%)	5.2	9.7	13.5
PROFITABILITY			
Return On Sales (%)	5.6	(4.6)	(12.1)
Return On Assets (%)	14.5	(3.3)	(15.5)
Return On Nw (%)	80.9	(6.5)	(23.5)

SIC 39 MISC MANUFACTURING
(NO BREAKDOWN)
2020 (49 Establishments)

	$	%
Cash	609,088	14.4
Accounts Receivable	972,849	23.0
Notes Receivable	4,230	0.1
Inventory	769,820	18.2
Other Current	321,462	7.6
Total Current	**2,677,449**	**63.3**
Fixed Assets	854,415	20.2
Other Non-current	697,914	16.5
Total Assets	**4,229,778**	**100.0**
Accounts Payable	4,978,449	117.7
Bank Loans	0	0.0
Notes Payable	29,608	0.7
Other Current	(2,152,957)	(50.9)
Total Current	**2,855,100**	**67.5**
Other Long Term	1,573,478	37.2
Deferred Credits	16,919	0.4
Net Worth	(215,719)	(5.1)
Total Liab & Net Worth	**4,229,778**	**100.0**
Net Sales	5,891,056	100.0
Gross Profit	2,486,026	42.2
Net Profit After Tax	235,642	4.0
Working Capital	(177,651)	—

	UQ	MED	LQ
Quick Ratio (times)	2.8	1.2	0.6
Current Ratio (times)	4.6	1.8	1.3
Curr Liab To Nw (%)	13.1	42.4	194.8
Curr Liab To Inv (%)	93.7	195.1	281.8
Total Liab To Nw (%)	23.7	149.5	333.6
Fixed Assets To Nw (%)	17.3	24.4	85.7
Coll Period (days)	25.4	48.9	72.5
Sales To Inv (times)	15.1	7.8	4.3
Assets To Sales (%)	49.8	71.8	117.3
Sales To Nwc (times)	7.7	4.7	2.6
Acct Pay To Sales (%)	2.8	5.9	11.3
Return On Sales (%)	7.5	4.1	(2.0)
Return On Assets (%)	11.8	4.5	(3.4)
Return On Nw (%)	34.4	13.8	(0.2)

SIC 3993 SIGNS,ADVT SPCLTIES
(NO BREAKDOWN)
2020 (15 Establishments)

	$	%
Cash	194,322	5.1
Accounts Receivable	1,455,511	38.2
Notes Receivable	0	0.0
Inventory	472,470	12.4
Other Current	270,527	7.1
Total Current	**2,392,830**	**62.8**
Fixed Assets	1,047,816	27.5
Other Non-current	369,593	9.7
Total Assets	**3,810,239**	**100.0**
Accounts Payable	369,593	9.7
Bank Loans	0	0.0
Notes Payable	11,431	0.3
Other Current	1,013,523	26.6
Total Current	**1,394,547**	**36.6**
Other Long Term	750,618	19.7
Deferred Credits	0	0.0
Net Worth	1,665,074	43.7
Total Liab & Net Worth	**3,810,239**	**100.0**
Net Sales	6,318,804	100.0
Gross Profit	3,007,751	47.6
Net Profit After Tax	379,128	6.0
Working Capital	998,283	—

	UQ	MED	LQ
Quick Ratio (times)	2.5	1.5	0.7
Current Ratio (times)	3.5	1.7	1.3
Curr Liab To Nw (%)	11.6	74.1	239.2
Curr Liab To Inv (%)	182.7	256.7	423.1
Total Liab To Nw (%)	36.0	137.6	347.6
Fixed Assets To Nw (%)	23.0	44.4	101.2
Coll Period (days)	41.6	53.1	94.2
Sales To Inv (times)	24.4	8.8	6.3
Assets To Sales (%)	50.1	60.3	79.4
Sales To Nwc (times)	8.1	5.3	3.4
Acct Pay To Sales (%)	1.6	5.6	9.1
Return On Sales (%)	9.3	4.9	0.8
Return On Assets (%)	13.1	7.6	1.7
Return On Nw (%)	62.6	19.9	9.4

SIC 3999 MFG INDUSTRIES, NEC
(NO BREAKDOWN)
2020 (12 Establishments)

	$	%
Cash	640,953	26.4
Accounts Receivable	240,357	9.9
Notes Receivable	7,284	0.3
Inventory	303,482	12.5
Other Current	378,744	15.6
Total Current	**1,570,820**	**64.7**
Fixed Assets	509,849	21.0
Other Non-current	347,183	14.3
Total Assets	**2,427,852**	**100.0**
Accounts Payable	10,867,066	447.6
Bank Loans	0	0.0
Notes Payable	60,696	2.5
Other Current	(7,225,288)	(297.6)
Total Current	**3,702,474**	**152.5**
Other Long Term	1,670,363	68.8
Deferred Credits	43,701	1.8
Net Worth	(2,988,686)	(123.1)
Total Liab & Net Worth	**2,427,852**	**100.0**
Net Sales	3,395,597	100.0
Gross Profit	1,297,118	38.2
Net Profit After Tax	336,164	9.9
Working Capital	(2,131,654)	—

	UQ	MED	LQ
Quick Ratio (times)	5.1	1.8	0.5
Current Ratio (times)	6.7	3.6	1.4
Curr Liab To Nw (%)	12.9	42.2	86.0
Curr Liab To Inv (%)	100.8	170.9	247.9
Total Liab To Nw (%)	13.1	220.9	338.7
Fixed Assets To Nw (%)	13.1	34.8	77.4
Coll Period (days)	16.3	42.6	53.7
Sales To Inv (times)	37.4	10.9	6.5
Assets To Sales (%)	36.7	71.5	180.7
Sales To Nwc (times)	8.8	5.0	3.3
Acct Pay To Sales (%)	2.1	3.7	5.9
Return On Sales (%)	5.8	3.9	(3.8)
Return On Assets (%)	14.3	3.3	(13.8)
Return On Nw (%)	41.6	10.1	(14.1)

Page 24

SIC 41 LOCAL PASSENGER TRAN
(NO BREAKDOWN)
2020 (34 Establishments)

	$	%
Cash	15,186,252	12.2
Accounts Receivable	9,086,856	7.3
Notes Receivable	0	0.0
Inventory	622,387	0.5
Other Current	17,177,893	13.8
Total Current	**42,073,388**	**33.8**
Fixed Assets	67,217,838	54.0
Other Non-current	15,186,252	12.2
Total Assets	**124,477,478**	**100.0**
Accounts Payable	4,854,622	3.9
Bank Loans	0	0.0
Notes Payable	0	0.0
Other Current	24,646,540	19.8
Total Current	**29,501,162**	**23.7**
Other Long Term	75,682,307	60.8
Deferred Credits	0	0.0
Net Worth	19,294,009	15.5
Total Liab & Net Worth	**124,477,478**	**100.0**
Net Sales	17,653,876	100.0
Gross Profit	8,562,130	48.5
Net Profit After Tax	(247,154)	(1.4)
Working Capital	12,572,226	---

RATIOS | UQ | MED | LQ

SOLVENCY
Quick Ratio (times)	2.6	0.8	0.3
Current Ratio (times)	5.3	2.3	1.0
Curr Liab To Nw (%)	8.2	19.1	76.2
Curr Liab To Inv (%)	522.2	920.5	999.9
Total Liab To Nw (%)	45.7	102.0	279.3
Fixed Assets To Nw (%)	82.0	103.0	212.7

EFFICIENCY
Coll Period (days)	12.3	34.3	47.9
Sales To Inv (times)	27.7	12.9	5.7
Assets To Sales (%)	136.9	705.1	999.9
Sales To Nwc (times)	7.3	2.2	0.3
Acct Pay To Sales (%)	4.9	14.9	39.3

PROFITABILITY
Return On Sales (%)	15.5	(3.1)	(23.8)
Return On Assets (%)	1.3	(1.8)	(10.9)
Return On Nw (%)	5.6	0.6	(88.0)

SIC 4111 LCL SUBURNAN TRANS
(NO BREAKDOWN)
2020 (18 Establishments)

	$	%
Cash	28,932,014	9.0
Accounts Receivable	1,928,801	0.6
Notes Receivable	0	0.0
Inventory	2,250,268	0.7
Other Current	62,364,562	19.4
Total Current	**95,475,645**	**29.7**
Fixed Assets	190,951,290	59.4
Other Non-current	35,039,883	10.9
Total Assets	**321,466,818**	**100.0**
Accounts Payable	9,965,471	3.1
Bank Loans	0	0.0
Notes Payable	0	0.0
Other Current	35,361,350	11.0
Total Current	**45,326,821**	**14.1**
Other Long Term	266,495,992	82.9
Deferred Credits	0	0.0
Net Worth	9,644,005	3.0
Total Liab & Net Worth	**321,466,818**	**100.0**
Net Sales	32,540,421	100.0
Gross Profit	0	0.0
Net Profit After Tax	1,431,779	4.4
Working Capital	50,148,824	---

RATIOS | UQ | MED | LQ

SOLVENCY
Quick Ratio (times)	1.0	0.5	0.2
Current Ratio (times)	5.2	1.7	1.0
Curr Liab To Nw (%)	7.7	16.0	84.1
Curr Liab To Inv (%)	510.3	871.5	999.9
Total Liab To Nw (%)	45.7	107.2	362.0
Fixed Assets To Nw (%)	97.2	164.3	256.6

EFFICIENCY
Coll Period (days)	9.9	29.2	43.8
Sales To Inv (times)	21.7	10.6	5.7
Assets To Sales (%)	695.0	987.9	999.9
Sales To Nwc (times)	6.7	1.6	0.3
Acct Pay To Sales (%)	7.5	25.3	39.3

PROFITABILITY
Return On Sales (%)	20.7	3.8	(17.6)
Return On Assets (%)	2.1	0.2	(3.1)
Return On Nw (%)	8.4	1.0	0.3

SIC 4119 LCL PASS TRANS NEC
(NO BREAKDOWN)
2020 (12 Establishments)

	$	%
Cash	798,885	18.3
Accounts Receivable	785,789	18.0
Notes Receivable	0	0.0
Inventory	8,731	0.2
Other Current	331,777	7.6
Total Current	**1,925,182**	**44.1**
Fixed Assets	1,715,639	39.3
Other Non-current	724,672	16.6
Total Assets	**4,365,493**	**100.0**
Accounts Payable	270,661	6.2
Bank Loans	0	0.0
Notes Payable	0	0.0
Other Current	1,663,252	38.1
Total Current	**1,933,913**	**44.3**
Other Long Term	1,510,461	34.6
Deferred Credits	0	0.0
Net Worth	921,119	21.1
Total Liab & Net Worth	**4,365,493**	**100.0**
Net Sales	6,029,686	100.0
Gross Profit	3,159,555	52.4
Net Profit After Tax	(1,857,143)	(30.8)
Working Capital	(8,731)	---

RATIOS | UQ | MED | LQ

SOLVENCY
Quick Ratio (times)	4.4	1.7	0.2
Current Ratio (times)	4.7	2.5	1.0
Curr Liab To Nw (%)	14.9	51.7	85.9
Curr Liab To Inv (%)	655.1	999.9	999.9
Total Liab To Nw (%)	72.8	109.5	276.9
Fixed Assets To Nw (%)	47.5	103.0	236.3

EFFICIENCY
Coll Period (days)	23.9	46.2	57.5
Sales To Inv (times)	828.5	415.3	2.1
Assets To Sales (%)	48.3	72.4	279.3
Sales To Nwc (times)	7.3	4.5	2.4
Acct Pay To Sales (%)	1.8	5.7	14.1

PROFITABILITY
Return On Sales (%)	(4.6)	(46.8)	(117.0)
Return On Assets (%)	(7.8)	(26.4)	(77.9)
Return On Nw (%)	(88.0)	(91.2)	(183.1)

SIC 42 TRUCKING & WAREHSNG
(NO BREAKDOWN)
2020 (82 Establishments)

	$	%
Cash	696,531	17.1
Accounts Receivable	928,707	22.8
Notes Receivable	20,366	0.5
Inventory	89,612	2.2
Other Current	472,501	11.6
Total Current	**2,207,717**	**54.2**
Fixed Assets	1,560,065	38.3
Other Non-current	305,496	7.5
Total Assets	**4,073,278**	**100.0**
Accounts Payable	378,815	9.3
Bank Loans	0	0.0
Notes Payable	48,879	1.2
Other Current	904,268	22.2
Total Current	**1,331,962**	**32.7**
Other Long Term	814,656	20.0
Deferred Credits	4,073	0.1
Net Worth	1,922,587	47.2
Total Liab & Net Worth	**4,073,278**	**100.0**
Net Sales	10,833,186	100.0
Gross Profit	4,073,278	37.6
Net Profit After Tax	509,160	4.7
Working Capital	875,755	---

RATIOS | UQ | MED | LQ

SOLVENCY
Quick Ratio (times)	2.8	1.6	0.8
Current Ratio (times)	3.9	2.2	1.3
Curr Liab To Nw (%)	13.3	34.8	84.6
Curr Liab To Inv (%)	137.5	797.2	999.9
Total Liab To Nw (%)	31.0	68.4	141.4
Fixed Assets To Nw (%)	35.9	61.2	99.8

EFFICIENCY
Coll Period (days)	20.1	30.3	44.2
Sales To Inv (times)	285.1	124.3	29.6
Assets To Sales (%)	22.1	37.6	77.5
Sales To Nwc (times)	17.7	9.0	4.2
Acct Pay To Sales (%)	1.7	2.7	4.3

PROFITABILITY
Return On Sales (%)	6.8	2.6	0.1
Return On Assets (%)	14.5	6.0	0.6
Return On Nw (%)	35.3	10.7	2.6

	SIC 4212 LCL TRCKG W/O STRGE (NO BREAKDOWN) 2020 (20 Establishments)		SIC 4213 TRCKG, EXCEPT LOCAL (NO BREAKDOWN) 2020 (28 Establishments)		SIC 4214 LCL TRCKG WTH STRGE (NO BREAKDOWN) 2020 (13 Establishments)		SIC 4225 GNRL WRHSG,STRGE (NO BREAKDOWN) 2020 (12 Establishments)	
	$	%	$	%	$	%	$	%
Cash	418,420	17.7	1,157,058	21.5	264,702	9.8	686,706	21.8
Accounts Receivable	404,236	17.1	1,313,126	24.4	894,045	33.1	856,808	27.2
Notes Receivable	9,456	0.4	53,817	1.0	2,701	0.1	0	0.0
Inventory	26,004	1.1	123,778	2.3	27,010	1.0	107,101	3.4
Other Current	205,664	8.7	532,784	9.9	372,744	13.8	516,605	16.4
Total Current	**1,063,780**	**45.0**	**3,180,563**	**59.1**	**1,561,202**	**57.8**	**2,167,220**	**68.8**
Fixed Assets	1,108,695	46.9	1,883,582	35.0	1,002,086	37.1	746,557	23.7
Other Non-current	191,481	8.1	317,518	5.9	137,753	5.1	236,252	7.5
Total Assets	**2,363,956**	**100.0**	**5,381,663**	**100.0**	**2,701,041**	**100.0**	**3,150,029**	**100.0**
Accounts Payable	82,738	3.5	694,235	12.9	318,723	11.8	324,453	10.3
Bank Loans	0	0.0	0	0.0	0	0.0	0	0.0
Notes Payable	73,283	3.1	48,435	0.9	13,505	0.5	0	0.0
Other Current	397,145	16.8	1,474,575	27.4	505,095	18.7	384,304	12.2
Total Current	**553,166**	**23.4**	**2,217,245**	**41.2**	**837,323**	**31.0**	**708,757**	**22.5**
Other Long Term	512,978	21.7	1,415,378	26.3	467,280	17.3	327,603	10.4
Deferred Credits	0	0.0	0	0.0	0	0.0	0	0.0
Net Worth	1,297,812	54.9	1,749,040	32.5	1,396,438	51.7	2,113,669	67.1
Total Liab & Net Worth	**2,363,956**	**100.0**	**5,381,663**	**100.0**	**2,701,041**	**100.0**	**3,150,029**	**100.0**
Net Sales	3,554,821	100.0	15,969,326	100.0	8,629,524	100.0	8,898,387	100.0
Gross Profit	1,557,012	43.8	5,477,479	34.3	3,857,397	44.7	1,850,864	20.8
Net Profit After Tax	188,406	5.3	718,620	4.5	(25,889)	(0.3)	952,127	10.7
Working Capital	510,614	---	963,318	---	723,879	---	1,458,463	---

RATIOS	UQ	MED	LQ	UQ	MED	LQ	UQ	MED	LQ	UQ	MED	LQ
SOLVENCY												
Quick Ratio (times)	2.8	1.8	0.8	2.6	1.9	1.1	1.9	1.3	0.6	5.4	1.9	1.4
Current Ratio (times)	3.9	2.2	1.2	4.0	2.4	1.5	2.4	1.4	1.2	7.0	4.5	2.0
Curr Liab To Nw (%)	13.3	23.8	72.1	18.4	34.8	66.1	29.3	84.2	155.0	8.0	29.1	80.8
Curr Liab To Inv (%)	236.7	656.4	965.0	160.7	655.7	999.9	566.3	999.9	999.9	264.1	700.0	999.9
Total Liab To Nw (%)	32.1	72.1	177.3	37.4	62.6	118.4	87.7	122.5	160.1	13.6	58.2	101.5
Fixed Assets To Nw (%)	41.6	77.7	154.8	24.0	51.0	89.2	46.8	71.1	133.5	6.8	37.8	49.0
EFFICIENCY												
Coll Period (days)	23.0	28.5	42.3	19.0	26.1	35.8	32.0	37.4	64.6	24.7	40.5	50.2
Sales To Inv (times)	178.4	112.5	70.0	171.3	91.3	51.4	367.4	271.6	110.7	289.9	206.1	71.2
Assets To Sales (%)	24.2	66.5	130.9	17.8	33.7	52.4	30.1	31.3	40.4	31.5	35.4	63.6
Sales To Nwc (times)	21.5	11.4	4.2	17.7	10.0	4.4	23.8	8.4	4.8	8.6	4.5	2.8
Acct Pay To Sales (%)	1.2	2.6	3.9	1.7	2.7	3.6	2.1	3.6	4.1	1.4	2.0	6.7
PROFITABILITY												
Return On Sales (%)	10.2	4.9	0.9	6.9	3.1	0.5	2.1	1.5	0.1	18.1	5.2	0.1
Return On Assets (%)	13.4	6.6	1.5	18.1	7.7	3.2	6.9	2.6	0.3	15.9	8.9	1.0
Return On Nw (%)	28.7	11.1	2.0	38.4	18.7	7.7	15.9	5.0	1.6	31.6	14.7	2.9

Page 25

SIC 4581 ARPTS.FLY FLDS.SVCS
(NO BREAKDOWN)
2020 (12 Establishments)

	$	%
Cash	14,042,966	4.0
Accounts Receivable	12,989,743	3.7
Notes Receivable	1,053,222	0.3
Inventory	702,148	0.2
Other Current	28,788,080	8.2
Total Current	**57,576,159**	**16.4**
Fixed Assets	262,603,455	74.8
Other Non-current	30,894,524	8.8
Total Assets	**351,074,138**	**100.0**
Accounts Payable	6,670,409	1.9
Bank Loans	0	0.0
Notes Payable	1,755,371	0.5
Other Current	12,638,668	3.6
Total Current	**21,064,448**	**6.0**
Other Long Term	126,035,616	35.9
Deferred Credits	0	0.0
Net Worth	203,974,074	58.1
Total Liab & Net Worth	**351,074,138**	**100.0**
Net Sales	35,110,925	100.0
Gross Profit	23,629,653	67.3
Net Profit After Tax	6,776,409	19.3
Working Capital	36,511,711	

RATIOS	UQ	MED	LQ
SOLVENCY			
Quick Ratio (times)	2.1	1.5	0.4
Current Ratio (times)	3.8	2.7	2.1
Curr Liab To Nw (%)	4.2	7.8	13.3
Curr Liab To Inv (%)	999.9	999.9	999.9
Total Liab To Nw (%)	19.2	45.5	129.0
Fixed Assets To Nw (%)	89.9	110.6	156.1
EFFICIENCY			
Coll Period (days)	14.6	22.7	61.9
Sales To Inv (times)	119.6	49.3	38.8
Assets To Sales (%)	735.0	999.9	999.9
Sales To Nwc (times)	1.8	1.4	1.1
Acct Pay To Sales (%)	4.4	13.0	24.6
PROFITABILITY			
Return On Sales (%)	37.7	22.7	6.9
Return On Assets (%)	4.1	2.4	1.5
Return On Nw (%)	5.7	4.4	2.5

SIC 47 TRANSPORTATION SVS
(NO BREAKDOWN)
2020 (84 Establishments)

	$	%
Cash	1,497,022	21.9
Accounts Receivable	2,166,922	31.7
Notes Receivable	13,671	0.2
Inventory	54,686	0.8
Other Current	704,078	10.3
Total Current	**4,436,379**	**64.9**
Fixed Assets	1,250,936	18.3
Other Non-current	1,148,400	16.8
Total Assets	**6,835,715**	**100.0**
Accounts Payable	1,421,829	20.8
Bank Loans	0	0.0
Notes Payable	232,414	3.4
Other Current	1,469,679	21.5
Total Current	**3,123,922**	**45.7**
Other Long Term	1,702,093	24.9
Deferred Credits	13,671	0.2
Net Worth	1,996,029	29.2
Total Liab & Net Worth	**6,835,715**	**100.0**
Net Sales	24,500,771	100.0
Gross Profit	6,786,714	27.7
Net Profit After Tax	1,862,059	7.6
Working Capital	1,312,457	

RATIOS	UQ	MED	LQ
SOLVENCY			
Quick Ratio (times)	1.9	1.2	0.6
Current Ratio (times)	2.8	1.5	1.1
Curr Liab To Nw (%)	27.0	88.3	193.5
Curr Liab To Inv (%)	999.9	999.9	999.9
Total Liab To Nw (%)	68.0	128.6	349.3
Fixed Assets To Nw (%)	5.3	24.9	88.8
EFFICIENCY			
Coll Period (days)	21.5	35.4	54.8
Sales To Inv (times)	521.0	67.6	43.4
Assets To Sales (%)	15.9	27.9	79.1
Sales To Nwc (times)	29.7	14.2	5.6
Acct Pay To Sales (%)	3.4	5.8	8.7
PROFITABILITY			
Return On Sales (%)	7.2	3.1	1.2
Return On Assets (%)	22.4	6.9	2.9
Return On Nw (%)	41.1	20.4	9.9

SIC 4724 TRAVEL AGENCIES
(NO BREAKDOWN)
2020 (11 Establishments)

	$	%
Cash	24,876,675	43.4
Accounts Receivable	8,082,053	14.1
Notes Receivable	0	0.0
Inventory	0	0.0
Other Current	4,241,645	7.4
Total Current	**37,200,373**	**64.9**
Fixed Assets	7,336,899	12.8
Other Non-current	12,782,255	22.3
Total Assets	**57,319,527**	**100.0**
Accounts Payable	2,923,296	5.1
Bank Loans	0	0.0
Notes Payable	8,082,053	14.1
Other Current	14,845,758	25.9
Total Current	**25,851,107**	**45.1**
Other Long Term	30,895,225	53.9
Deferred Credits	802,473	1.4
Net Worth	(229,278)	(0.4)
Total Liab & Net Worth	**57,319,527**	**100.0**
Net Sales	127,094,295	100.0
Gross Profit	59,861,413	47.1
Net Profit After Tax	16,522,258	13.0
Working Capital	11,349,266	

RATIOS	UQ	MED	LQ
SOLVENCY			
Quick Ratio (times)	2.6	1.2	0.6
Current Ratio (times)	2.9	1.3	0.9
Curr Liab To Nw (%)	30.1	59.1	102.3
Curr Liab To Inv (%)	999.9	999.9	999.9
Total Liab To Nw (%)	70.9	149.3	286.8
Fixed Assets To Nw (%)	10.7	21.1	39.7
EFFICIENCY			
Coll Period (days)	15.9	32.5	50.2
Sales To Inv (times)	67.6	67.6	67.6
Assets To Sales (%)	8.4	45.1	177.5
Sales To Nwc (times)	15.9	12.1	5.5
Acct Pay To Sales (%)	0.3	0.7	9.6
PROFITABILITY			
Return On Sales (%)	17.4	6.4	2.0
Return On Assets (%)	32.5	6.4	2.7
Return On Nw (%)	34.4	13.3	10.3

SIC 4731 FRGT TRANS ARNGMNT
(NO BREAKDOWN)
2020 (54 Establishments)

	$	%
Cash	811,113	19.8
Accounts Receivable	1,724,640	42.1
Notes Receivable	4,097	0.1
Inventory	0	0.0
Other Current	376,881	9.2
Total Current	**2,916,731**	**71.2**
Fixed Assets	675,928	16.5
Other Non-current	503,873	12.3
Total Assets	**4,096,532**	**100.0**
Accounts Payable	1,147,029	28.0
Bank Loans	0	0.0
Notes Payable	81,931	2.0
Other Current	876,657	21.4
Total Current	**2,105,617**	**51.4**
Other Long Term	540,743	13.2
Deferred Credits	0	0.0
Net Worth	1,450,172	35.4
Total Liab & Net Worth	**4,096,532**	**100.0**
Net Sales	20,279,861	100.0
Gross Profit	3,974,853	19.6
Net Profit After Tax	770,635	3.8
Working Capital	811,114	

RATIOS	UQ	MED	LQ
SOLVENCY			
Quick Ratio (times)	1.9	1.3	0.9
Current Ratio (times)	2.0	1.5	1.1
Curr Liab To Nw (%)	34.1	93.1	204.2
Curr Liab To Inv (%)	942.6	999.9	999.9
Total Liab To Nw (%)	68.0	116.5	354.4
Fixed Assets To Nw (%)	4.1	19.5	84.2
EFFICIENCY			
Coll Period (days)	25.9	40.5	54.8
Sales To Inv (times)	661.5	465.3	46.3
Assets To Sales (%)	15.3	20.2	41.5
Sales To Nwc (times)	33.3	17.5	10.3
Acct Pay To Sales (%)	4.2	6.2	8.9
PROFITABILITY			
Return On Sales (%)	4.6	2.4	0.8
Return On Assets (%)	16.0	8.0	2.9
Return On Nw (%)	39.8	19.8	7.3

	SIC 48 COMMUNICATION (NO BREAKDOWN) 2020 (115 Establishments)		SIC 4812 RDIO TELPHON COMM (NO BREAKDOWN) 2020 (14 Establishments)		SIC 4813 TEL COMM.EXC RDIO (NO BREAKDOWN) 2020 (56 Establishments)		SIC 4833 TEL BRDCSTG STNS (NO BREAKDOWN) 2020 (11 Establishments)	
	$	%	$	%	$	%	$	%
Cash	14,024,110	15.7	10,000,447	11.4	2,812,554	19.4	4,493,369	20.0
Accounts Receivable	14,202,761	15.9	11,579,465	13.2	3,030,019	20.9	943,608	4.2
Notes Receivable	0	0.0	0	0.0	0	0.0	0	0.0
Inventory	3,215,719	3.6	13,772,545	15.7	260,959	1.8	0	0.0
Other Current	6,878,067	7.7	2,543,973	2.9	1,377,281	9.5	2,718,488	12.1
Total Current	**38,320,657**	**42.9**	**37,896,430**	**43.2**	**7,480,813**	**51.6**	**8,155,465**	**36.3**
Fixed Assets	19,115,666	21.4	13,772,545	15.7	3,218,489	22.2	3,662,096	16.3
Other Non-current	31,889,218	35.7	36,054,242	41.1	3,798,398	26.2	10,649,286	47.4
Total Assets	**89,325,541**	**100.0**	**87,723,217**	**100.0**	**14,497,700**	**100.0**	**22,466,847**	**100.0**
Accounts Payable	17,954,434	20.1	14,825,224	16.9	4,450,794	30.7	629,072	2.8
Bank Loans	0	0.0	0	0.0	0	0.0	0	0.0
Notes Payable	1,429,209	1.6	175,446	0.2	376,940	2.6	0	0.0
Other Current	41,893,678	46.9	13,772,545	15.7	9,872,934	68.1	6,470,452	28.8
Total Current	**61,277,321**	**68.6**	**28,773,215**	**32.8**	**14,700,668**	**101.4**	**7,099,524**	**31.6**
Other Long Term	33,407,752	37.4	16,228,795	18.5	5,378,646	37.1	5,504,377	24.5
Deferred Credits	625,279	0.7	1,140,402	1.3	57,991	0.4	0	0.0
Net Worth	(5,984,811)	(6.7)	41,580,805	47.4	(5,639,605)	(38.9)	9,862,946	43.9
Total Liab & Net Worth	**89,325,541**	**100.0**	**87,723,217**	**100.0**	**14,497,700**	**100.0**	**22,466,847**	**100.0**
Net Sales	59,155,987	100.0	69,787,762	100.0	16,326,239	100.0	9,365,088	100.0
Gross Profit	26,442,726	44.7	29,520,223	42.3	6,563,148	40.2	6,237,149	66.6
Net Profit After Tax	177,468	0.3	(767,665)	(1.1)	(326,525)	(2.0)	683,651	7.3
Working Capital	(22,956,664)	---	9,123,215	---	(7,219,855)	---	1,055,941	---

RATIOS	UQ	MED	LQ	UQ	MED	LQ	UQ	MED	LQ	UQ	MED	LQ
SOLVENCY												
Quick Ratio (times)	1.9	0.9	0.5	1.4	0.6	0.3	2.3	0.9	0.5	2.6	1.6	1.1
Current Ratio (times)	2.6	1.3	0.7	1.7	1.3	0.7	3.0	1.2	0.7	5.3	2.7	1.7
Curr Liab To Nw (%)	17.7	36.1	74.6	20.5	48.4	108.2	18.1	49.7	101.6	7.1	13.3	22.7
Curr Liab To Inv (%)	215.7	591.2	999.9	141.4	443.3	999.9	310.4	613.1	999.9	999.9	999.9	999.9
Total Liab To Nw (%)	39.7	119.1	268.5	53.4	118.4	201.9	56.0	119.1	287.9	7.2	18.6	272.6
Fixed Assets To Nw (%)	9.8	28.0	80.0	3.2	20.0	65.3	6.5	27.8	126.7	27.6	31.0	46.8
EFFICIENCY												
Coll Period (days)	19.0	37.6	70.5	15.0	34.0	45.3	16.5	28.9	55.5	14.1	70.3	93.3
Sales To Inv (times)	58.7	28.3	7.1	46.7	32.0	4.6	79.1	33.6	16.0	822.5	822.5	822.5
Assets To Sales (%)	36.1	151.0	278.6	34.9	125.7	289.0	29.7	88.8	247.4	178.0	239.9	302.4
Sales To Nwc (times)	15.0	5.9	3.3	23.6	7.6	4.4	28.5	8.7	4.1	6.6	5.0	4.1
Acct Pay To Sales (%)	2.4	6.1	14.8	3.1	8.0	15.6	3.2	6.1	12.0	1.0	2.0	2.6
PROFITABILITY												
Return On Sales (%)	9.0	0.8	(9.6)	7.7	(1.3)	(17.3)	3.9	0.6	(12.7)	12.0	10.2	(3.1)
Return On Assets (%)	6.5	1.3	(10.2)	4.0	(1.0)	(8.1)	8.2	0.8	(9.4)	4.2	3.0	(3.9)
Return On Nw (%)	17.4	5.0	(9.1)	11.3	(0.8)	(26.8)	26.2	6.1	(5.3)	12.2	5.0	(4.2)

Page 27

Page 28

SIC 4899 COMMNCTN SVCS,NEC
(NO BREAKDOWN)
2020 (17 Establishments)

	$	%
Cash	16,750,107	9.9
Accounts Receivable	29,270,389	17.3
Notes Receivable	0	0.0
Inventory	8,290,457	4.9
Other Current	12,858,668	7.6
Total Current	**67,169,621**	**39.7**
Fixed Assets	55,495,304	32.8
Other Non-current	46,528,075	27.5
Total Assets	**169,193,000**	**100.0**
Accounts Payable	22,502,669	13.3
Bank Loans	0	0.0
Notes Payable	3,214,667	1.9
Other Current	76,644,429	45.3
Total Current	**102,361,765**	**60.5**
Other Long Term	60,571,094	35.8
Deferred Credits	4,399,018	2.6
Net Worth	1,861,123	1.1
Total Liab & Net Worth	**169,193,000**	**100.0**
Net Sales	155,508,272	100.0
Gross Profit	65,002,458	41.8
Net Profit After Tax	(5,131,773)	(3.3)
Working Capital	(35,192,144)	—

RATIOS	UQ	MED	LQ
SOLVENCY			
Quick Ratio (times)	1.1	0.8	0.4
Current Ratio (times)	2.2	1.5	0.5
Curr Liab To Nw (%)	12.8	32.6	95.0
Curr Liab To Inv (%)	162.9	371.2	864.6
Total Liab To Nw (%)	21.3	83.0	163.6
Fixed Assets To Nw (%)	14.8	42.7	78.9
EFFICIENCY			
Coll Period (days)	37.1	58.2	80.5
Sales To Inv (times)	25.6	8.9	6.8
Assets To Sales (%)	68.4	108.8	295.4
Sales To Nwc (times)	7.9	5.6	3.8
Acct Pay To Sales (%)	2.1	5.5	22.8
PROFITABILITY			
Return On Sales (%)	6.8	(6.6)	(23.4)
Return On Assets (%)	1.8	(5.6)	(16.0)
Return On Nw (%)	38.4	(3.6)	(26.5)

SIC 49 ELEC,GAS,SANITARY SV
(NO BREAKDOWN)
2020 (564 Establishments)

	$	%
Cash	12,785,464	8.1
Accounts Receivable	7,576,571	4.8
Notes Receivable	315,690	0.2
Inventory	1,894,143	1.2
Other Current	11,049,167	7.0
Total Current	**33,621,035**	**21.3**
Fixed Assets	102,125,868	64.7
Other Non-current	22,098,333	14.0
Total Assets	**157,845,236**	**100.0**
Accounts Payable	45,617,273	28.9
Bank Loans	0	0.0
Notes Payable	23,518,940	14.9
Other Current	(29,201,368)	(18.5)
Total Current	**39,934,845**	**25.3**
Other Long Term	65,505,773	41.5
Deferred Credits	2,999,059	1.9
Net Worth	49,405,559	31.3
Total Liab & Net Worth	**157,845,236**	**100.0**
Net Sales	36,386,638	100.0
Gross Profit	16,810,627	46.2
Net Profit After Tax	4,912,196	13.5
Working Capital	(6,313,810)	—

RATIOS	UQ	MED	LQ
SOLVENCY			
Quick Ratio (times)	2.4	0.8	0.4
Current Ratio (times)	3.9	1.8	0.9
Curr Liab To Nw (%)	7.2	16.0	31.7
Curr Liab To Inv (%)	441.5	821.5	999.9
Total Liab To Nw (%)	47.2	115.8	198.8
Fixed Assets To Nw (%)	97.0	137.8	218.8
EFFICIENCY			
Coll Period (days)	21.9	32.1	44.5
Sales To Inv (times)	58.9	29.9	16.1
Assets To Sales (%)	264.4	433.8	691.8
Sales To Nwc (times)	6.9	2.6	1.0
Acct Pay To Sales (%)	3.7	6.8	10.6
PROFITABILITY			
Return On Sales (%)	20.0	11.2	3.7
Return On Assets (%)	4.3	2.8	1.3
Return On Nw (%)	9.6	6.1	2.7

SIC 4911 ELECTRIC SERVICES
(NO BREAKDOWN)
2020 (200 Establishments)

	$	%
Cash	22,850,821	6.1
Accounts Receivable	17,606,370	4.7
Notes Receivable	749,207	0.2
Inventory	6,368,262	1.7
Other Current	23,974,631	6.4
Total Current	**71,549,291**	**19.1**
Fixed Assets	245,739,974	65.6
Other Non-current	57,314,354	15.3
Total Assets	**374,603,619**	**100.0**
Accounts Payable	285,822,561	76.3
Bank Loans	0	0.0
Notes Payable	154,711,295	41.3
Other Current	(245,365,371)	(65.5)
Total Current	**195,168,485**	**52.1**
Other Long Term	201,162,144	53.7
Deferred Credits	10,488,901	2.8
Net Worth	(32,215,911)	(8.6)
Total Liab & Net Worth	**374,603,619**	**100.0**
Net Sales	115,298,128	100.0
Gross Profit	50,500,580	43.8
Net Profit After Tax	9,569,745	8.3
Working Capital	(123,619,194)	—

RATIOS	UQ	MED	LQ
SOLVENCY			
Quick Ratio (times)	1.1	0.5	0.3
Current Ratio (times)	2.2	1.1	0.8
Curr Liab To Nw (%)	14.8	21.6	37.0
Curr Liab To Inv (%)	427.0	686.3	999.9
Total Liab To Nw (%)	90.0	167.2	220.8
Fixed Assets To Nw (%)	120.1	182.1	244.1
EFFICIENCY			
Coll Period (days)	20.8	29.6	37.2
Sales To Inv (times)	44.4	23.9	13.7
Assets To Sales (%)	231.7	324.9	466.1
Sales To Nwc (times)	15.1	4.9	3.0
Acct Pay To Sales (%)	5.6	7.5	10.4
PROFITABILITY			
Return On Sales (%)	13.2	8.3	4.0
Return On Assets (%)	3.6	2.7	1.5
Return On Nw (%)	10.1	7.4	4.3

SIC 4941 WATER SUPPLY
(NO BREAKDOWN)
2020 (169 Establishments)

	$	%
Cash	5,666,095	9.3
Accounts Receivable	1,279,441	2.1
Notes Receivable	0	0.0
Inventory	304,629	0.5
Other Current	4,630,356	7.6
Total Current	**11,880,521**	**19.5**
Fixed Assets	43,135,430	70.8
Other Non-current	5,909,798	9.7
Total Assets	**60,925,749**	**100.0**
Accounts Payable	670,183	1.1
Bank Loans	0	0.0
Notes Payable	60,926	0.1
Other Current	2,802,584	4.6
Total Current	**3,533,693**	**5.8**
Other Long Term	20,349,200	33.4
Deferred Credits	60,926	0.1
Net Worth	36,981,930	60.7
Total Liab & Net Worth	**60,925,749**	**100.0**
Net Sales	8,632,155	100.0
Gross Profit	5,334,672	61.8
Net Profit After Tax	1,631,477	18.9
Working Capital	8,346,828	—

RATIOS	UQ	MED	LQ
SOLVENCY			
Quick Ratio (times)	4.3	2.2	0.8
Current Ratio (times)	6.8	4.2	2.2
Curr Liab To Nw (%)	4.4	7.1	12.5
Curr Liab To Inv (%)	553.6	953.6	999.9
Total Liab To Nw (%)	30.0	54.7	123.2
Fixed Assets To Nw (%)	94.1	116.5	150.8
EFFICIENCY			
Coll Period (days)	25.9	33.2	46.4
Sales To Inv (times)	64.8	35.0	23.1
Assets To Sales (%)	481.3	705.8	893.4
Sales To Nwc (times)	2.0	1.0	0.7
Acct Pay To Sales (%)	2.9	5.2	9.2
PROFITABILITY			
Return On Sales (%)	29.2	16.2	6.6
Return On Assets (%)	4.4	2.5	0.9
Return On Nw (%)	7.0	4.5	1.6

SIC 4952 SEWERAGE SYSTEMS
(NO BREAKDOWN)
2020 (35 Establishments)

	$	%
Cash	18,050,346	12.5
Accounts Receivable	3,898,875	2.7
Notes Receivable	144,403	0.1
Inventory	144,403	0.1
Other Current	12,707,443	8.8
Total Current	**34,945,470**	**24.2**
Fixed Assets	99,637,910	69.0
Other Non-current	9,819,388	6.8
Total Assets	**144,402,768**	**100.0**
Accounts Payable	2,454,847	1.7
Bank Loans	0	0.0
Notes Payable	0	0.0
Other Current	8,375,361	5.8
Total Current	**10,830,208**	**7.5**
Other Long Term	60,215,954	41.7
Deferred Credits	0	0.0
Net Worth	73,356,606	50.8
Total Liab & Net Worth	**144,402,768**	**100.0**
Net Sales	19,638,619	100.0
Gross Profit	9,681,839	49.3
Net Profit After Tax	5,518,452	28.1
Working Capital	24,115,262	---

RATIOS
	UQ	MED	LQ
SOLVENCY			
Quick Ratio (times)	4.0	2.1	1.0
Current Ratio (times)	6.9	3.9	2.2
Curr Liab To Nw (%)	4.5	10.2	18.0
Curr Liab To Inv (%)	999.9	999.9	999.9
Total Liab To Nw (%)	53.1	73.2	141.7
Fixed Assets To Nw (%)	96.2	137.6	187.9
EFFICIENCY			
Coll Period (days)	21.9	35.8	52.6
Sales To Inv (times)	200.6	94.3	47.0
Assets To Sales (%)	600.8	735.3	979.8
Sales To Nwc (times)	1.6	1.0	0.7
Acct Pay To Sales (%)	2.5	6.4	13.4
PROFITABILITY			
Return On Sales (%)	40.4	27.4	14.7
Return On Assets (%)	6.0	3.7	2.1
Return On Nw (%)	11.7	6.8	3.6

SIC 4953 REFUSE SYSTEMS
(NO BREAKDOWN)
2020 (40 Establishments)

	$	%
Cash	5,901,836	11.1
Accounts Receivable	6,965,230	13.1
Notes Receivable	531,697	1.0
Inventory	1,276,073	2.4
Other Current	4,997,952	9.4
Total Current	**19,672,788**	**37.0**
Fixed Assets	21,002,030	39.5
Other Non-current	12,494,878	23.5
Total Assets	**53,169,696**	**100.0**
Accounts Payable	4,094,067	7.7
Bank Loans	0	0.0
Notes Payable	372,188	0.7
Other Current	6,858,890	12.9
Total Current	**11,325,145**	**21.3**
Other Long Term	13,239,255	24.9
Deferred Credits	0	0.0
Net Worth	28,605,296	53.8
Total Liab & Net Worth	**53,169,696**	**100.0**
Net Sales	39,738,188	100.0
Gross Profit	12,994,387	32.7
Net Profit After Tax	2,463,768	6.2
Working Capital	8,347,643	---

	UQ	MED	LQ
Quick Ratio (times)	2.5	1.1	0.4
Current Ratio (times)	3.3	1.7	0.9
Curr Liab To Nw (%)	16.0	36.8	92.0
Curr Liab To Inv (%)	398.5	999.9	999.9
Total Liab To Nw (%)	49.9	129.8	247.6
Fixed Assets To Nw (%)	17.3	73.1	170.7
Coll Period (days)	21.2	38.7	65.3
Sales To Inv (times)	84.1	63.4	37.5
Assets To Sales (%)	53.4	133.8	320.4
Sales To Nwc (times)	19.5	5.0	1.6
Acct Pay To Sales (%)	4.5	8.0	12.2
Return On Sales (%)	9.5	1.8	(0.5)
Return On Assets (%)	3.4	1.4	(0.3)
Return On Nw (%)	11.6	3.3	0.3

SIC 4959 SANITARY SVCS,NEC
(NO BREAKDOWN)
2020 (15 Establishments)

	$	%
Cash	1,464,669	6.9
Accounts Receivable	5,710,087	26.9
Notes Receivable	0	0.0
Inventory	297,179	1.4
Other Current	2,844,431	13.4
Total Current	**10,316,366**	**48.6**
Fixed Assets	8,214,884	38.7
Other Non-current	2,695,840	12.7
Total Assets	**21,227,090**	**100.0**
Accounts Payable	3,035,474	14.3
Bank Loans	0	0.0
Notes Payable	275,952	1.3
Other Current	2,738,295	12.9
Total Current	**6,049,721**	**28.5**
Other Long Term	5,731,314	27.0
Deferred Credits	21,227	0.1
Net Worth	9,424,828	44.4
Total Liab & Net Worth	**21,227,090**	**100.0**
Net Sales	29,078,205	100.0
Gross Profit	8,665,305	29.8
Net Profit After Tax	1,482,988	5.1
Working Capital	4,266,645	---

	UQ	MED	LQ
Quick Ratio (times)	1.9	1.4	0.8
Current Ratio (times)	2.2	1.9	1.4
Curr Liab To Nw (%)	33.3	49.2	101.7
Curr Liab To Inv (%)	718.9	999.9	999.9
Total Liab To Nw (%)	82.4	108.2	145.3
Fixed Assets To Nw (%)	52.5	67.4	115.4
Coll Period (days)	45.6	71.9	110.6
Sales To Inv (times)	142.6	67.9	15.1
Assets To Sales (%)	47.8	73.0	531.4
Sales To Nwc (times)	9.2	6.1	2.4
Acct Pay To Sales (%)	6.7	8.6	12.1
Return On Sales (%)	6.3	2.0	(5.4)
Return On Assets (%)	10.8	3.3	(0.3)
Return On Nw (%)	34.7	7.1	(0.5)

SIC 50 WHOLESALE TRADE
(NO BREAKDOWN)
2020 (549 Establishments)

	$	%
Cash	1,065,204	15.5
Accounts Receivable	1,807,410	26.3
Notes Receivable	20,617	0.3
Inventory	2,020,451	29.4
Other Current	467,315	6.8
Total Current	**5,380,997**	**78.3**
Fixed Assets	804,057	11.7
Other Non-current	687,228	10.0
Total Assets	**6,872,282**	**100.0**
Accounts Payable	1,566,880	22.8
Bank Loans	6,872	0.1
Notes Payable	219,913	3.2
Other Current	3,766,011	54.8
Total Current	**5,559,676**	**80.9**
Other Long Term	968,992	14.1
Deferred Credits	6,872	0.1
Net Worth	336,742	4.9
Total Liab & Net Worth	**6,872,282**	**100.0**
Net Sales	16,170,075	100.0
Gross Profit	4,511,451	27.9
Net Profit After Tax	662,973	4.1
Working Capital	(178,679)	---

	UQ	MED	LQ
Quick Ratio (times)	1.9	1.0	0.6
Current Ratio (times)	3.7	2.0	1.4
Curr Liab To Nw (%)	30.1	72.2	164.4
Curr Liab To Inv (%)	60.7	108.8	223.6
Total Liab To Nw (%)	41.1	107.5	227.4
Fixed Assets To Nw (%)	4.9	14.8	36.3
Coll Period (days)	25.0	38.7	53.1
Sales To Inv (times)	18.4	8.0	4.4
Assets To Sales (%)	27.1	42.5	63.5
Sales To Nwc (times)	11.5	6.2	3.7
Acct Pay To Sales (%)	3.2	5.7	9.8
Return On Sales (%)	6.3	2.6	0.7
Return On Assets (%)	15.6	5.6	1.7
Return On Nw (%)	32.8	14.0	5.1

Page 29

SIC 5013 MTR VHCL SPLS, PRTS
(NO BREAKDOWN)
2020 (14 Establishments)

	$	%
Cash	369,706	12.4
Accounts Receivable	790,097	26.5
Notes Receivable	0	0.0
Inventory	915,320	30.7
Other Current	304,113	10.2
Total Current	**2,379,236**	**79.8**
Fixed Assets	119,260	4.0
Other Non-current	483,003	16.2
Total Assets	**2,981,499**	**100.0**
Accounts Payable	524,744	17.6
Bank Loans	0	0.0
Notes Payable	101,371	3.4
Other Current	530,707	17.8
Total Current	**1,156,822**	**38.8**
Other Long Term	330,946	11.1
Deferred Credits	0	0.0
Net Worth	1,493,731	50.1
Total Liab & Net Worth	**2,981,499**	**100.0**
Net Sales	8,592,216	100.0
Gross Profit	2,508,927	29.2
Net Profit After Tax	421,019	4.9
Working Capital	1,222,414	---

RATIOS	UQ	MED	LQ
SOLVENCY			
Quick Ratio (times)	1.8	0.7	0.4
Current Ratio (times)	3.1	1.6	1.4
Curr Liab To Nw (%)	33.8	75.7	173.0
Curr Liab To Inv (%)	76.8	117.3	152.4
Total Liab To Nw (%)	34.6	91.6	245.3
Fixed Assets To Nw (%)	0.8	14.3	21.8
EFFICIENCY			
Coll Period (days)	18.1	37.8	50.6
Sales To Inv (times)	10.7	7.9	5.6
Assets To Sales (%)	28.9	34.7	45.5
Sales To Nwc (times)	12.6	8.0	4.8
Acct Pay To Sales (%)	3.8	6.4	9.2
PROFITABILITY			
Return On Sales (%)	3.6	1.6	0.5
Return On Assets (%)	18.5	4.4	0.5
Return On Nw (%)	31.1	10.2	2.2

SIC 5021 FURNITURE
(NO BREAKDOWN)
2020 (12 Establishments)

	$	%
Cash	842,138	20.3
Accounts Receivable	1,622,048	39.1
Notes Receivable	0	0.0
Inventory	547,597	13.2
Other Current	298,689	7.2
Total Current	**3,310,472**	**79.8**
Fixed Assets	410,698	9.9
Other Non-current	427,291	10.3
Total Assets	**4,148,461**	**100.0**
Accounts Payable	829,692	20.0
Bank Loans	0	0.0
Notes Payable	99,563	2.4
Other Current	1,149,124	27.7
Total Current	**2,078,379**	**50.1**
Other Long Term	539,300	13.0
Deferred Credits	0	0.0
Net Worth	1,530,782	36.9
Total Liab & Net Worth	**4,148,461**	**100.0**
Net Sales	17,653,026	100.0
Gross Profit	4,572,134	25.9
Net Profit After Tax	282,448	1.6
Working Capital	1,232,093	---

RATIOS	UQ	MED	LQ
SOLVENCY			
Quick Ratio (times)	2.2	1.3	1.0
Current Ratio (times)	2.7	1.6	1.2
Curr Liab To Nw (%)	54.1	152.7	406.8
Curr Liab To Inv (%)	157.1	323.7	882.9
Total Liab To Nw (%)	85.5	169.8	429.1
Fixed Assets To Nw (%)	9.3	16.0	79.2
EFFICIENCY			
Coll Period (days)	19.0	44.0	59.9
Sales To Inv (times)	167.6	45.6	27.7
Assets To Sales (%)	21.6	23.5	45.7
Sales To Nwc (times)	14.6	12.8	7.3
Acct Pay To Sales (%)	2.0	3.5	5.8
PROFITABILITY			
Return On Sales (%)	6.2	1.8	0.2
Return On Assets (%)	27.4	4.7	1.0
Return On Nw (%)	39.6	17.0	4.7

SIC 5023 HOMEFURNISHINGS
(NO BREAKDOWN)
2020 (11 Establishments)

	$	%
Cash	474,805	12.4
Accounts Receivable	1,064,482	27.8
Notes Receivable	0	0.0
Inventory	1,420,586	37.1
Other Current	172,308	4.5
Total Current	**3,132,181**	**81.8**
Fixed Assets	130,188	3.4
Other Non-current	566,703	14.8
Total Assets	**3,829,072**	**100.0**
Accounts Payable	945,781	24.7
Bank Loans	0	0.0
Notes Payable	72,752	1.9
Other Current	298,668	7.8
Total Current	**1,317,201**	**34.4**
Other Long Term	271,864	7.1
Deferred Credits	0	0.0
Net Worth	2,240,007	58.5
Total Liab & Net Worth	**3,829,072**	**100.0**
Net Sales	15,377,799	100.0
Gross Profit	5,397,607	35.1
Net Profit After Tax	584,356	3.8
Working Capital	1,814,980	---

RATIOS	UQ	MED	LQ
SOLVENCY			
Quick Ratio (times)	4.2	1.2	0.7
Current Ratio (times)	6.1	2.6	1.5
Curr Liab To Nw (%)	13.8	62.9	179.7
Curr Liab To Inv (%)	41.2	106.3	127.1
Total Liab To Nw (%)	13.8	62.9	226.0
Fixed Assets To Nw (%)	1.5	3.5	13.2
EFFICIENCY			
Coll Period (days)	16.1	35.0	50.1
Sales To Inv (times)	13.7	8.4	6.8
Assets To Sales (%)	18.3	24.9	32.7
Sales To Nwc (times)	22.9	12.4	6.6
Acct Pay To Sales (%)	4.9	6.6	11.9
PROFITABILITY			
Return On Sales (%)	7.9	3.0	(0.3)
Return On Assets (%)	43.3	18.7	(1.0)
Return On Nw (%)	75.7	60.2	1.3

SIC 5031 LBR.PLYWD.MILLWRK
(NO BREAKDOWN)
2020 (26 Establishments)

	$	%
Cash	848,030	5.3
Accounts Receivable	5,168,183	32.3
Notes Receivable	80,003	0.5
Inventory	5,264,187	32.9
Other Current	1,152,041	7.2
Total Current	**12,512,444**	**78.2**
Fixed Assets	1,872,066	11.7
Other Non-current	1,616,058	10.1
Total Assets	**16,000,568**	**100.0**
Accounts Payable	2,640,094	16.5
Bank Loans	0	0.0
Notes Payable	64,002	0.4
Other Current	5,136,182	32.1
Total Current	**7,840,278**	**49.0**
Other Long Term	3,120,111	19.5
Deferred Credits	0	0.0
Net Worth	5,040,179	31.5
Total Liab & Net Worth	**16,000,568**	**100.0**
Net Sales	43,479,804	100.0
Gross Profit	8,869,880	20.4
Net Profit After Tax	782,636	1.8
Working Capital	4,672,166	---

RATIOS	UQ	MED	LQ
SOLVENCY			
Quick Ratio (times)	1.2	0.8	0.6
Current Ratio (times)	2.9	1.9	1.3
Curr Liab To Nw (%)	55.0	121.4	172.3
Curr Liab To Inv (%)	64.6	108.1	150.9
Total Liab To Nw (%)	77.2	168.6	308.1
Fixed Assets To Nw (%)	9.1	17.7	36.8
EFFICIENCY			
Coll Period (days)	26.7	31.8	43.3
Sales To Inv (times)	12.1	8.3	6.5
Assets To Sales (%)	22.3	36.8	50.1
Sales To Nwc (times)	19.3	7.7	5.8
Acct Pay To Sales (%)	2.0	4.6	7.2
PROFITABILITY			
Return On Sales (%)	2.9	1.0	0.0
Return On Assets (%)	6.5	3.0	0.1
Return On Nw (%)	15.3	8.9	1.6

Page 31

SIC 5045 CMPTRS,PERIPH SFTWR
(NO BREAKDOWN)
2020 (32 Establishments)

	$	%
Cash	1,818,402	25.2
Accounts Receivable	1,941,072	26.9
Notes Receivable	0	0.0
Inventory	1,053,519	14.6
Other Current	974,144	13.5
Total Current	**5,787,137**	**80.2**
Fixed Assets	259,772	3.6
Other Non-current	1,168,972	16.2
Total Assets	**7,215,881**	**100.0**
Accounts Payable	3,110,045	43.1
Bank Loans	0	0.0
Notes Payable	1,616,357	22.4
Other Current	16,466,640	228.2
Total Current	**21,193,042**	**293.7**
Other Long Term	577,271	8.0
Deferred Credits	50,511	0.7
Net Worth	(14,604,943)	(202.4)
Total Liab & Net Worth	**7,215,881**	**100.0**
Net Sales	18,889,741	100.0
Gross Profit	4,779,104	25.3
Net Profit After Tax	793,369	4.2
Working Capital	(15,405,905)	---

RATIOS	UQ	MED	LQ
SOLVENCY			
Quick Ratio (times)	1.5	1.0	0.7
Current Ratio (times)	2.3	1.5	1.2
Curr Liab To Nw (%)	22.1	76.7	171.9
Curr Liab To Inv (%)	136.1	420.7	795.8
Total Liab To Nw (%)	27.1	89.1	208.0
Fixed Assets To Nw (%)	2.0	6.9	15.9
EFFICIENCY			
Coll Period (days)	16.4	44.9	61.7
Sales To Inv (times)	43.4	17.8	9.2
Assets To Sales (%)	24.3	38.2	60.5
Sales To Nwc (times)	14.2	6.2	4.3
Acct Pay To Sales (%)	3.2	7.7	17.1
PROFITABILITY			
Return On Sales (%)	5.9	2.9	0.5
Return On Assets (%)	13.4	5.4	0.9
Return On Nw (%)	28.9	12.1	2.3

SIC 5046 CMMRCL EQUIP, NEC
(NO BREAKDOWN)
2020 (12 Establishments)

	$	%
Cash	258,578	10.4
Accounts Receivable	872,700	35.1
Notes Receivable	0	0.0
Inventory	601,691	24.2
Other Current	154,152	6.2
Total Current	**1,887,121**	**75.9**
Fixed Assets	435,107	17.5
Other Non-current	164,098	6.6
Total Assets	**2,486,326**	**100.0**
Accounts Payable	551,964	22.2
Bank Loans	0	0.0
Notes Payable	7,459	0.3
Other Current	847,838	34.1
Total Current	**1,407,261**	**56.6**
Other Long Term	271,009	10.9
Deferred Credits	0	0.0
Net Worth	808,056	32.5
Total Liab & Net Worth	**2,486,326**	**100.0**
Net Sales	8,287,753	100.0
Gross Profit	2,792,973	33.7
Net Profit After Tax	505,553	6.1
Working Capital	479,860	---

RATIOS	UQ	MED	LQ
SOLVENCY			
Quick Ratio (times)	2.1	1.0	0.3
Current Ratio (times)	2.4	1.6	1.0
Curr Liab To Nw (%)	54.3	146.2	740.2
Curr Liab To Inv (%)	119.0	148.4	299.0
Total Liab To Nw (%)	57.9	159.9	740.2
Fixed Assets To Nw (%)	3.7	10.1	39.1
EFFICIENCY			
Coll Period (days)	33.2	38.0	65.7
Sales To Inv (times)	21.1	11.0	4.3
Assets To Sales (%)	18.2	30.0	39.5
Sales To Nwc (times)	19.4	8.3	5.6
Acct Pay To Sales (%)	2.2	4.3	6.7
PROFITABILITY			
Return On Sales (%)	9.3	5.6	1.5
Return On Assets (%)	42.6	16.1	5.0
Return On Nw (%)	75.8	29.8	26.0

SIC 5047 MEDICAL HOSP EQUIP
(NO BREAKDOWN)
2020 (28 Establishments)

	$	%
Cash	867,649	22.4
Accounts Receivable	863,776	22.3
Notes Receivable	81,342	2.1
Inventory	732,079	18.9
Other Current	197,546	5.1
Total Current	**2,742,392**	**70.8**
Fixed Assets	546,154	14.1
Other Non-current	584,889	15.1
Total Assets	**3,873,435**	**100.0**
Accounts Payable	933,498	24.1
Bank Loans	0	0.0
Notes Payable	38,734	1.0
Other Current	751,447	19.4
Total Current	**1,723,679**	**44.5**
Other Long Term	1,069,068	27.6
Deferred Credits	0	0.0
Net Worth	1,080,688	27.9
Total Liab & Net Worth	**3,873,435**	**100.0**
Net Sales	7,700,666	100.0
Gross Profit	2,772,240	36.0
Net Profit After Tax	423,537	5.5
Working Capital	1,018,713	---

RATIOS	UQ	MED	LQ
SOLVENCY			
Quick Ratio (times)	3.0	1.0	0.6
Current Ratio (times)	4.2	1.6	1.1
Curr Liab To Nw (%)	27.1	62.3	256.3
Curr Liab To Inv (%)	123.6	296.4	753.6
Total Liab To Nw (%)	50.9	153.6	402.2
Fixed Assets To Nw (%)	10.5	56.6	125.3
EFFICIENCY			
Coll Period (days)	26.0	41.3	53.1
Sales To Inv (times)	40.1	19.1	7.3
Assets To Sales (%)	18.1	50.3	84.7
Sales To Nwc (times)	33.1	9.2	3.3
Acct Pay To Sales (%)	4.0	7.4	10.6
PROFITABILITY			
Return On Sales (%)	7.2	3.3	1.0
Return On Assets (%)	23.3	10.6	1.9
Return On Nw (%)	51.9	19.8	5.6

SIC 5051 METLS SVC CNTRS,OFF
(NO BREAKDOWN)
2020 (40 Establishments)

	$	%
Cash	2,982,768	12.1
Accounts Receivable	5,743,678	23.3
Notes Receivable	0	0.0
Inventory	9,564,579	38.8
Other Current	1,873,474	7.6
Total Current	**20,164,499**	**81.8**
Fixed Assets	2,613,004	10.6
Other Non-current	1,873,474	7.6
Total Assets	**24,650,977**	**100.0**
Accounts Payable	3,253,929	13.2
Bank Loans	147,906	0.6
Notes Payable	123,255	0.5
Other Current	3,574,391	14.5
Total Current	**7,099,481**	**28.8**
Other Long Term	4,486,478	18.2
Deferred Credits	0	0.0
Net Worth	13,065,018	53.0
Total Liab & Net Worth	**24,650,977**	**100.0**
Net Sales	53,589,080	100.0
Gross Profit	11,950,365	22.3
Net Profit After Tax	2,625,865	4.9
Working Capital	13,065,018	---

RATIOS	UQ	MED	LQ
SOLVENCY			
Quick Ratio (times)	2.0	1.3	0.8
Current Ratio (times)	5.7	3.6	2.1
Curr Liab To Nw (%)	16.7	44.5	118.1
Curr Liab To Inv (%)	32.5	59.8	106.5
Total Liab To Nw (%)	28.5	106.8	205.9
Fixed Assets To Nw (%)	6.0	14.8	26.1
EFFICIENCY			
Coll Period (days)	31.3	37.4	47.1
Sales To Inv (times)	7.9	5.3	3.8
Assets To Sales (%)	32.5	46.0	74.1
Sales To Nwc (times)	7.4	4.4	2.4
Acct Pay To Sales (%)	2.6	4.6	9.0
PROFITABILITY			
Return On Sales (%)	6.2	1.8	0.6
Return On Assets (%)	11.0	5.8	1.1
Return On Nw (%)	32.3	13.0	4.0

Page 32

SIC 5063 ELEC APPRATUS, EQUIP
(NO BREAKDOWN)
2020 (39 Establishments)

	$	%
Cash	1,071,307	11.5
Accounts Receivable	3,185,975	34.2
Notes Receivable	27,947	0.3
Inventory	2,654,979	28.5
Other Current	857,047	9.2
Total Current	**7,797,255**	**83.7**
Fixed Assets	838,415	9.0
Other Non-current	680,047	7.3
Total Assets	**9,315,717**	**100.0**
Accounts Payable	2,049,458	22.0
Bank Loans	9,316	0.1
Notes Payable	186,314	2.0
Other Current	2,012,195	21.6
Total Current	**4,257,283**	**45.7**
Other Long Term	1,471,883	15.8
Deferred Credits	0	0.0
Net Worth	3,586,551	38.5
Total Liab & Net Worth	**9,315,717**	**100.0**
Net Sales	24,644,754	100.0
Gross Profit	6,777,307	27.5
Net Profit After Tax	197,158	0.8
Working Capital	3,539,972	—

RATIOS	UQ	MED	LQ
SOLVENCY			
Quick Ratio (times)	1.9	1.3	0.9
Current Ratio (times)	3.8	2.2	1.5
Curr Liab To Nw (%)	35.9	82.7	142.3
Curr Liab To Inv (%)	69.5	114.0	210.7
Total Liab To Nw (%)	38.8	113.2	186.9
Fixed Assets To Nw (%)	4.2	10.7	24.1
EFFICIENCY			
Coll Period (days)	33.3	49.6	59.2
Sales To Inv (times)	13.7	10.0	5.1
Assets To Sales (%)	32.8	37.8	51.3
Sales To Nwc (times)	9.1	6.0	3.1
Acct Pay To Sales (%)	4.0	6.6	9.9
PROFITABILITY			
Return On Sales (%)	3.9	2.0	0.8
Return On Assets (%)	11.8	5.3	1.5
Return On Nw (%)	27.7	12.0	4.5

SIC 5065 ELEC PARTS, EQUIP
(NO BREAKDOWN)
2020 (59 Establishments)

	$	%
Cash	1,749,640	18.2
Accounts Receivable	3,749,228	39.0
Notes Receivable	0	0.0
Inventory	2,701,367	28.1
Other Current	(173,041)	(1.8)
Total Current	**8,027,194**	**83.5**
Fixed Assets	884,433	9.2
Other Non-current	701,779	7.3
Total Assets	**9,613,406**	**100.0**
Accounts Payable	2,884,022	30.0
Bank Loans	9,613	0.1
Notes Payable	182,655	1.9
Other Current	2,499,485	26.0
Total Current	**5,575,775**	**58.0**
Other Long Term	644,098	6.7
Deferred Credits	19,227	0.2
Net Worth	3,374,306	35.1
Total Liab & Net Worth	**9,613,406**	**100.0**
Net Sales	28,274,724	100.0
Gross Profit	6,983,857	24.7
Net Profit After Tax	961,341	3.4
Working Capital	2,451,419	—

RATIOS	UQ	MED	LQ
SOLVENCY			
Quick Ratio (times)	1.8	1.0	0.7
Current Ratio (times)	2.7	1.7	1.2
Curr Liab To Nw (%)	40.9	84.0	248.8
Curr Liab To Inv (%)	90.5	222.7	408.8
Total Liab To Nw (%)	56.3	111.4	249.9
Fixed Assets To Nw (%)	3.4	12.7	20.2
EFFICIENCY			
Coll Period (days)	35.1	47.7	59.3
Sales To Inv (times)	39.1	9.9	6.1
Assets To Sales (%)	24.0	34.0	51.3
Sales To Nwc (times)	18.3	8.1	4.3
Acct Pay To Sales (%)	5.3	9.4	15.4
PROFITABILITY			
Return On Sales (%)	6.3	1.3	0.5
Return On Assets (%)	17.3	4.4	1.7
Return On Nw (%)	45.2	16.7	5.3

SIC 5072 HARDWARE
(NO BREAKDOWN)
2020 (11 Establishments)

	$	%
Cash	1,778,552	13.7
Accounts Receivable	2,570,462	19.8
Notes Receivable	0	0.0
Inventory	5,179,871	39.9
Other Current	324,553	2.5
Total Current	**9,853,438**	**75.9**
Fixed Assets	1,635,749	12.6
Other Non-current	1,492,945	11.5
Total Assets	**12,982,132**	**100.0**
Accounts Payable	1,791,534	13.8
Bank Loans	0	0.0
Notes Payable	38,946	0.3
Other Current	2,142,052	16.5
Total Current	**3,972,532**	**30.6**
Other Long Term	2,025,213	15.6
Deferred Credits	0	0.0
Net Worth	6,984,387	53.8
Total Liab & Net Worth	**12,982,132**	**100.0**
Net Sales	24,540,892	100.0
Gross Profit	7,362,268	30.0
Net Profit After Tax	1,055,258	4.3
Working Capital	5,880,906	—

RATIOS	UQ	MED	LQ
SOLVENCY			
Quick Ratio (times)	3.0	0.8	0.5
Current Ratio (times)	5.2	3.0	1.4
Curr Liab To Nw (%)	23.7	54.4	113.5
Curr Liab To Inv (%)	41.6	91.1	117.3
Total Liab To Nw (%)	25.4	97.8	298.2
Fixed Assets To Nw (%)	7.6	17.1	57.0
EFFICIENCY			
Coll Period (days)	26.3	39.8	44.9
Sales To Inv (times)	8.8	6.3	3.8
Assets To Sales (%)	46.4	52.9	68.5
Sales To Nwc (times)	11.5	5.2	2.8
Acct Pay To Sales (%)	7.1	7.4	10.3
PROFITABILITY			
Return On Sales (%)	5.2	3.5	1.0
Return On Assets (%)	8.2	5.6	4.4
Return On Nw (%)	28.1	20.0	5.4

SIC 5074 PLMBG HDRNC, HTG SUP
(NO BREAKDOWN)
2020 (13 Establishments)

	$	%
Cash	538,419	17.6
Accounts Receivable	504,768	16.5
Notes Receivable	0	0.0
Inventory	994,239	32.5
Other Current	217,203	7.1
Total Current	**2,254,629**	**73.7**
Fixed Assets	431,347	14.1
Other Non-current	373,222	12.2
Total Assets	**3,059,198**	**100.0**
Accounts Payable	364,045	11.9
Bank Loans	0	0.0
Notes Payable	30,592	1.0
Other Current	602,662	19.7
Total Current	**997,299**	**32.6**
Other Long Term	412,991	13.5
Deferred Credits	0	0.0
Net Worth	1,648,908	53.9
Total Liab & Net Worth	**3,059,198**	**100.0**
Net Sales	6,167,738	100.0
Gross Profit	1,887,328	30.6
Net Profit After Tax	259,045	4.2
Working Capital	1,257,330	—

RATIOS	UQ	MED	LQ
SOLVENCY			
Quick Ratio (times)	2.3	0.8	0.6
Current Ratio (times)	4.7	2.4	1.4
Curr Liab To Nw (%)	23.0	50.6	109.9
Curr Liab To Inv (%)	39.9	75.8	132.1
Total Liab To Nw (%)	23.0	83.1	120.7
Fixed Assets To Nw (%)	8.2	21.7	46.5
EFFICIENCY			
Coll Period (days)	19.4	28.5	41.1
Sales To Inv (times)	8.3	6.1	3.5
Assets To Sales (%)	34.5	49.6	85.2
Sales To Nwc (times)	10.9	6.3	2.2
Acct Pay To Sales (%)	5.3	6.7	10.0
PROFITABILITY			
Return On Sales (%)	4.9	1.5	(0.4)
Return On Assets (%)	11.9	2.9	0.1
Return On Nw (%)	15.2	5.9	4.0

SIC 5075 WRM AIR HTG.AC
(NO BREAKDOWN)
2020 (10 Establishments)

	$	%
Cash	3,597,959	23.7
Accounts Receivable	3,947,128	26.0
Notes Receivable	0	0.0
Inventory	3,871,222	25.5
Other Current	667,975	4.4
Total Current	**12,084,284**	**79.6**
Fixed Assets	1,275,226	8.4
Other Non-current	1,821,751	12.0
Total Assets	**15,181,261**	**100.0**
Accounts Payable	3,339,877	22.0
Bank Loans	0	0.0
Notes Payable	0	0.0
Other Current	3,992,672	26.3
Total Current	**7,332,549**	**48.3**
Other Long Term	1,487,764	9.8
Deferred Credits	0	0.0
Net Worth	6,360,948	41.9
Total Liab & Net Worth	**15,181,261**	**100.0**
Net Sales	46,425,875	100.0
Gross Profit	11,745,746	25.3
Net Profit After Tax	4,317,606	9.3
Working Capital	4,751,735	—

RATIOS	UQ	MED	LQ
SOLVENCY		
Quick Ratio (times)	1.3	1.2	0.7
Current Ratio (times)	2.9	1.9	1.2
Curr Liab To Nw (%)	36.3	57.9	259.5
Curr Liab To Inv (%)	84.2	143.6	254.3
Total Liab To Nw (%)	49.1	61.0	367.7
Fixed Assets To Nw (%)	6.0	8.1	27.7
EFFICIENCY		
Coll Period (days)	26.7	38.7	44.2
Sales To Inv (times)	11.1	9.0	7.7
Assets To Sales (%)	29.0	32.7	43.8
Sales To Nwc (times)	9.1	6.9	4.6
Acct Pay To Sales (%)	2.4	7.4	12.3
PROFITABILITY		
Return On Sales (%)	9.9	5.2	2.5
Return On Assets (%)	20.8	13.8	7.9
Return On Nw (%)	49.3	32.8	17.2

SIC 5082 CONSTR, MINNG MACH
(NO BREAKDOWN)
2020 (15 Establishments)

	$	%
Cash	2,200,469	8.2
Accounts Receivable	4,374,104	16.3
Notes Receivable	53,670	0.2
Inventory	10,626,657	39.6
Other Current	590,370	2.2
Total Current	**17,845,270**	**66.5**
Fixed Assets	7,621,138	28.4
Other Non-current	1,368,584	5.1
Total Assets	**26,834,992**	**100.0**
Accounts Payable	2,119,964	7.9
Bank Loans	0	0.0
Notes Payable	429,360	1.6
Other Current	7,325,953	27.3
Total Current	**9,875,277**	**36.8**
Other Long Term	5,930,533	22.1
Deferred Credits	0	0.0
Net Worth	11,029,182	41.1
Total Liab & Net Worth	**26,834,992**	**100.0**
Net Sales	34,986,952	100.0
Gross Profit	9,726,373	27.8
Net Profit After Tax	1,014,622	2.9
Working Capital	7,969,993	—

RATIOS	UQ	MED	LQ
SOLVENCY		
Quick Ratio (times)	1.0	0.4	0.2
Current Ratio (times)	3.1	1.7	1.3
Curr Liab To Nw (%)	45.4	87.9	134.9
Curr Liab To Inv (%)	50.5	102.4	122.6
Total Liab To Nw (%)	52.0	138.4	235.4
Fixed Assets To Nw (%)	12.9	63.7	94.8
EFFICIENCY		
Coll Period (days)	15.2	27.4	51.9
Sales To Inv (times)	7.1	2.8	2.2
Assets To Sales (%)	56.4	76.7	91.9
Sales To Nwc (times)	7.6	6.5	3.4
Acct Pay To Sales (%)	2.7	4.3	7.0
PROFITABILITY		
Return On Sales (%)	5.0	3.6	0.1
Return On Assets (%)	7.8	4.2	0.1
Return On Nw (%)	15.9	14.4	0.3

SIC 5083 FARM,GRDN MACH
(NO BREAKDOWN)
2020 (24 Establishments)

	$	%
Cash	805,175	7.5
Accounts Receivable	869,588	8.1
Notes Receivable	32,207	0.3
Inventory	7,547,169	70.3
Other Current	246,920	2.3
Total Current	**9,501,059**	**88.5**
Fixed Assets	858,853	8.0
Other Non-current	375,748	3.5
Total Assets	**10,735,660**	**100.0**
Accounts Payable	891,060	8.3
Bank Loans	0	0.0
Notes Payable	1,180,923	11.0
Other Current	2,823,478	26.3
Total Current	**4,895,461**	**45.6**
Other Long Term	1,148,715	10.7
Deferred Credits	10,736	0.1
Net Worth	4,680,748	43.6
Total Liab & Net Worth	**10,735,660**	**100.0**
Net Sales	22,506,625	100.0
Gross Profit	4,366,285	19.4
Net Profit After Tax	427,626	1.9
Working Capital	4,605,598	—

RATIOS	UQ	MED	LQ
SOLVENCY		
Quick Ratio (times)	0.9	0.2	0.1
Current Ratio (times)	2.7	1.6	1.4
Curr Liab To Nw (%)	60.5	127.5	213.4
Curr Liab To Inv (%)	54.7	71.3	82.0
Total Liab To Nw (%)	84.9	191.7	264.4
Fixed Assets To Nw (%)	7.3	18.9	25.4
EFFICIENCY		
Coll Period (days)	5.1	11.2	19.4
Sales To Inv (times)	4.2	2.4	1.7
Assets To Sales (%)	46.0	47.7	73.2
Sales To Nwc (times)	7.1	6.0	3.8
Acct Pay To Sales (%)	1.5	2.2	5.1
PROFITABILITY		
Return On Sales (%)	3.0	1.4	1.0
Return On Assets (%)	5.2	2.8	1.8
Return On Nw (%)	14.1	8.1	4.7

SIC 5084 INDL MCHNRY.EQPT
(NO BREAKDOWN)
2020 (71 Establishments)

	$	%
Cash	702,032	20.3
Accounts Receivable	857,655	24.8
Notes Receivable	3,458	0.1
Inventory	785,031	22.7
Other Current	314,703	9.1
Total Current	**2,662,879**	**77.0**
Fixed Assets	494,535	14.3
Other Non-current	300,871	8.7
Total Assets	**3,458,285**	**100.0**
Accounts Payable	556,784	16.1
Bank Loans	3,458	0.1
Notes Payable	48,416	1.4
Other Current	1,580,436	45.7
Total Current	**2,189,094**	**63.3**
Other Long Term	591,367	17.1
Deferred Credits	3,458	0.1
Net Worth	674,366	19.5
Total Liab & Net Worth	**3,458,285**	**100.0**
Net Sales	8,194,988	100.0
Gross Profit	2,458,496	30.0
Net Profit After Tax	401,554	4.9
Working Capital	473,785	—

RATIOS	UQ	MED	LQ
SOLVENCY		
Quick Ratio (times)	2.5	1.1	0.7
Current Ratio (times)	3.3	2.3	1.4
Curr Liab To Nw (%)	34.2	57.5	123.8
Curr Liab To Inv (%)	66.9	110.0	218.2
Total Liab To Nw (%)	44.0	92.4	152.6
Fixed Assets To Nw (%)	5.1	15.3	41.2
EFFICIENCY		
Coll Period (days)	24.9	41.3	53.5
Sales To Inv (times)	15.0	9.3	4.5
Assets To Sales (%)	26.6	42.2	60.4
Sales To Nwc (times)	9.6	5.7	3.7
Acct Pay To Sales (%)	3.6	6.0	9.1
PROFITABILITY		
Return On Sales (%)	6.2	2.7	1.0
Return On Assets (%)	13.4	4.9	2.1
Return On Nw (%)	26.9	12.1	5.0

SIC 5085 INDUSTRIAL SUPPLIES
(NO BREAKDOWN)
2020 (35 Establishments)

	$	%
Cash	997,973	12.6
Accounts Receivable	2,265,240	28.6
Notes Receivable	71,284	0.9
Inventory	2,352,364	29.7
Other Current	506,907	6.4
Total Current	**6,193,768**	**78.2**
Fixed Assets	974,212	12.3
Other Non-current	752,439	9.5
Total Assets	**7,920,419**	**100.0**
Accounts Payable	982,132	12.4
Bank Loans	0	0.0
Notes Payable	126,727	1.6
Other Current	934,609	11.8
Total Current	**2,043,468**	**25.8**
Other Long Term	966,291	12.2
Deferred Credits	0	0.0
Net Worth	4,910,660	62.0
Total Liab & Net Worth	**7,920,419**	**100.0**
Net Sales	15,653,002	100.0
Gross Profit	5,102,879	32.6
Net Profit After Tax	923,527	5.9
Working Capital	4,150,300	—

RATIOS	UQ	MED	LQ
SOLVENCY			
Quick Ratio (times)	2.5	1.7	1.0
Current Ratio (times)	5.5	2.8	2.0
Curr Liab To Nw (%)	19.9	39.2	80.2
Curr Liab To Inv (%)	39.9	86.2	123.4
Total Liab To Nw (%)	21.5	54.0	140.0
Fixed Assets To Nw (%)	3.4	15.3	32.1
EFFICIENCY			
Coll Period (days)	37.2	45.1	54.8
Sales To Inv (times)	10.0	6.6	4.8
Assets To Sales (%)	32.2	50.6	64.6
Sales To Nwc (times)	6.0	4.5	3.2
Acct Pay To Sales (%)	3.7	4.8	6.8
PROFITABILITY			
Return On Sales (%)	9.0	4.9	1.9
Return On Assets (%)	16.2	9.8	3.5
Return On Nw (%)	29.7	14.6	7.7

SIC 5088 TRNSPRTN EQPT.SUPPL
(NO BREAKDOWN)
2020 (16 Establishments)

	$	%
Cash	412,886	8.7
Accounts Receivable	1,390,524	29.3
Notes Receivable	0	0.0
Inventory	1,969,514	41.5
Other Current	374,919	7.9
Total Current	**4,147,843**	**87.4**
Fixed Assets	512,548	10.8
Other Non-current	85,425	1.8
Total Assets	**4,745,816**	**100.0**
Accounts Payable	802,043	16.9
Bank Loans	0	0.0
Notes Payable	71,187	1.5
Other Current	1,072,555	22.6
Total Current	**1,945,785**	**41.0**
Other Long Term	379,665	8.0
Deferred Credits	0	0.0
Net Worth	2,420,366	51.0
Total Liab & Net Worth	**4,745,816**	**100.0**
Net Sales	12,896,239	100.0
Gross Profit	3,868,872	30.0
Net Profit After Tax	1,070,388	8.3
Working Capital	2,202,058	—

RATIOS	UQ	MED	LQ
SOLVENCY			
Quick Ratio (times)	2.3	1.0	0.5
Current Ratio (times)	4.4	2.5	1.7
Curr Liab To Nw (%)	34.0	84.1	229.7
Curr Liab To Inv (%)	61.9	96.3	156.7
Total Liab To Nw (%)	34.0	86.2	231.7
Fixed Assets To Nw (%)	1.2	5.9	19.5
EFFICIENCY			
Coll Period (days)	31.4	37.4	45.8
Sales To Inv (times)	11.0	6.3	3.6
Assets To Sales (%)	28.3	36.8	64.9
Sales To Nwc (times)	9.4	5.2	3.6
Acct Pay To Sales (%)	3.5	6.1	8.3
PROFITABILITY			
Return On Sales (%)	9.9	6.7	5.0
Return On Assets (%)	34.8	18.6	8.9
Return On Nw (%)	62.2	38.7	24.7

SIC 5099 DURABLE GOODS, NEC
(NO BREAKDOWN)
2020 (11 Establishments)

	$	%
Cash	141,045	5.6
Accounts Receivable	453,359	18.0
Notes Receivable	0	0.0
Inventory	889,088	35.3
Other Current	261,941	10.4
Total Current	**1,745,433**	**69.3**
Fixed Assets	538,994	21.4
Other Non-current	234,235	9.3
Total Assets	**2,518,662**	**100.0**
Accounts Payable	1,664,836	66.1
Bank Loans	30,224	1.2
Notes Payable	0	0.0
Other Current	3,526,126	140.0
Total Current	**5,221,186**	**207.3**
Other Long Term	468,471	18.6
Deferred Credits	0	0.0
Net Worth	(3,170,995)	(125.9)
Total Liab & Net Worth	**2,518,662**	**100.0**
Net Sales	6,249,782	100.0
Gross Profit	1,987,431	31.8
Net Profit After Tax	112,496	1.8
Working Capital	(3,475,753)	—

RATIOS	UQ	MED	LQ
SOLVENCY			
Quick Ratio (times)	0.7	0.4	0.2
Current Ratio (times)	1.8	1.3	1.3
Curr Liab To Nw (%)	141.3	172.4	200.4
Curr Liab To Inv (%)	77.4	112.5	461.2
Total Liab To Nw (%)	141.3	204.9	257.4
Fixed Assets To Nw (%)	6.4	40.6	66.3
EFFICIENCY			
Coll Period (days)	15.0	37.6	45.6
Sales To Inv (times)	27.5	5.2	4.4
Assets To Sales (%)	31.9	40.3	45.0
Sales To Nwc (times)	15.0	11.0	5.4
Acct Pay To Sales (%)	2.9	3.9	15.7
PROFITABILITY			
Return On Sales (%)	6.1	1.1	(0.4)
Return On Assets (%)	14.1	2.2	(1.2)
Return On Nw (%)	37.4	16.9	3.1

SIC 51 WHLE TRD NONDURBL GDS
(NO BREAKDOWN)
2020 (381 Establishments)

	$	%
Cash	1,408,025	14.6
Accounts Receivable	2,555,662	26.5
Notes Receivable	38,576	0.4
Inventory	2,189,190	22.7
Other Current	790,808	8.2
Total Current	**6,982,261**	**72.4**
Fixed Assets	1,678,057	17.4
Other Non-current	983,689	10.2
Total Assets	**9,644,007**	**100.0**
Accounts Payable	1,948,089	20.2
Bank Loans	19,288	0.2
Notes Payable	212,168	2.2
Other Current	2,816,051	29.2
Total Current	**4,995,596**	**51.8**
Other Long Term	1,475,533	15.3
Deferred Credits	0	0.0
Net Worth	3,172,878	32.9
Total Liab & Net Worth	**9,644,007**	**100.0**
Net Sales	29,313,091	100.0
Gross Profit	6,273,001	21.4
Net Profit After Tax	820,767	2.8
Working Capital	1,986,665	—

RATIOS	UQ	MED	LQ
SOLVENCY			
Quick Ratio (times)	2.0	1.0	0.6
Current Ratio (times)	3.7	1.8	1.3
Curr Liab To Nw (%)	27.6	72.2	162.3
Curr Liab To Inv (%)	83.9	150.8	351.2
Total Liab To Nw (%)	46.4	115.3	257.2
Fixed Assets To Nw (%)	6.2	29.4	71.0
EFFICIENCY			
Coll Period (days)	16.8	28.1	42.3
Sales To Inv (times)	28.7	12.9	6.6
Assets To Sales (%)	20.5	32.9	55.2
Sales To Nwc (times)	20.3	10.5	5.0
Acct Pay To Sales (%)	2.3	4.8	8.4
PROFITABILITY			
Return On Sales (%)	4.0	1.7	0.3
Return On Assets (%)	12.1	5.2	0.9
Return On Nw (%)	29.5	12.0	3.2

Page 35

SIC 5122 DRGS,PRPRTRS,SNDRS
(NO BREAKDOWN)
2020 (28 Establishments)

	$	%
Cash	2,019,188	23.6
Accounts Receivable	1,890,849	22.1
Notes Receivable	0	0.0
Inventory	2,156,082	25.2
Other Current	821,364	9.6
Total Current	**6,887,483**	**80.5**
Fixed Assets	564,688	6.6
Other Non-current	1,103,709	12.9
Total Assets	**8,555,880**	**100.0**
Accounts Payable	2,352,867	27.5
Bank Loans	0	0.0
Notes Payable	367,903	4.3
Other Current	1,882,293	22.0
Total Current	**4,603,063**	**53.8**
Other Long Term	1,942,185	22.7
Deferred Credits	0	0.0
Net Worth	2,010,632	23.5
Total Liab & Net Worth	**8,555,880**	**100.0**
Net Sales	25,770,723	100.0
Gross Profit	8,272,402	32.1
Net Profit After Tax	(103,083)	(0.4)
Working Capital	2,284,420	—

RATIOS	UQ	MED	LQ
SOLVENCY			
Quick Ratio (times)	4.2	1.1	0.5
Current Ratio (times)	5.1	1.9	1.1
Curr Liab To Nw (%)	14.2	103.5	314.9
Curr Liab To Inv (%)	82.4	188.3	399.3
Total Liab To Nw (%)	24.5	119.1	547.1
Fixed Assets To Nw (%)	4.2	7.4	35.1
EFFICIENCY			
Coll Period (days)	14.1	27.7	39.5
Sales To Inv (times)	17.5	10.9	7.2
Assets To Sales (%)	22.7	33.2	73.1
Sales To Nwc (times)	12.5	5.1	4.1
Acct Pay To Sales (%)	4.2	6.9	15.9
PROFITABILITY			
Return On Sales (%)	3.8	0.9	(0.7)
Return On Assets (%)	8.2	2.2	(4.7)
Return On Nw (%)	30.5	15.7	(2.2)

SIC 5137 WMNS,CLDRNS CLTHNG
(NO BREAKDOWN)
2020 (11 Establishments)

	$	%
Cash	1,076,519	13.8
Accounts Receivable	1,997,021	25.6
Notes Receivable	0	0.0
Inventory	2,995,531	38.4
Other Current	1,185,731	15.2
Total Current	**7,254,802**	**93.0**
Fixed Assets	429,047	5.5
Other Non-current	117,013	1.5
Total Assets	**7,800,862**	**100.0**
Accounts Payable	1,708,389	21.9
Bank Loans	0	0.0
Notes Payable	0	0.0
Other Current	2,433,869	31.2
Total Current	**4,142,258**	**53.1**
Other Long Term	132,614	1.7
Deferred Credits	0	0.0
Net Worth	3,525,990	45.2
Total Liab & Net Worth	**7,800,862**	**100.0**
Net Sales	21,197,995	100.0
Gross Profit	7,694,872	36.3
Net Profit After Tax	932,712	4.4
Working Capital	3,112,544	—

RATIOS	UQ	MED	LQ
SOLVENCY			
Quick Ratio (times)	1.3	0.7	0.6
Current Ratio (times)	2.5	1.5	1.3
Curr Liab To Nw (%)	67.7	189.3	273.4
Curr Liab To Inv (%)	53.2	108.4	126.9
Total Liab To Nw (%)	77.5	189.3	275.3
Fixed Assets To Nw (%)	3.8	5.5	18.3
EFFICIENCY			
Coll Period (days)	32.3	53.7	63.4
Sales To Inv (times)	7.5	6.1	3.9
Assets To Sales (%)	20.2	36.8	39.8
Sales To Nwc (times)	10.9	9.4	5.0
Acct Pay To Sales (%)	4.8	6.2	9.5
PROFITABILITY			
Return On Sales (%)	7.1	2.6	0.5
Return On Assets (%)	22.5	7.5	1.2
Return On Nw (%)	42.8	17.1	5.3

SIC 5141 GROCERIES,GNRL LNE
(NO BREAKDOWN)
2020 (28 Establishments)

	$	%
Cash	1,937,728	11.3
Accounts Receivable	6,121,848	35.7
Notes Receivable	0	0.0
Inventory	3,429,607	20.0
Other Current	840,253	4.9
Total Current	**12,329,436**	**71.9**
Fixed Assets	2,246,392	13.1
Other Non-current	2,572,206	15.0
Total Assets	**17,148,034**	**100.0**
Accounts Payable	4,046,936	23.6
Bank Loans	0	0.0
Notes Payable	34,296	0.2
Other Current	2,520,761	14.7
Total Current	**6,601,993**	**38.5**
Other Long Term	1,920,580	11.2
Deferred Credits	0	0.0
Net Worth	8,625,461	50.3
Total Liab & Net Worth	**17,148,034**	**100.0**
Net Sales	86,171,025	100.0
Gross Profit	12,322,457	14.3
Net Profit After Tax	1,378,736	1.6
Working Capital	5,727,443	—

RATIOS	UQ	MED	LQ
SOLVENCY			
Quick Ratio (times)	1.9	1.2	0.7
Current Ratio (times)	2.8	1.9	1.6
Curr Liab To Nw (%)	42.7	65.7	123.5
Curr Liab To Inv (%)	62.4	113.1	199.2
Total Liab To Nw (%)	54.2	107.1	176.3
Fixed Assets To Nw (%)	7.3	22.0	66.1
EFFICIENCY			
Coll Period (days)	16.4	21.5	39.8
Sales To Inv (times)	26.9	17.3	12.2
Assets To Sales (%)	12.7	19.9	26.7
Sales To Nwc (times)	22.0	18.0	10.4
Acct Pay To Sales (%)	3.2	5.2	6.7
PROFITABILITY			
Return On Sales (%)	2.5	1.0	0.4
Return On Assets (%)	13.9	3.4	1.8
Return On Nw (%)	27.0	9.8	3.2

SIC 5147 MEATS,MEAT PRDTS
(NO BREAKDOWN)
2020 (10 Establishments)

	$	%
Cash	886,980	16.6
Accounts Receivable	1,426,649	26.7
Notes Receivable	90,835	1.7
Inventory	1,207,575	22.6
Other Current	176,327	3.3
Total Current	**3,788,366**	**70.9**
Fixed Assets	785,458	14.7
Other Non-current	769,429	14.4
Total Assets	**5,343,253**	**100.0**
Accounts Payable	555,698	10.4
Bank Loans	0	0.0
Notes Payable	0	0.0
Other Current	913,697	17.1
Total Current	**1,469,395**	**27.5**
Other Long Term	854,920	16.0
Deferred Credits	0	0.0
Net Worth	3,018,938	56.5
Total Liab & Net Worth	**5,343,253**	**100.0**
Net Sales	16,750,009	100.0
Gross Profit	2,428,751	14.5
Net Profit After Tax	385,250	2.3
Working Capital	2,318,971	—

RATIOS	UQ	MED	LQ
SOLVENCY			
Quick Ratio (times)	2.4	1.7	0.7
Current Ratio (times)	6.0	2.6	1.4
Curr Liab To Nw (%)	17.3	38.9	77.8
Curr Liab To Inv (%)	74.9	129.2	164.9
Total Liab To Nw (%)	15.3	40.4	114.7
Fixed Assets To Nw (%)	1.8	29.8	68.4
EFFICIENCY			
Coll Period (days)	16.4	29.6	35.0
Sales To Inv (times)	25.3	12.9	11.2
Assets To Sales (%)	21.6	31.9	35.0
Sales To Nwc (times)	18.4	13.2	6.3
Acct Pay To Sales (%)	1.7	2.5	4.4
PROFITABILITY			
Return On Sales (%)	3.7	1.8	0.1
Return On Assets (%)	17.3	7.9	0.7
Return On Nw (%)	20.8	12.8	10.4

SIC 5148 FRSH FRTS,VGTBLES
(NO BREAKDOWN)
2020 (43 Establishments)

	$	%
Cash	1,080,213	14.7
Accounts Receivable	2,917,310	39.7
Notes Receivable	29,394	0.4
Inventory	551,129	7.5
Other Current	984,683	13.4
Total Current	**5,562,729**	**75.7**
Fixed Assets	1,227,181	16.7
Other Non-current	558,477	7.6
Total Assets	**7,348,387**	**100.0**
Accounts Payable	2,123,684	28.9
Bank Loans	0	0.0
Notes Payable	7,348	0.1
Other Current	1,263,923	17.2
Total Current	**3,394,955**	**46.2**
Other Long Term	712,793	9.7
Deferred Credits	0	0.0
Net Worth	3,240,639	44.1
Total Liab & Net Worth	**7,348,387**	**100.0**
Net Sales	35,845,790	100.0
Gross Profit	5,376,869	15.0
Net Profit After Tax	573,533	1.6
Working Capital	2,167,774	—

RATIOS

	UQ	MED	LQ
SOLVENCY			
Quick Ratio (times)	1.7	1.2	0.9
Current Ratio (times)	3.0	1.6	1.3
Curr Liab To Nw (%)	24.3	100.6	155.9
Curr Liab To Inv (%)	186.8	513.3	999.9
Total Liab To Nw (%)	56.1	109.7	184.6
Fixed Assets To Nw (%)	4.0	11.6	47.1
EFFICIENCY			
Coll Period (days)	23.0	29.2	37.6
Sales To Inv (times)	123.7	65.9	28.5
Assets To Sales (%)	13.7	20.5	34.4
Sales To Nwc (times)	33.1	12.2	5.8
Acct Pay To Sales (%)	3.5	5.3	8.4
PROFITABILITY			
Return On Sales (%)	2.5	1.2	0.1
Return On Assets (%)	12.0	3.4	0.4
Return On Nw (%)	23.7	11.5	2.0

SIC 5149 GRCRS,RLTD PRDS,NEC
(NO BREAKDOWN)
2020 (28 Establishments)

	$	%
Cash	1,039,910	20.0
Accounts Receivable	1,097,105	21.1
Notes Receivable	0	0.0
Inventory	1,076,307	20.7
Other Current	395,166	7.6
Total Current	**3,608,488**	**69.4**
Fixed Assets	972,316	18.7
Other Non-current	618,746	11.9
Total Assets	**5,199,550**	**100.0**
Accounts Payable	1,258,291	24.2
Bank Loans	0	0.0
Notes Payable	57,195	1.1
Other Current	7,326,166	140.9
Total Current	**8,641,652**	**166.2**
Other Long Term	1,487,071	28.6
Deferred Credits	0	0.0
Net Worth	(4,929,173)	(94.8)
Total Liab & Net Worth	**5,199,550**	**100.0**
Net Sales	17,103,783	100.0
Gross Profit	5,250,861	30.7
Net Profit After Tax	632,840	3.7
Working Capital	(5,033,164)	—

RATIOS

	UQ	MED	LQ
SOLVENCY			
Quick Ratio (times)	2.7	1.1	0.7
Current Ratio (times)	4.6	1.7	1.1
Curr Liab To Nw (%)	18.2	57.4	199.1
Curr Liab To Inv (%)	120.5	179.5	346.1
Total Liab To Nw (%)	81.8	172.5	416.1
Fixed Assets To Nw (%)	10.2	36.9	92.6
EFFICIENCY			
Coll Period (days)	19.0	25.2	29.9
Sales To Inv (times)	19.6	14.8	8.9
Assets To Sales (%)	20.5	30.4	51.2
Sales To Nwc (times)	23.2	13.7	5.4
Acct Pay To Sales (%)	2.8	6.7	9.5
PROFITABILITY			
Return On Sales (%)	8.3	2.7	(1.3)
Return On Assets (%)	30.8	3.1	(3.8)
Return On Nw (%)	55.3	24.8	(6.8)

SIC 5153 GRAIN,FIELD BEANS
(NO BREAKDOWN)
2020 (29 Establishments)

	$	%
Cash	1,091,319	8.1
Accounts Receivable	1,293,415	9.6
Notes Receivable	13,473	0.1
Inventory	4,782,943	35.5
Other Current	929,643	6.9
Total Current	**8,110,793**	**60.2**
Fixed Assets	4,419,170	32.8
Other Non-current	943,115	7.0
Total Assets	**13,473,078**	**100.0**
Accounts Payable	1,010,481	7.5
Bank Loans	0	0.0
Notes Payable	1,293,415	9.6
Other Current	3,152,701	23.4
Total Current	**5,456,597**	**40.5**
Other Long Term	1,832,338	13.6
Deferred Credits	0	0.0
Net Worth	6,184,143	45.9
Total Liab & Net Worth	**13,473,078**	**100.0**
Net Sales	24,407,750	100.0
Gross Profit	2,416,367	9.9
Net Profit After Tax	292,893	1.2
Working Capital	2,654,196	—

RATIOS

	UQ	MED	LQ
SOLVENCY			
Quick Ratio (times)	0.7	0.3	0.1
Current Ratio (times)	2.0	1.4	1.2
Curr Liab To Nw (%)	43.6	103.4	147.6
Curr Liab To Inv (%)	88.9	106.2	134.2
Total Liab To Nw (%)	75.3	136.1	212.1
Fixed Assets To Nw (%)	50.4	72.2	96.4
EFFICIENCY			
Coll Period (days)	7.9	9.9	26.0
Sales To Inv (times)	9.1	5.4	3.6
Assets To Sales (%)	32.8	55.2	76.1
Sales To Nwc (times)	14.1	10.5	7.6
Acct Pay To Sales (%)	0.6	2.1	5.0
PROFITABILITY			
Return On Sales (%)	2.3	1.0	0.1
Return On Assets (%)	4.0	1.5	0.1
Return On Nw (%)	8.5	3.1	0.4

SIC 5169 CHEM,ALLD PRDTS,NEC
(NO BREAKDOWN)
2020 (25 Establishments)

	$	%
Cash	1,432,954	8.3
Accounts Receivable	4,799,533	27.8
Notes Receivable	69,058	0.4
Inventory	4,143,482	24.0
Other Current	1,208,516	7.0
Total Current	**11,653,543**	**67.5**
Fixed Assets	3,211,198	18.6
Other Non-current	2,399,767	13.9
Total Assets	**17,264,508**	**100.0**
Accounts Payable	2,952,231	17.1
Bank Loans	0	0.0
Notes Payable	86,323	0.5
Other Current	2,624,205	15.2
Total Current	**5,662,759**	**32.8**
Other Long Term	2,106,270	12.2
Deferred Credits	0	0.0
Net Worth	9,495,479	55.0
Total Liab & Net Worth	**17,264,508**	**100.0**
Net Sales	42,211,511	100.0
Gross Profit	9,877,494	23.4
Net Profit After Tax	1,477,403	3.5
Working Capital	5,990,784	—

RATIOS

	UQ	MED	LQ
SOLVENCY			
Quick Ratio (times)	1.5	1.2	0.9
Current Ratio (times)	2.8	1.9	1.6
Curr Liab To Nw (%)	24.3	60.8	97.6
Curr Liab To Inv (%)	73.4	126.8	249.6
Total Liab To Nw (%)	29.7	87.7	157.3
Fixed Assets To Nw (%)	6.1	39.5	65.7
EFFICIENCY			
Coll Period (days)	35.8	43.8	67.9
Sales To Inv (times)	15.7	10.2	6.7
Assets To Sales (%)	30.4	40.9	71.0
Sales To Nwc (times)	10.3	7.2	4.3
Acct Pay To Sales (%)	4.9	6.9	9.0
PROFITABILITY			
Return On Sales (%)	5.3	2.1	0.5
Return On Assets (%)	8.1	3.1	1.8
Return On Nw (%)	14.4	10.1	2.0

SIC 5171 PETRO BLK STNS.TMNL
(NO BREAKDOWN)
2020 (15 Establishments)

	$	%
Cash	2,264,519	13.8
Accounts Receivable	3,807,017	23.2
Notes Receivable	114,867	0.7
Inventory	2,133,242	13.0
Other Current	918,935	5.6
Total Current	**9,238,580**	**56.3**
Fixed Assets	5,562,839	33.9
Other Non-current	1,608,137	9.8
Total Assets	**16,409,556**	**100.0**
Accounts Payable	2,149,652	13.1
Bank Loans	0	0.0
Notes Payable	246,143	1.5
Other Current	1,608,137	9.8
Total Current	**4,003,932**	**24.4**
Other Long Term	3,675,740	22.4
Deferred Credits	0	0.0
Net Worth	8,729,884	53.2
Total Liab & Net Worth	**16,409,556**	**100.0**
Net Sales	70,427,279	100.0
Gross Profit	10,423,237	14.8
Net Profit After Tax	4,789,055	6.8
Working Capital	5,234,648	—

RATIOS	UQ	MED	LQ
SOLVENCY			
Quick Ratio (times)	3.3	1.6	0.9
Current Ratio (times)	4.1	2.2	1.1
Curr Liab To Nw (%)	23.1	30.0	66.2
Curr Liab To Inv (%)	87.0	228.6	384.3
Total Liab To Nw (%)	45.9	72.7	197.5
Fixed Assets To Nw (%)	28.2	47.1	108.6
EFFICIENCY			
Coll Period (days)	11.7	18.6	36.2
Sales To Inv (times)	62.2	28.9	14.8
Assets To Sales (%)	17.0	23.3	52.3
Sales To Nwc (times)	13.9	11.8	7.8
Acct Pay To Sales (%)	2.3	2.8	3.8
PROFITABILITY			
Return On Sales (%)	2.7	1.1	0.2
Return On Assets (%)	8.5	4.6	1.2
Return On Nw (%)	25.6	7.8	1.8

SIC 5172 PETRO PRDTS.NEC
(NO BREAKDOWN)
2020 (34 Establishments)

	$	%
Cash	1,578,813	14.8
Accounts Receivable	2,773,591	26.0
Notes Receivable	53,338	0.5
Inventory	1,344,125	12.6
Other Current	704,065	6.6
Total Current	**6,453,932**	**60.5**
Fixed Assets	2,944,273	27.6
Other Non-current	1,269,452	11.9
Total Assets	**10,667,657**	**100.0**
Accounts Payable	1,760,163	16.5
Bank Loans	21,335	0.2
Notes Payable	106,677	1.0
Other Current	1,888,176	17.7
Total Current	**3,776,351**	**35.4**
Other Long Term	2,368,219	22.2
Deferred Credits	0	0.0
Net Worth	4,523,087	42.4
Total Liab & Net Worth	**10,667,657**	**100.0**
Net Sales	43,364,459	100.0
Gross Profit	7,025,042	16.2
Net Profit After Tax	1,040,747	2.4
Working Capital	2,677,581	—

RATIOS	UQ	MED	LQ
SOLVENCY			
Quick Ratio (times)	2.4	1.0	0.7
Current Ratio (times)	3.3	1.7	1.1
Curr Liab To Nw (%)	23.1	70.5	155.4
Curr Liab To Inv (%)	172.9	305.7	550.4
Total Liab To Nw (%)	47.9	136.3	324.1
Fixed Assets To Nw (%)	18.2	56.4	132.2
EFFICIENCY			
Coll Period (days)	9.4	21.5	29.0
Sales To Inv (times)	94.3	57.5	19.7
Assets To Sales (%)	11.2	24.6	32.8
Sales To Nwc (times)	45.1	20.8	10.5
Acct Pay To Sales (%)	2.2	2.8	5.5
PROFITABILITY			
Return On Sales (%)	3.1	1.5	0.7
Return On Assets (%)	14.1	6.0	3.0
Return On Nw (%)	33.8	18.3	7.3

SIC 5191 FARM SUPPLIES
(NO BREAKDOWN)
2020 (34 Establishments)

	$	%
Cash	1,347,910	12.1
Accounts Receivable	1,927,178	17.3
Notes Receivable	133,677	1.2
Inventory	2,862,917	25.7
Other Current	1,035,997	9.3
Total Current	**7,307,679**	**65.6**
Fixed Assets	2,551,004	22.9
Other Non-current	1,281,072	11.5
Total Assets	**11,139,755**	**100.0**
Accounts Payable	1,526,146	13.7
Bank Loans	0	0.0
Notes Payable	835,482	7.5
Other Current	2,940,895	26.4
Total Current	**5,302,523**	**47.6**
Other Long Term	813,202	7.3
Deferred Credits	0	0.0
Net Worth	5,024,030	45.1
Total Liab & Net Worth	**11,139,755**	**100.0**
Net Sales	24,164,328	100.0
Gross Profit	4,373,743	18.1
Net Profit After Tax	338,301	1.4
Working Capital	2,005,156	—

RATIOS	UQ	MED	LQ
SOLVENCY			
Quick Ratio (times)	1.2	0.6	0.4
Current Ratio (times)	2.4	1.6	1.4
Curr Liab To Nw (%)	25.2	55.2	127.1
Curr Liab To Inv (%)	96.9	137.3	189.4
Total Liab To Nw (%)	36.6	77.9	149.6
Fixed Assets To Nw (%)	23.7	31.7	62.9
EFFICIENCY			
Coll Period (days)	15.3	22.7	34.3
Sales To Inv (times)	15.2	9.8	5.9
Assets To Sales (%)	34.2	46.1	65.7
Sales To Nwc (times)	18.4	9.0	5.6
Acct Pay To Sales (%)	2.3	4.7	8.2
PROFITABILITY			
Return On Sales (%)	3.7	2.3	0.5
Return On Assets (%)	6.9	5.1	1.0
Return On Nw (%)	11.9	7.7	2.9

SIC 5199 NNDRBL GDS.NEC
(NO BREAKDOWN)
2020 (27 Establishments)

	$	%
Cash	2,075,179	24.4
Accounts Receivable	2,160,228	25.4
Notes Receivable	76,544	0.9
Inventory	2,228,267	26.2
Other Current	391,222	4.6
Total Current	**6,931,440**	**81.5**
Fixed Assets	927,027	10.9
Other Non-current	646,367	7.6
Total Assets	**8,504,834**	**100.0**
Accounts Payable	1,964,617	23.1
Bank Loans	0	0.0
Notes Payable	178,602	2.1
Other Current	1,896,577	22.3
Total Current	**4,039,796**	**47.5**
Other Long Term	705,901	8.3
Deferred Credits	0	0.0
Net Worth	3,759,137	44.2
Total Liab & Net Worth	**8,504,834**	**100.0**
Net Sales	20,493,576	100.0
Gross Profit	5,451,291	26.6
Net Profit After Tax	1,106,653	5.4
Working Capital	2,891,644	—

RATIOS	UQ	MED	LQ
SOLVENCY			
Quick Ratio (times)	2.9	0.8	0.6
Current Ratio (times)	4.5	1.9	1.3
Curr Liab To Nw (%)	28.0	56.6	263.4
Curr Liab To Inv (%)	59.7	143.2	269.8
Total Liab To Nw (%)	32.9	118.8	263.4
Fixed Assets To Nw (%)	4.6	12.7	42.8
EFFICIENCY			
Coll Period (days)	16.5	32.5	49.5
Sales To Inv (times)	13.8	7.8	6.5
Assets To Sales (%)	33.4	41.5	57.3
Sales To Nwc (times)	12.3	7.8	3.6
Acct Pay To Sales (%)	2.9	6.1	11.4
PROFITABILITY			
Return On Sales (%)	5.7	2.8	1.0
Return On Assets (%)	11.4	5.3	3.7
Return On Nw (%)	49.0	15.7	8.3

Page 38

	SIC 52 BLD MTLS HDW GDN SUP (NO BREAKDOWN) 2020 (78 Establishments)					SIC 5211 LMBR,BLDNG MTRLS (NO BREAKDOWN) 2020 (41 Establishments)					SIC 5251 HARDWARE STORES (NO BREAKDOWN) 2020 (26 Establishments)					SIC 53 GEN MERCHANDISE (NO BREAKDOWN) 2020 (39 Establishments)	
	$	%				$	%				$	%				$	%
Cash	802,181	14.8				769,513	15.3				987,103	12.7				29,949,616	15.7
Accounts Receivable	1,046,088	19.3				1,171,872	23.3				1,111,463	14.3				5,341,333	2.8
Notes Receivable	21,681	0.4				25,147	0.5				23,317	0.3				0	0.0
Inventory	1,669,405	30.8				1,413,288	28.1				2,945,765	37.9				88,322,752	46.3
Other Current	298,108	5.5				206,210	4.1				287,582	3.7				10,301,141	5.4
Total Current	**3,837,463**	**70.8**				**3,586,030**	**71.3**				**5,355,230**	**68.9**				**133,914,842**	**70.2**
Fixed Assets	970,206	17.9				1,005,899	20.0				1,158,098	14.9				41,395,329	21.7
Other Non-current	612,476	11.3				437,566	8.7				1,259,139	16.2				15,451,712	8.1
Total Assets	**5,420,145**	**100.0**				**5,029,495**	**100.0**				**7,772,467**	**100.0**				**190,761,883**	**100.0**
Accounts Payable	569,115	10.5				492,891	9.8				785,019	10.1				35,481,710	18.6
Bank Loans	0	0.0				0	0.0				0	0.0				0	0.0
Notes Payable	65,042	1.2				60,354	1.2				124,359	1.6				0	0.0
Other Current	715,459	13.2				699,099	13.9				777,247	10.0				80,119,991	42.0
Total Current	**1,349,616**	**24.9**				**1,252,344**	**24.9**				**1,686,625**	**21.7**				**115,601,701**	**60.6**
Other Long Term	552,855	10.2				573,363	11.4				699,523	9.0				24,799,045	13.0
Deferred Credits	0	0.0				0	0.0				7,772	0.1				0	0.0
Net Worth	3,517,674	64.9				3,203,788	63.7				5,378,547	69.2				50,361,137	26.4
Total Liab & Net Worth	**5,420,145**	**100.0**				**5,029,495**	**100.0**				**7,772,467**	**100.0**				**190,761,883**	**100.0**
Net Sales	11,106,855	100.0				11,834,106	100.0				14,366,852	100.0				386,157,658	100.0
Gross Profit	3,309,843	29.8				3,420,057	28.9				4,468,091	31.1				128,590,500	33.3
Net Profit After Tax	333,206	3.0				295,853	2.5				502,840	3.5				7,723,153	2.0
Working Capital	2,487,847	---				2,333,686	---				3,668,605	---				18,313,141	---

RATIOS	UQ	MED	LQ	UQ	MED	LQ	UQ	MED	LQ	UQ	MED	LQ
SOLVENCY												
Quick Ratio (times)	2.7	1.5	0.7	2.9	2.2	1.0	2.0	1.2	0.5	0.9	0.4	0.2
Current Ratio (times)	5.3	3.4	1.8	5.3	3.5	1.9	6.0	3.6	2.3	2.9	2.0	1.3
Curr Liab To Nw (%)	14.8	28.1	62.3	14.0	27.3	63.4	13.5	25.6	46.9	37.1	54.6	97.3
Curr Liab To Inv (%)	45.6	75.9	119.0	53.2	83.1	120.0	27.6	49.9	99.1	51.3	71.4	125.0
Total Liab To Nw (%)	22.2	40.3	94.2	23.5	39.3	93.8	18.2	44.0	84.6	43.9	74.8	191.3
Fixed Assets To Nw (%)	7.7	20.5	42.0	8.1	24.3	43.1	7.0	15.5	23.1	3.9	39.9	104.0
EFFICIENCY												
Coll Period (days)	15.2	25.6	46.4	22.3	32.7	44.5	10.1	23.4	53.3	1.9	3.7	6.2
Sales To Inv (times)	11.4	7.1	4.4	11.9	7.8	5.7	7.7	4.8	3.6	9.7	5.6	4.3
Assets To Sales (%)	34.1	48.8	62.8	33.3	42.5	52.5	38.6	54.1	76.9	30.8	49.4	59.7
Sales To Nwc (times)	6.8	5.1	3.2	7.2	5.1	3.6	6.7	5.2	2.4	12.2	7.0	3.5
Acct Pay To Sales (%)	2.9	3.7	6.7	2.7	3.7	5.9	2.9	4.0	7.6	4.6	7.6	12.7
PROFITABILITY												
Return On Sales (%)	4.2	2.7	0.9	3.8	2.2	0.8	4.4	2.9	0.8	4.7	2.4	0.0
Return On Assets (%)	8.6	5.0	1.8	8.8	4.7	1.8	6.9	4.8	1.7	11.6	5.4	(0.1)
Return On Nw (%)	13.3	7.3	3.3	13.3	7.5	2.7	10.9	6.4	3.3	23.5	12.3	2.2

Page 39

SIC 5311 DEPARTMENT STORES
(NO BREAKDOWN)
2020 (22 Establishments)

	$	%
Cash	5,134,376	13.6
Accounts Receivable	1,245,841	3.3
Notes Receivable	0	0.0
Inventory	19,820,203	52.5
Other Current	1,359,100	3.6
Total Current	**27,559,520**	**73.0**
Fixed Assets	9,211,675	24.4
Other Non-current	981,572	2.6
Total Assets	**37,752,767**	**100.0**
Accounts Payable	7,626,059	20.2
Bank Loans	0	0.0
Notes Payable	0	0.0
Other Current	5,813,926	15.4
Total Current	**13,439,985**	**35.6**
Other Long Term	4,907,860	13.0
Deferred Credits	37,753	0.1
Net Worth	19,367,169	51.3
Total Liab & Net Worth	**37,752,767**	**100.0**
Net Sales	72,185,023	100.0
Gross Profit	24,831,648	34.4
Net Profit After Tax	1,804,626	2.5
Working Capital	14,119,535	---

RATIOS
	UQ	MED	LQ
SOLVENCY			
Quick Ratio (times)	0.8	0.4	0.2
Current Ratio (times)	3.0	2.3	1.4
Curr Liab To Nw (%)	44.6	55.6	115.1
Curr Liab To Inv (%)	50.6	65.4	96.2
Total Liab To Nw (%)	49.1	75.4	215.1
Fixed Assets To Nw (%)	4.2	39.9	132.7
EFFICIENCY			
Coll Period (days)	2.9	4.0	8.0
Sales To Inv (times)	7.0	4.9	2.7
Assets To Sales (%)	41.9	52.3	61.6
Sales To Nwc (times)	10.9	5.4	3.1
Acct Pay To Sales (%)	4.9	11.6	14.2
PROFITABILITY			
Return On Sales (%)	4.7	2.5	0.7
Return On Assets (%)	10.2	5.4	2.3
Return On Nw (%)	21.0	11.2	3.6

SIC 54 FOOD STORES
(NO BREAKDOWN)
2020 (46 Establishments)

	$	%
Cash	1,272,912	13.5
Accounts Receivable	1,065,475	11.3
Notes Receivable	9,429	0.1
Inventory	1,932,940	20.5
Other Current	744,889	7.9
Total Current	**5,025,645**	**53.3**
Fixed Assets	3,083,276	32.7
Other Non-current	1,320,057	14.0
Total Assets	**9,428,978**	**100.0**
Accounts Payable	1,640,642	17.4
Bank Loans	0	0.0
Notes Payable	37,716	0.4
Other Current	2,442,105	25.9
Total Current	**4,120,463**	**43.7**
Other Long Term	2,046,089	21.7
Deferred Credits	18,858	0.2
Net Worth	3,243,568	34.4
Total Liab & Net Worth	**9,428,978**	**100.0**
Net Sales	26,264,563	100.0
Gross Profit	7,459,136	28.4
Net Profit After Tax	892,995	3.4
Working Capital	905,182	---

RATIOS
	UQ	MED	LQ
SOLVENCY			
Quick Ratio (times)	1.2	0.6	0.2
Current Ratio (times)	2.7	1.7	1.0
Curr Liab To Nw (%)	26.0	39.7	71.6
Curr Liab To Inv (%)	86.6	124.2	222.5
Total Liab To Nw (%)	36.3	70.3	164.9
Fixed Assets To Nw (%)	31.4	62.2	128.0
EFFICIENCY			
Coll Period (days)	1.8	6.9	20.1
Sales To Inv (times)	35.1	19.6	12.2
Assets To Sales (%)	22.4	35.9	53.0
Sales To Nwc (times)	28.3	11.9	6.3
Acct Pay To Sales (%)	2.0	4.0	6.6
PROFITABILITY			
Return On Sales (%)	4.4	2.2	0.8
Return On Assets (%)	9.9	6.2	3.4
Return On Nw (%)	20.9	10.1	6.2

SIC 5411 GROCERY STORES
(NO BREAKDOWN)
2020 (26 Establishments)

	$	%
Cash	3,122,895	10.2
Accounts Receivable	3,031,046	9.9
Notes Receivable	30,617	0.1
Inventory	6,276,408	20.5
Other Current	1,316,514	4.3
Total Current	**13,777,480**	**45.0**
Fixed Assets	11,113,834	36.3
Other Non-current	5,725,308	18.7
Total Assets	**30,616,622**	**100.0**
Accounts Payable	4,500,643	14.7
Bank Loans	0	0.0
Notes Payable	122,466	0.4
Other Current	5,939,626	19.4
Total Current	**10,562,735**	**34.5**
Other Long Term	6,031,474	19.7
Deferred Credits	0	0.0
Net Worth	14,022,413	45.8
Total Liab & Net Worth	**30,616,622**	**100.0**
Net Sales	86,001,747	100.0
Gross Profit	19,350,393	22.5
Net Profit After Tax	1,892,038	2.2
Working Capital	3,214,745	---

RATIOS
	UQ	MED	LQ
SOLVENCY			
Quick Ratio (times)	1.2	0.6	0.2
Current Ratio (times)	3.1	1.9	1.0
Curr Liab To Nw (%)	13.9	29.0	48.0
Curr Liab To Inv (%)	74.1	112.6	212.8
Total Liab To Nw (%)	29.2	58.3	173.4
Fixed Assets To Nw (%)	43.4	69.0	127.4
EFFICIENCY			
Coll Period (days)	1.7	5.5	9.7
Sales To Inv (times)	31.9	20.1	12.8
Assets To Sales (%)	26.2	35.6	48.3
Sales To Nwc (times)	19.2	14.2	5.7
Acct Pay To Sales (%)	2.3	3.6	4.8
PROFITABILITY			
Return On Sales (%)	2.9	2.0	0.8
Return On Assets (%)	9.1	5.8	3.6
Return On Nw (%)	14.5	9.7	6.4

SIC 55 AUTO DEALER SVC STATN
(NO BREAKDOWN)
2020 (114 Establishments)

	$	%
Cash	2,805,947	18.2
Accounts Receivable	1,279,635	8.3
Notes Receivable	0	0.0
Inventory	5,550,225	36.0
Other Current	601,274	3.9
Total Current	**10,237,081**	**66.4**
Fixed Assets	3,083,458	20.0
Other Non-current	2,096,752	13.6
Total Assets	**15,417,291**	**100.0**
Accounts Payable	1,850,075	12.0
Bank Loans	0	0.0
Notes Payable	601,274	3.9
Other Current	3,715,567	24.1
Total Current	**6,166,916**	**40.0**
Other Long Term	2,466,767	16.0
Deferred Credits	15,417	0.1
Net Worth	6,768,191	43.9
Total Liab & Net Worth	**15,417,291**	**100.0**
Net Sales	48,943,781	100.0
Gross Profit	11,354,957	23.2
Net Profit After Tax	538,382	1.1
Working Capital	4,070,165	---

RATIOS
	UQ	MED	LQ
SOLVENCY			
Quick Ratio (times)	1.2	0.7	0.3
Current Ratio (times)	3.7	1.6	1.2
Curr Liab To Nw (%)	21.5	70.3	164.2
Curr Liab To Inv (%)	76.9	104.2	127.9
Total Liab To Nw (%)	45.0	110.0	328.3
Fixed Assets To Nw (%)	5.4	27.3	84.2
EFFICIENCY			
Coll Period (days)	3.7	9.1	18.6
Sales To Inv (times)	27.0	7.5	4.4
Assets To Sales (%)	19.1	31.5	56.7
Sales To Nwc (times)	25.3	9.9	5.7
Acct Pay To Sales (%)	1.3	2.8	5.3
PROFITABILITY			
Return On Sales (%)	3.3	1.6	0.5
Return On Assets (%)	11.6	4.3	1.2
Return On Nw (%)	24.8	11.4	4.6

Page 40

SIC 5511 NEW,USED CAR DLRS
(NO BREAKDOWN)
2020 (35 Establishments)

	$	%
Cash	4,288,506	16.4
Accounts Receivable	1,699,713	6.5
Notes Receivable	0	0.0
Inventory	11,113,506	42.5
Other Current	653,735	2.5
Total Current	**17,755,460**	**67.9**
Fixed Assets	2,458,046	9.4
Other Non-current	5,935,920	22.7
Total Assets	**26,149,426**	**100.0**
Accounts Payable	627,586	2.4
Bank Loans	0	0.0
Notes Payable	1,568,966	6.0
Other Current	9,806,035	37.5
Total Current	**12,002,587**	**45.9**
Other Long Term	3,634,770	13.9
Deferred Credits	26,149	0.1
Net Worth	10,485,920	40.1
Total Liab & Net Worth	**26,149,426**	**100.0**
Net Sales	59,838,503	100.0
Gross Profit	14,241,564	23.8
Net Profit After Tax	(1,675,478)	(2.8)
Working Capital	5,752,873	---

RATIOS

	UQ	MED	LQ
SOLVENCY			
Quick Ratio (times)	0.7	0.6	0.3
Current Ratio (times)	1.6	1.5	1.2
Curr Liab To Nw (%)	74.6	137.0	177.1
Curr Liab To Inv (%)	100.9	107.6	123.5
Total Liab To Nw (%)	89.3	140.7	298.9
Fixed Assets To Nw (%)	1.8	6.3	56.4
EFFICIENCY			
Coll Period (days)	5.1	9.1	15.0
Sales To Inv (times)	6.7	6.3	5.2
Assets To Sales (%)	31.2	43.7	54.8
Sales To Nwc (times)	25.5	20.3	6.9
Acct Pay To Sales (%)	1.2	1.5	3.0
PROFITABILITY			
Return On Sales (%)	2.7	1.9	1.0
Return On Assets (%)	4.5	3.3	1.5
Return On Nw (%)	18.9	14.8	6.0

SIC 5531 AUTO,HOME SPPL STRS
(NO BREAKDOWN)
2020 (25 Establishments)

	$	%
Cash	1,012,270	18.9
Accounts Receivable	739,118	13.8
Notes Receivable	5,356	0.1
Inventory	2,115,592	39.5
Other Current	101,763	1.9
Total Current	**3,974,099**	**74.2**
Fixed Assets	1,124,745	21.0
Other Non-current	257,084	4.8
Total Assets	**5,355,928**	**100.0**
Accounts Payable	1,226,508	22.9
Bank Loans	0	0.0
Notes Payable	37,491	0.7
Other Current	664,135	12.4
Total Current	**1,928,134**	**36.0**
Other Long Term	696,271	13.0
Deferred Credits	10,712	0.2
Net Worth	2,720,811	50.8
Total Liab & Net Worth	**5,355,928**	**100.0**
Net Sales	16,789,743	100.0
Gross Profit	5,322,349	31.7
Net Profit After Tax	638,010	3.8
Working Capital	2,045,965	---

	UQ	MED	LQ
Quick Ratio (times)	2.3	1.0	0.3
Current Ratio (times)	4.1	2.2	1.3
Curr Liab To Nw (%)	25.7	55.4	155.1
Curr Liab To Inv (%)	47.0	98.0	123.6
Total Liab To Nw (%)	28.3	83.2	228.8
Fixed Assets To Nw (%)	6.8	25.6	68.0
Coll Period (days)	8.6	17.9	25.9
Sales To Inv (times)	11.9	7.2	4.6
Assets To Sales (%)	23.6	31.9	51.3
Sales To Nwc (times)	12.7	7.9	5.3
Acct Pay To Sales (%)	5.7	8.4	15.5
Return On Sales (%)	5.8	3.3	1.0
Return On Assets (%)	15.2	6.5	3.0
Return On Nw (%)	29.0	14.0	7.0

SIC 5541 GASLNE SVC STATIONS
(NO BREAKDOWN)
2020 (32 Establishments)

	$	%
Cash	1,991,172	21.1
Accounts Receivable	802,131	8.5
Notes Receivable	(28,311)	(0.3)
Inventory	1,660,883	17.6
Other Current	632,269	6.7
Total Current	**5,058,144**	**53.6**
Fixed Assets	3,491,629	37.0
Other Non-current	887,063	9.4
Total Assets	**9,436,836**	**100.0**
Accounts Payable	1,698,630	18.0
Bank Loans	0	0.0
Notes Payable	358,600	3.8
Other Current	1,179,605	12.5
Total Current	**3,236,835**	**34.3**
Other Long Term	1,679,757	17.8
Deferred Credits	0	0.0
Net Worth	4,520,244	47.9
Total Liab & Net Worth	**9,436,836**	**100.0**
Net Sales	57,541,683	100.0
Gross Profit	9,149,128	15.9
Net Profit After Tax	978,209	1.7
Working Capital	1,821,309	---

	UQ	MED	LQ
Quick Ratio (times)	2.0	0.9	0.5
Current Ratio (times)	3.7	2.5	1.2
Curr Liab To Nw (%)	11.8	32.3	63.1
Curr Liab To Inv (%)	86.5	115.1	200.5
Total Liab To Nw (%)	21.5	61.6	90.1
Fixed Assets To Nw (%)	28.8	72.1	113.9
Coll Period (days)	0.7	5.5	11.3
Sales To Inv (times)	41.2	31.3	20.4
Assets To Sales (%)	13.1	16.4	24.8
Sales To Nwc (times)	52.2	19.7	9.6
Acct Pay To Sales (%)	1.1	2.3	3.3
Return On Sales (%)	2.3	1.1	0.5
Return On Assets (%)	13.6	4.5	1.5
Return On Nw (%)	22.4	7.7	4.2

SIC 56 APPAREL ACCES STORES
(NO BREAKDOWN)
2020 (75 Establishments)

	$	%
Cash	23,241,666	15.9
Accounts Receivable	5,554,612	3.8
Notes Receivable	0	0.0
Inventory	60,662,210	41.5
Other Current	11,986,268	8.2
Total Current	**101,444,756**	**69.4**
Fixed Assets	31,281,236	21.4
Other Non-current	13,448,008	9.2
Total Assets	**146,174,000**	**100.0**
Accounts Payable	20,464,360	14.0
Bank Loans	438,522	0.3
Notes Payable	584,696	0.4
Other Current	82,295,962	56.3
Total Current	**103,783,540**	**71.0**
Other Long Term	39,466,980	27.0
Deferred Credits	0	0.0
Net Worth	2,923,480	2.0
Total Liab & Net Worth	**146,174,000**	**100.0**
Net Sales	294,112,676	100.0
Gross Profit	122,939,099	41.8
Net Profit After Tax	7,058,704	2.4
Working Capital	(2,338,784)	---

	UQ	MED	LQ
Quick Ratio (times)	1.0	0.7	0.2
Current Ratio (times)	3.6	2.1	1.7
Curr Liab To Nw (%)	30.5	51.6	105.4
Curr Liab To Inv (%)	53.1	85.6	121.4
Total Liab To Nw (%)	45.2	85.1	183.8
Fixed Assets To Nw (%)	14.9	36.3	76.4
Coll Period (days)	0.7	3.3	8.4
Sales To Inv (times)	9.1	5.8	3.6
Assets To Sales (%)	38.7	49.7	68.3
Sales To Nwc (times)	10.7	6.2	3.3
Acct Pay To Sales (%)	4.3	6.3	9.4
Return On Sales (%)	5.9	2.1	0.0
Return On Assets (%)	10.2	3.7	0.2
Return On Nw (%)	21.0	9.6	1.3

	SIC 5611 MNS.BYS CLTHNG STRS (NO BREAKDOWN) 2020 (21 Establishments)			SIC 5621 WOMENS CLTHNG STRS (NO BREAKDOWN) 2020 (15 Establishments)			SIC 5651 FMLY CLTHNG STRS (NO BREAKDOWN) 2020 (13 Establishments)			SIC 5661 SHOE STORES (NO BREAKDOWN) 2020 (15 Establishments)	
	$		%	$		%	$		%	$	%
Cash	4,400,191		13.2	45,528,840		19.6	1,052,390		15.7	25,206,117	15.7
Accounts Receivable	1,800,078		5.4	7,897,860		3.4	113,953		1.7	5,458,650	3.4
Notes Receivable	0		0.0	0		0.0	6,703		0.1	0	0.0
Inventory	14,400,627		43.2	69,919,290		30.1	3,137,062		46.8	83,164,133	51.8
Other Current	2,900,127		8.7	19,512,360		8.4	542,953		8.1	8,509,071	5.3
Total Current	**23,501,023**		**70.5**	**142,858,350**		**61.5**	**4,853,061**		**72.4**	**122,337,971**	**76.2**
Fixed Assets	7,100,309		21.3	53,426,700		23.0	1,595,343		23.8	29,059,282	18.1
Other Non-current	2,733,452		8.2	36,004,950		15.5	254,719		3.8	9,151,266	5.7
Total Assets	**33,334,784**		**100.0**	**232,290,000**		**100.0**	**6,703,123**		**100.0**	**160,548,519**	**100.0**
Accounts Payable	4,633,535		13.9	42,973,650		18.5	898,218		13.4	16,697,046	10.4
Bank Loans	0		0.0	0		0.0	0		0.0	0	0.0
Notes Payable	0		0.0	0		0.0	80,437		1.2	2,408,228	1.5
Other Current	4,433,526		13.3	520,097,310		223.9	1,347,329		20.1	18,302,531	11.4
Total Current	**9,067,061**		**27.2**	**563,070,960**		**242.4**	**2,325,984**		**34.7**	**37,407,805**	**23.3**
Other Long Term	5,933,592		17.8	66,434,940		28.6	1,173,046		17.5	6,261,392	3.9
Deferred Credits	0		0.0	0		0.0	0		0.0	0	0.0
Net Worth	18,334,131		55.0	(397,215,900)		(171.0)	3,204,093		47.8	116,879,322	72.8
Total Liab & Net Worth	**33,334,784**		**100.0**	**232,290,000**		**100.0**	**6,703,123**		**100.0**	**160,548,519**	**100.0**
Net Sales	62,895,819		100.0	600,232,558		100.0	14,201,532		100.0	296,762,512	100.0
Gross Profit	27,862,848		44.3	258,100,000		43.0	5,495,993		38.7	116,924,430	39.4
Net Profit After Tax	2,390,041		3.8	(7,202,791)		(1.2)	28,403		0.2	11,870,500	4.0
Working Capital	14,433,962		---	(420,212,610)		---	2,527,077		---	84,930,166	---
RATIOS	UQ	MED	LQ	UQ	MED	LQ	UQ	MED	LQ	UQ MED	LQ
SOLVENCY											
Quick Ratio (times)	1.3	0.6	0.2	0.7	0.4	0.2	0.8	0.3	0.1	1.7 1.0	0.3
Current Ratio (times)	3.9	2.2	1.9	2.0	1.4	1.2	2.8	1.8	1.6	6.5 3.6	2.3
Curr Liab To Nw (%)	26.0	44.4	57.5	48.6	168.6	266.9	59.5	77.8	107.9	15.9 29.9	50.0
Curr Liab To Inv (%)	43.3	71.8	102.7	109.6	118.0	145.7	47.0	114.8	171.9	17.9 58.7	69.8
Total Liab To Nw (%)	35.4	61.9	168.4	84.2	223.6	343.9	83.7	95.5	181.2	23.5 52.4	61.3
Fixed Assets To Nw (%)	12.5	38.4	58.2	27.9	64.0	154.2	14.1	45.2	100.6	13.9 28.2	34.8
EFFICIENCY											
Coll Period (days)	1.1	3.7	8.4	2.6	4.9	10.1	0.7	2.6	3.3	0.4 0.7	18.3
Sales To Inv (times)	9.3	5.1	3.2	10.0	7.9	5.8	9.7	6.9	2.8	6.0 4.5	3.2
Assets To Sales (%)	46.8	53.0	81.9	34.1	38.7	50.3	38.2	47.2	91.2	40.1 54.1	80.3
Sales To Nwc (times)	8.0	6.2	2.7	27.3	10.3	6.6	12.0	5.2	2.4	6.0 4.7	2.7
Acct Pay To Sales (%)	4.5	6.9	8.9	5.7	6.9	10.2	3.8	4.5	7.4	4.1 4.8	10.6
PROFITABILITY											
Return On Sales (%)	5.0	1.9	0.5	2.9	0.5	(7.1)	4.1	2.2	0.9	7.9 3.3	0.2
Return On Assets (%)	7.8	3.7	1.2	5.4	0.9	(17.2)	7.9	4.6	0.7	16.2 6.1	0.5
Return On Nw (%)	14.8	8.1	2.6	27.3	4.9	(52.8)	31.7	9.1	1.5	23.0 9.2	0.7

Page 42

	SIC 57 FURN,HOME FURNISHGS (NO BREAKDOWN) 2020 (107 Establishments)		SIC 5712 FURNITURE STORES (NO BREAKDOWN) 2020 (51 Establishments)		SIC 5713 FLR CVRNG STRS (NO BREAKDOWN) 2020 (11 Establishments)		SIC 5731 RDO,TV,ELECTRNC STR (NO BREAKDOWN) 2020 (10 Establishments)	
	$	%	$	%	$	%	$	%
Cash	286,232	15.7	245,258	15.7	115,292	8.9	443,539	18.0
Accounts Receivable	351,865	19.3	204,642	13.1	243,539	18.8	736,768	29.9
Notes Receivable	9,116	0.5	12,497	0.8	0	0.0	0	0.0
Inventory	656,329	36.0	670,165	42.9	353,649	27.3	943,753	38.3
Other Current	87,510	4.8	59,363	3.8	216,335	16.7	32,033	1.3
Total Current	**1,391,052**	**76.3**	**1,191,925**	**76.3**	**928,815**	**71.7**	**2,156,093**	**87.5**
Fixed Assets	251,593	13.8	262,442	16.8	209,858	16.2	160,167	6.5
Other Non-current	180,490	9.9	107,789	6.9	156,745	12.1	147,846	6.0
Total Assets	**1,823,135**	**100.0**	**1,562,156**	**100.0**	**1,295,418**	**100.0**	**2,464,106**	**100.0**
Accounts Payable	309,933	17.0	165,589	10.6	159,336	12.3	522,390	21.2
Bank Loans	0	0.0	0	0.0	3,886	0.3	0	0.0
Notes Payable	21,878	1.2	12,497	0.8	63,475	4.9	12,321	0.5
Other Current	401,089	22.0	395,225	25.3	205,973	15.9	495,285	20.1
Total Current	**732,900**	**40.2**	**573,311**	**36.7**	**432,670**	**33.4**	**1,029,996**	**41.8**
Other Long Term	260,709	14.3	181,210	11.6	169,699	13.1	219,306	8.9
Deferred Credits	0	0.0	0	0.0	0	0.0	0	0.0
Net Worth	829,526	45.5	807,635	51.7	693,049	53.5	1,214,804	49.3
Total Liab & Net Worth	**1,823,135**	**100.0**	**1,562,156**	**100.0**	**1,295,418**	**100.0**	**2,464,106**	**100.0**
Net Sales	4,162,409	100.0	3,201,139	100.0	3,669,739	100.0	4,889,099	100.0
Gross Profit	1,648,314	39.6	1,434,110	44.8	1,291,748	35.2	1,882,303	38.5
Net Profit After Tax	133,197	3.2	64,023	2.0	135,780	3.7	523,134	10.7
Working Capital	658,152	---	618,614	---	496,145	---	1,126,097	---

RATIOS	UQ	MED	LQ	UQ	MED	LQ	UQ	MED	LQ	UQ	MED	LQ
SOLVENCY												
Quick Ratio (times)	1.7	0.8	0.4	2.2	0.7	0.3	1.5	1.1	0.3	1.6	0.9	0.6
Current Ratio (times)	3.8	2.1	1.4	4.2	2.6	1.7	3.1	2.1	1.7	3.6	1.9	1.6
Curr Liab To Nw (%)	30.1	68.7	129.3	17.4	37.8	110.9	50.8	73.0	85.3	46.4	82.6	129.3
Curr Liab To Inv (%)	49.9	94.9	180.9	35.6	66.2	133.0	61.3	120.3	585.9	72.7	93.7	137.7
Total Liab To Nw (%)	37.4	102.1	202.7	22.6	62.4	174.1	53.6	86.1	163.0	46.4	127.3	169.6
Fixed Assets To Nw (%)	6.4	17.9	37.9	5.9	17.4	37.0	20.2	27.6	53.3	4.2	11.1	24.1
EFFICIENCY												
Coll Period (days)	6.4	19.4	59.1	3.3	9.7	42.0	10.6	13.1	58.0	37.5	84.2	103.0
Sales To Inv (times)	11.4	6.8	3.8	8.3	4.6	3.3	34.1	9.3	4.8	10.8	6.9	3.6
Assets To Sales (%)	26.4	43.8	66.3	34.3	48.8	71.1	33.0	35.3	45.1	26.3	50.4	68.3
Sales To Nwc (times)	13.1	6.4	3.3	10.5	4.2	2.4	12.2	6.8	5.1	13.1	4.3	2.7
Acct Pay To Sales (%)	3.5	5.5	9.2	2.7	4.5	6.3	3.6	5.3	5.9	7.4	9.7	20.7
PROFITABILITY												
Return On Sales (%)	5.4	2.5	0.5	4.6	1.6	(0.1)	5.9	2.5	1.9	20.4	7.3	2.8
Return On Assets (%)	12.6	5.1	1.2	9.6	2.4	0.0	10.7	6.6	4.4	39.5	13.4	6.3
Return On Nw (%)	40.9	13.2	2.1	28.6	4.5	0.2	22.9	16.9	10.1	69.1	43.4	20.1

Page 43

SIC 5734 COMPTR.SOFTWRE STRS
(NO BREAKDOWN)
2020 (17 Establishments)

	$	%
Cash	881,945	22.6
Accounts Receivable	1,459,501	37.4
Notes Receivable	23,414	0.6
Inventory	542,435	13.9
Other Current	113,170	2.9
Total Current	**3,020,465**	**77.4**
Fixed Assets	277,071	7.1
Other Non-current	604,874	15.5
Total Assets	**3,902,410**	**100.0**
Accounts Payable	1,166,821	29.9
Bank Loans	0	0.0
Notes Payable	11,707	0.3
Other Current	729,750	18.7
Total Current	**1,908,278**	**48.9**
Other Long Term	905,360	23.2
Deferred Credits	0	0.0
Net Worth	1,088,772	27.9
Total Liab & Net Worth	**3,902,410**	**100.0**
Net Sales	16,260,042	100.0
Gross Profit	4,878,013	30.0
Net Profit After Tax	585,362	3.6
Working Capital	1,112,187	--

RATIOS	UQ	MED	LQ
SOLVENCY			
Quick Ratio (times)	2.2	1.4	0.9
Current Ratio (times)	2.3	1.6	1.3
Curr Liab To Nw (%)	58.5	121.6	200.0
Curr Liab To Inv (%)	180.9	352.7	999.9
Total Liab To Nw (%)	72.9	172.6	231.4
Fixed Assets To Nw (%)	2.7	13.1	23.1
EFFICIENCY			
Coll Period (days)	22.3	32.9	43.7
Sales To Inv (times)	103.8	59.0	9.3
Assets To Sales (%)	14.7	24.0	30.2
Sales To Nwc (times)	30.4	10.2	8.6
Acct Pay To Sales (%)	5.6	8.1	12.3
PROFITABILITY			
Return On Sales (%)	5.3	2.8	1.4
Return On Assets (%)	25.1	13.0	3.4
Return On Nw (%)	46.4	35.4	21.9

SIC 58 EATING,DRINKG PLACES
(NO BREAKDOWN)
2020 (69 Establishments)

	$	%
Cash	31,194,335	15.1
Accounts Receivable	15,080,705	7.3
Notes Receivable	0	0.0
Inventory	9,709,495	4.7
Other Current	8,883,155	4.3
Total Current	**64,867,690**	**31.4**
Fixed Assets	81,187,905	39.3
Other Non-current	60,529,405	29.3
Total Assets	**206,585,000**	**100.0**
Accounts Payable	16,733,385	8.1
Bank Loans	0	0.0
Notes Payable	206,585	0.1
Other Current	48,134,305	23.3
Total Current	**65,074,275**	**31.5**
Other Long Term	97,508,120	47.2
Deferred Credits	1,239,510	0.6
Net Worth	42,763,095	20.7
Total Liab & Net Worth	**206,585,000**	**100.0**
Net Sales	244,190,307	100.0
Gross Profit	136,502,382	55.9
Net Profit After Tax	17,825,892	7.3
Working Capital	(206,585)	--

RATIOS	UQ	MED	LQ
SOLVENCY			
Quick Ratio (times)	1.0	0.5	0.3
Current Ratio (times)	1.6	0.8	0.5
Curr Liab To Nw (%)	23.9	53.8	75.7
Curr Liab To Inv (%)	599.7	999.9	999.9
Total Liab To Nw (%)	70.1	132.6	269.3
Fixed Assets To Nw (%)	51.6	107.4	155.9
EFFICIENCY			
Coll Period (days)	3.5	9.9	20.3
Sales To Inv (times)	164.2	69.7	46.8
Assets To Sales (%)	41.5	84.6	110.3
Sales To Nwc (times)	20.6	9.6	4.3
Acct Pay To Sales (%)	2.1	3.4	4.8
PROFITABILITY			
Return On Sales (%)	9.6	4.4	(0.3)
Return On Assets (%)	13.4	4.6	(0.4)
Return On Nw (%)	31.4	9.3	(2.6)

SIC 5812 EATING PLACES
(NO BREAKDOWN)
2020 (63 Establishments)

	$	%
Cash	50,264,729	15.1
Accounts Receivable	25,964,562	7.8
Notes Receivable	0	0.0
Inventory	16,643,950	5.0
Other Current	12,649,402	3.8
Total Current	**105,522,643**	**31.7**
Fixed Assets	129,489,931	38.9
Other Non-current	97,866,426	29.4
Total Assets	**332,879,000**	**100.0**
Accounts Payable	28,294,715	8.5
Bank Loans	0	0.0
Notes Payable	0	0.0
Other Current	75,896,412	22.8
Total Current	**104,191,127**	**31.3**
Other Long Term	160,780,557	48.3
Deferred Credits	4,660,306	1.4
Net Worth	63,247,010	19.0
Total Liab & Net Worth	**332,879,000**	**100.0**
Net Sales	393,473,995	100.0
Gross Profit	213,262,905	54.2
Net Profit After Tax	25,969,284	6.6
Working Capital	1,331,516	--

RATIOS	UQ	MED	LQ
SOLVENCY			
Quick Ratio (times)	1.0	0.5	0.3
Current Ratio (times)	1.6	0.8	0.5
Curr Liab To Nw (%)	30.9	54.0	75.7
Curr Liab To Inv (%)	587.9	999.9	999.9
Total Liab To Nw (%)	73.1	135.3	269.3
Fixed Assets To Nw (%)	52.8	106.7	155.9
EFFICIENCY			
Coll Period (days)	3.3	9.1	19.4
Sales To Inv (times)	172.4	74.0	46.8
Assets To Sales (%)	40.8	84.6	106.2
Sales To Nwc (times)	16.4	7.2	3.4
Acct Pay To Sales (%)	2.1	3.4	4.8
PROFITABILITY			
Return On Sales (%)	9.2	4.2	(0.6)
Return On Assets (%)	12.3	4.2	(0.6)
Return On Nw (%)	28.2	7.5	(2.6)

SIC 59 MISC RETAIL STORES
(NO BREAKDOWN)
2020 (228 Establishments)

	$	%
Cash	1,487,047	19.0
Accounts Receivable	907,881	11.6
Notes Receivable	0	0.0
Inventory	2,175,784	27.8
Other Current	438,287	5.6
Total Current	**5,008,999**	**64.0**
Fixed Assets	1,573,139	20.1
Other Non-current	1,244,423	15.9
Total Assets	**7,826,561**	**100.0**
Accounts Payable	4,406,354	56.3
Bank Loans	23,480	0.3
Notes Payable	101,745	1.3
Other Current	6,566,484	83.9
Total Current	**11,098,063**	**141.8**
Other Long Term	2,019,253	25.8
Deferred Credits	7,827	0.1
Net Worth	(5,298,582)	(67.7)
Total Liab & Net Worth	**7,826,561**	**100.0**
Net Sales	17,125,954	100.0
Gross Profit	5,976,958	34.9
Net Profit After Tax	291,141	1.7
Working Capital	(6,089,064)	--

RATIOS	UQ	MED	LQ
SOLVENCY			
Quick Ratio (times)	1.6	0.8	0.3
Current Ratio (times)	3.6	1.8	1.2
Curr Liab To Nw (%)	22.9	56.5	131.2
Curr Liab To Inv (%)	58.7	107.3	307.3
Total Liab To Nw (%)	33.6	88.4	247.7
Fixed Assets To Nw (%)	8.5	29.2	67.6
EFFICIENCY			
Coll Period (days)	4.4	16.1	31.8
Sales To Inv (times)	22.8	8.5	4.5
Assets To Sales (%)	27.3	45.7	71.2
Sales To Nwc (times)	13.9	6.6	3.6
Acct Pay To Sales (%)	2.5	4.5	9.2
PROFITABILITY			
Return On Sales (%)	6.1	1.5	(0.2)
Return On Assets (%)	11.2	4.2	(0.8)
Return On Nw (%)	26.2	10.2	0.7

Page 44

SIC 5912 DRG STRS,PRPRTRY ST
(NO BREAKDOWN)
2020 (21 Establishments)

	$	%
Cash	18,128,649	23.1
Accounts Receivable	10,516,186	13.4
Notes Receivable	0	0.0
Inventory	11,379,455	14.5
Other Current	2,982,202	3.8
Total Current	**43,006,492**	**54.8**
Fixed Assets	12,399,682	15.8
Other Non-current	23,072,826	29.4
Total Assets	**78,479,000**	**100.0**
Accounts Payable	38,690,147	49.3
Bank Loans	78,479	0.1
Notes Payable	0	0.0
Other Current	75,418,319	96.1
Total Current	**114,186,945**	**145.5**
Other Long Term	24,250,011	30.9
Deferred Credits	235,437	0.3
Net Worth	(60,193,393)	(76.7)
Total Liab & Net Worth	**78,479,000**	**100.0**
Net Sales	130,363,787	100.0
Gross Profit	37,805,498	29.0
Net Profit After Tax	521,455	0.4
Working Capital	(71,180,453)	—

RATIOS	UQ	MED	LQ
SOLVENCY			
Quick Ratio (times)	1.3	0.8	0.5
Current Ratio (times)	3.0	1.5	0.8
Curr Liab To Nw (%)	25.6	74.6	116.3
Curr Liab To Inv (%)	127.7	237.7	691.9
Total Liab To Nw (%)	97.7	202.2	329.5
Fixed Assets To Nw (%)	4.4	18.8	85.5
EFFICIENCY			
Coll Period (days)	19.0	30.5	45.6
Sales To Inv (times)	38.1	16.6	9.1
Assets To Sales (%)	22.6	60.2	127.0
Sales To Nwc (times)	12.8	7.6	4.4
Acct Pay To Sales (%)	4.0	6.0	12.2
PROFITABILITY			
Return On Sales (%)	3.1	1.1	(3.9)
Return On Assets (%)	7.1	3.3	(3.6)
Return On Nw (%)	25.6	13.5	(1.5)

SIC 5941 SPTG GDS,BCYLE SHPS
(NO BREAKDOWN)
2020 (12 Establishments)

	$	%
Cash	3,217,464	6.8
Accounts Receivable	1,750,679	3.7
Notes Receivable	0	0.0
Inventory	21,575,935	45.6
Other Current	4,069,146	8.6
Total Current	**30,613,224**	**64.7**
Fixed Assets	10,835,283	22.9
Other Non-current	5,867,140	12.4
Total Assets	**47,315,647**	**100.0**
Accounts Payable	4,021,830	8.5
Bank Loans	0	0.0
Notes Payable	0	0.0
Other Current	16,040,004	33.9
Total Current	**20,061,834**	**42.4**
Other Long Term	8,422,185	17.8
Deferred Credits	47,316	0.1
Net Worth	18,784,312	39.7
Total Liab & Net Worth	**47,315,647**	**100.0**
Net Sales	86,658,694	100.0
Gross Profit	27,990,758	32.3
Net Profit After Tax	1,906,491	2.2
Working Capital	10,551,390	—

RATIOS	UQ	MED	LQ
SOLVENCY			
Quick Ratio (times)	1.2	0.4	0.1
Current Ratio (times)	5.8	2.1	1.4
Curr Liab To Nw (%)	14.5	32.0	123.5
Curr Liab To Inv (%)	36.3	72.0	91.2
Total Liab To Nw (%)	14.5	40.7	281.9
Fixed Assets To Nw (%)	9.9	34.0	82.2
EFFICIENCY			
Coll Period (days)	1.1	3.7	5.8
Sales To Inv (times)	5.3	4.0	3.4
Assets To Sales (%)	47.3	54.6	63.5
Sales To Nwc (times)	12.4	6.5	4.2
Acct Pay To Sales (%)	2.9	4.9	8.4
PROFITABILITY			
Return On Sales (%)	4.2	2.8	0.3
Return On Assets (%)	8.1	4.3	0.4
Return On Nw (%)	16.8	11.3	3.9

SIC 5942 BOOK STORES
(NO BREAKDOWN)
2020 (11 Establishments)

	$	%
Cash	1,954,192	29.6
Accounts Receivable	316,896	4.8
Notes Receivable	0	0.0
Inventory	1,366,614	20.7
Other Current	699,812	10.6
Total Current	**4,337,514**	**65.7**
Fixed Assets	1,003,504	15.2
Other Non-current	1,260,982	19.1
Total Assets	**6,602,000**	**100.0**
Accounts Payable	660,200	10.0
Bank Loans	0	0.0
Notes Payable	0	0.0
Other Current	845,056	12.8
Total Current	**1,505,256**	**22.8**
Other Long Term	1,663,704	25.2
Deferred Credits	85,826	1.3
Net Worth	3,347,214	50.7
Total Liab & Net Worth	**6,602,000**	**100.0**
Net Sales	11,810,376	100.0
Gross Profit	4,854,065	41.1
Net Profit After Tax	(531,467)	(4.5)
Working Capital	2,832,258	—

RATIOS	UQ	MED	LQ
SOLVENCY			
Quick Ratio (times)	5.2	1.5	0.5
Current Ratio (times)	7.6	2.5	1.6
Curr Liab To Nw (%)	6.4	38.4	70.8
Curr Liab To Inv (%)	47.6	83.8	130.6
Total Liab To Nw (%)	6.4	61.8	72.2
Fixed Assets To Nw (%)	5.6	11.3	23.1
EFFICIENCY			
Coll Period (days)	3.9	15.0	36.2
Sales To Inv (times)	5.5	4.8	4.4
Assets To Sales (%)	40.9	55.9	133.9
Sales To Nwc (times)	9.5	3.6	1.0
Acct Pay To Sales (%)	2.6	6.2	10.5
PROFITABILITY			
Return On Sales (%)	5.6	(0.3)	(1.8)
Return On Assets (%)	10.2	(0.5)	(1.9)
Return On Nw (%)	9.9	(0.4)	(3.4)

SIC 5944 JEWELRY STORES
(NO BREAKDOWN)
2020 (15 Establishments)

	$	%
Cash	994,638	12.3
Accounts Receivable	444,757	5.5
Notes Receivable	0	0.0
Inventory	5,514,984	68.2
Other Current	315,373	3.9
Total Current	**7,269,752**	**89.9**
Fixed Assets	485,189	6.0
Other Non-current	331,546	4.1
Total Assets	**8,086,487**	**100.0**
Accounts Payable	938,032	11.6
Bank Loans	0	0.0
Notes Payable	97,038	1.2
Other Current	1,253,406	15.5
Total Current	**2,288,476**	**28.3**
Other Long Term	291,113	3.6
Deferred Credits	0	0.0
Net Worth	5,506,898	68.1
Total Liab & Net Worth	**8,086,487**	**100.0**
Net Sales	11,470,194	100.0
Gross Profit	5,184,528	45.2
Net Profit After Tax	435,867	3.8
Working Capital	4,981,276	—

RATIOS	UQ	MED	LQ
SOLVENCY			
Quick Ratio (times)	2.4	1.0	0.4
Current Ratio (times)	13.2	5.3	2.8
Curr Liab To Nw (%)	8.2	22.3	77.1
Curr Liab To Inv (%)	10.4	29.6	42.2
Total Liab To Nw (%)	8.2	29.4	106.3
Fixed Assets To Nw (%)	1.4	3.7	8.9
EFFICIENCY			
Coll Period (days)	0.7	11.4	43.4
Sales To Inv (times)	2.7	1.9	1.7
Assets To Sales (%)	64.6	70.5	97.5
Sales To Nwc (times)	2.8	1.8	1.5
Acct Pay To Sales (%)	2.9	6.6	11.9
PROFITABILITY			
Return On Sales (%)	6.9	1.5	0.6
Return On Assets (%)	9.9	1.9	0.7
Return On Nw (%)	13.1	9.6	0.8

	SIC 5961 CTLG,ML-ORDER HSES (NO BREAKDOWN) 2020 (33 Establishments)				SIC 5983 FUEL OIL DEALERS (NO BREAKDOWN) 2020 (24 Establishments)				SIC 5999 MISC RTL STRS.NEC (NO BREAKDOWN) 2020 (68 Establishments)				SIC 61 CREDIT AGENC EX BANK (NO BREAKDOWN) 2020 (24 Establishments)	
	$			%	$			%	$			%	$	%
Cash	3,473,898			25.3	1,689,140			27.5	609,821			15.9	2,972,579	31.4
Accounts Receivable	1,318,159			9.6	1,025,769			16.7	605,986			15.8	454,407	4.8
Notes Receivable	0			0.0	6,142			0.1	0			0.0	246,137	2.6
Inventory	2,814,818			20.5	792,360			12.9	1,154,442			30.1	160,936	1.7
Other Current	480,579			3.5	528,241			8.6	161,085			4.2	2,395,103	25.3
Total Current	**8,087,454**			**58.9**	**4,041,652**			**65.8**	**2,531,334**			**66.0**	**6,229,162**	**65.8**
Fixed Assets	2,801,087			20.4	1,560,151			25.4	759,400			19.8	965,615	10.2
Other Non-current	2,842,280			20.7	540,525			8.8	544,620			14.2	2,272,034	24.0
Total Assets	**13,730,821**			**100.0**	**6,142,328**			**100.0**	**3,835,354**			**100.0**	**9,466,811**	**100.0**
Accounts Payable	8,416,993			61.3	1,099,477			17.9	4,732,827			123.4	22,815,015	241.0
Bank Loans	0			0.0	0			0.0	26,847			0.7	0	0.0
Notes Payable	151,039			1.1	116,704			1.9	107,390			2.8	22,616,211	238.9
Other Current	30,688,385			223.5	1,394,308			22.7	4,241,902			110.6	1,107,617	11.7
Total Current	**39,256,417**			**285.9**	**2,610,489**			**42.5**	**9,108,966**			**237.5**	**46,538,843**	**491.6**
Other Long Term	9,597,844			69.9	522,098			8.5	548,455			14.3	16,831,990	177.8
Deferred Credits	0			0.0	0			0.0	0			0.0	9,467	0.1
Net Worth	(35,123,440)			(255.8)	3,009,741			49.0	(5,822,067)			(151.8)	(53,913,489)	(569.5)
Total Liab & Net Worth	**13,730,821**			**100.0**	**6,142,328**			**100.0**	**3,835,354**			**100.0**	**9,466,811**	**100.0**
Net Sales	35,388,714			100.0	20,542,903			100.0	8,561,058			100.0	2,748,784	100.0
Gross Profit	12,775,326			36.1	3,553,922			17.3	3,099,103			36.2	1,731,734	63.0
Net Profit After Tax	176,944			0.5	431,401			2.1	231,149			2.7	574,496	20.9
Working Capital	(31,168,963)			---	1,431,163			---	(6,577,632)			---	(40,309,681)	---
RATIOS	UQ	MED	LQ		UQ	MED	LQ		UQ	MED	LQ		UQ MED	LQ
SOLVENCY														
Quick Ratio (times)	1.1	0.6	0.3		1.3	1.1	0.7		1.9	0.7	0.3		2.1 1.0	0.1
Current Ratio (times)	2.4	1.5	0.9		2.1	1.5	1.1		3.1	1.9	1.0		4.4 2.3	0.9
Curr Liab To Nw (%)	46.4	88.9	141.7		38.2	80.1	168.6		16.5	56.8	141.2		10.9 28.7	75.7
Curr Liab To Inv (%)	104.2	147.2	247.8		183.3	372.4	715.9		58.7	96.2	241.9		74.7 197.0	999.9
Total Liab To Nw (%)	66.3	159.2	263.0		53.7	85.4	211.0		26.8	89.6	237.5		29.1 130.8	197.0
Fixed Assets To Nw (%)	6.4	13.9	47.8		27.1	56.8	79.1		14.8	32.8	67.4		1.4 7.8	51.0
EFFICIENCY														
Coll Period (days)	4.4	8.4	25.2		9.7	13.3	21.9		6.6	19.4	42.3		28.2 37.2	59.9
Sales To Inv (times)	24.3	13.4	6.3		55.3	34.4	19.8		16.0	7.7	4.1		999.9 13.8	0.3
Assets To Sales (%)	20.7	38.8	67.5		17.7	29.9	40.7		27.5	44.8	56.9		117.4 344.4	999.9
Sales To Nwc (times)	22.8	7.4	5.7		27.5	17.8	6.6		11.0	6.3	3.6		2.3 1.7	0.2
Acct Pay To Sales (%)	4.6	7.2	10.9		2.0	3.3	4.8		2.0	3.9	9.3		3.3 5.3	5.9
PROFITABILITY														
Return On Sales (%)	7.4	2.9	(4.9)		3.5	0.9	0.5		7.0	1.8	0.2		24.2 8.0	(0.5)
Return On Assets (%)	14.2	6.1	(12.1)		7.2	5.1	2.8		13.9	4.0	0.1		2.7 1.1	(9.5)
Return On Nw (%)	59.6	16.4	9.7		23.0	8.2	5.7		35.9	7.9	2.3		7.9 4.9	2.4

Page 45

Page 46

	SIC 62 SEC,COM BROKERS,SVS (NO BREAKDOWN) 2020 (18 Establishments)			SIC 65 REAL ESTATE (NO BREAKDOWN) 2020 (104 Establishments)		SIC 6512 NRSDNTL BLDG OPTRS (NO BREAKDOWN) 2020 (12 Establishments)		SIC 6513 APMNT BLDG OPRTRS (NO BREAKDOWN) 2020 (35 Establishments)	
	$	%		$	%	$	%	$	%
Cash	34,615,451	22.3		1,926,111	13.8	9,853,652	22.3	516,048	7.3
Accounts Receivable	20,955,542	13.5		851,397	6.1	6,407,083	14.5	77,761	1.1
Notes Receivable	0	0.0		69,787	0.5	44,187	0.1	0	0.0
Inventory	4,812,013	3.1		181,445	1.3	972,109	2.2	0	0.0
Other Current	24,836,199	16.0		1,493,434	10.7	2,076,779	4.7	777,607	11.0
Total Current	**85,219,205**	**54.9**		**4,522,174**	**32.4**	**19,353,810**	**43.8**	**1,371,416**	**19.4**
Fixed Assets	14,280,814	9.2		6,211,011	44.5	19,618,930	44.4	4,425,292	62.6
Other Non-current	55,726,219	35.9		3,224,142	23.1	5,214,040	11.8	1,272,448	18.0
Total Assets	**155,226,238**	**100.0**		**13,957,327**	**100.0**	**44,186,780**	**100.0**	**7,069,156**	**100.0**
Accounts Payable	133,494,565	86.0		795,568	5.7	5,965,215	13.5	106,037	1.5
Bank Loans	0	0.0		0	0.0	0	0.0	0	0.0
Notes Payable	716,679,541	461.7		111,659	0.8	1,369,790	3.1	0	0.0
Other Current	(422,681,047)	(272.3)		11,235,647	80.5	234,631,802	531.0	940,198	13.3
Total Current	**427,493,059**	**275.4**		**12,142,874**	**87.0**	**241,966,807**	**547.6**	**1,046,235**	**14.8**
Other Long Term	35,391,583	22.8		5,401,486	38.7	5,302,414	12.0	4,510,121	63.8
Deferred Credits	0	0.0		111,659	0.8	0	0.0	120,176	1.7
Net Worth	(307,658,404)	(198.2)		(3,698,692)	(26.5)	(203,082,441)	(459.6)	1,392,624	19.7
Total Liab & Net Worth	**155,226,238**	**100.0**		**13,957,327**	**100.0**	**44,186,780**	**100.0**	**7,069,156**	**100.0**
Net Sales	73,047,641	100.0		4,122,069	100.0	18,101,917	100.0	1,193,308	100.0
Gross Profit	28,853,818	39.5		1,690,048	41.0	7,222,665	39.9	284,007	23.8
Net Profit After Tax	4,894,192	6.7		272,057	6.6	6,227,059	34.4	(52,506)	(4.4)
Working Capital	(342,273,854)	---		(7,620,700)	---	(222,612,997)	---	325,181	---

RATIOS	UQ	MED	LQ	UQ	MED	LQ	UQ	MED	LQ	UQ	MED	LQ
SOLVENCY												
Quick Ratio (times)	2.3	1.2	0.1	3.0	0.9	0.4	12.8	2.1	0.8	1.9	0.8	0.3
Current Ratio (times)	4.6	1.7	1.0	5.5	1.7	0.7	20.6	2.8	1.0	5.1	1.4	0.7
Curr Liab To Nw (%)	11.4	19.2	271.2	4.2	20.6	80.5	0.6	7.6	19.8	1.6	7.1	171.9
Curr Liab To Inv (%)	295.3	319.5	493.3	157.4	984.1	999.9	792.1	999.9	999.9	546.6	999.9	999.9
Total Liab To Nw (%)	19.5	63.6	317.1	20.8	74.8	220.0	4.2	28.2	75.6	5.2	62.9	597.8
Fixed Assets To Nw (%)	2.1	4.4	10.1	19.2	66.9	125.5	65.2	97.3	102.7	68.2	107.5	262.5
EFFICIENCY												
Coll Period (days)	35.0	42.4	53.3	3.7	15.0	48.6	7.2	30.3	69.7	1.7	6.9	18.7
Sales To Inv (times)	37.2	26.7	4.6	347.3	196.7	8.2	755.2	415.2	179.5	374.7	374.7	374.7
Assets To Sales (%)	121.5	212.5	442.4	102.1	338.6	739.3	30.8	244.1	999.9	316.0	592.4	851.9
Sales To Nwc (times)	7.7	3.8	2.2	18.9	2.2	0.9	6.6	0.9	0.6	22.6	6.7	1.4
Acct Pay To Sales (%)	2.3	4.8	10.1	1.5	4.7	10.2	2.8	6.7	15.7	1.9	3.4	7.5
PROFITABILITY												
Return On Sales (%)	21.2	14.9	0.6	14.8	3.0	(11.8)	66.0	(3.9)	4.6	7.4	(3.9)	(23.1)
Return On Assets (%)	7.3	2.8	(14.7)	8.2	2.2	(2.6)	23.1	(0.7)	4.5	2.8	0.7	(2.6)
Return On Nw (%)	13.5	11.1	2.8	21.6	7.8	(3.4)	23.1	20.6	7.5	10.8	1.9	(6.8)

Page 47

SIC 6531 RL ESTE AGNTS,MGRS
(NO BREAKDOWN)
2020 (39 Establishments)

	$	%
Cash	1,971,078	16.8
Accounts Receivable	903,411	7.7
Notes Receivable	105,593	0.9
Inventory	211,187	1.8
Other Current	1,490,042	12.7
Total Current	**4,681,311**	**39.9**
Fixed Assets	4,024,285	34.3
Other Non-current	3,027,014	25.8
Total Assets	**11,732,610**	**100.0**
Accounts Payable	821,283	7.0
Bank Loans	0	0.0
Notes Payable	129,059	1.1
Other Current	3,965,622	33.8
Total Current	**4,915,964**	**41.9**
Other Long Term	3,484,585	29.7
Deferred Credits	35,198	0.3
Net Worth	3,296,863	28.1
Total Liab & Net Worth	**11,732,610**	**100.0**
Net Sales	4,769,354	100.0
Gross Profit	2,184,364	45.8
Net Profit After Tax	367,240	7.7
Working Capital	(234,653)	---

RATIOS	UQ	MED	LQ
SOLVENCY			
Quick Ratio (times)	2.3	0.8	0.3
Current Ratio (times)	4.1	1.4	0.7
Curr Liab To Nw (%)	13.0	25.7	105.5
Curr Liab To Inv (%)	191.1	968.2	999.9
Total Liab To Nw (%)	36.6	156.4	201.2
Fixed Assets To Nw (%)	14.1	41.1	120.4
EFFICIENCY			
Coll Period (days)	5.1	17.7	67.9
Sales To Inv (times)	288.9	131.1	5.9
Assets To Sales (%)	76.0	246.0	412.8
Sales To Nwc (times)	22.8	2.2	1.4
Acct Pay To Sales (%)	1.1	3.5	8.6
PROFITABILITY			
Return On Sales (%)	7.3	2.0	(8.1)
Return On Assets (%)	7.7	3.2	(6.6)
Return On Nw (%)	21.6	11.1	(4.2)

SIC 6552 SBDVDRS,DVLPRS,NEC
(NO BREAKDOWN)
2020 (12 Establishments)

	$	%
Cash	5,749,763	13.6
Accounts Receivable	4,143,212	9.8
Notes Receivable	380,499	0.9
Inventory	253,666	0.6
Other Current	5,411,542	12.8
Total Current	**15,938,682**	**37.7**
Fixed Assets	15,727,294	37.2
Other Non-current	10,611,695	25.1
Total Assets	**42,277,671**	**100.0**
Accounts Payable	3,593,602	8.5
Bank Loans	0	0.0
Notes Payable	0	0.0
Other Current	6,341,651	15.0
Total Current	**9,935,253**	**23.5**
Other Long Term	12,260,524	29.0
Deferred Credits	126,833	0.3
Net Worth	19,955,061	47.2
Total Liab & Net Worth	**42,277,671**	**100.0**
Net Sales	8,784,058	100.0
Gross Profit	3,188,613	36.3
Net Profit After Tax	26,352	0.3
Working Capital	6,003,429	---

RATIOS	UQ	MED	LQ
SOLVENCY			
Quick Ratio (times)	3.3	1.0	0.4
Current Ratio (times)	6.2	1.7	0.9
Curr Liab To Nw (%)	8.8	30.3	127.1
Curr Liab To Inv (%)	478.7	478.7	478.7
Total Liab To Nw (%)	39.0	69.7	269.4
Fixed Assets To Nw (%)	20.5	62.9	151.2
EFFICIENCY			
Coll Period (days)	3.7	57.3	69.7
Sales To Inv (times)	25.1	25.1	25.1
Assets To Sales (%)	213.8	481.3	880.4
Sales To Nwc (times)	13.5	3.6	0.6
Acct Pay To Sales (%)	5.0	9.4	19.4
PROFITABILITY			
Return On Sales (%)	18.9	11.0	(24.9)
Return On Assets (%)	10.9	2.8	(1.6)
Return On Nw (%)	15.0	4.7	(1.8)

SIC 67 HOLDG,RE INVESTM COS
(NO BREAKDOWN)
2020 (127 Establishments)

	$	%
Cash	6,638,740	26.7
Accounts Receivable	696,197	2.8
Notes Receivable	24,864	0.1
Inventory	348,099	1.4
Other Current	3,207,481	12.9
Total Current	**10,915,381**	**43.9**
Fixed Assets	2,287,506	9.2
Other Non-current	11,661,307	46.9
Total Assets	**24,864,194**	**100.0**
Accounts Payable	99,058,949	398.4
Bank Loans	149,185	0.6
Notes Payable	50,424,585	202.8
Other Current	37,147,106	149.4
Total Current	**186,779,825**	**751.2**
Other Long Term	34,014,218	136.8
Deferred Credits	0	0.0
Net Worth	(195,929,849)	(788.0)
Total Liab & Net Worth	**24,864,194**	**100.0**
Net Sales	12,296,832	100.0
Gross Profit	5,890,183	47.9
Net Profit After Tax	553,357	4.5
Working Capital	(175,864,444)	---

RATIOS	UQ	MED	LQ
SOLVENCY			
Quick Ratio (times)	3.6	0.7	0.1
Current Ratio (times)	4.3	1.3	0.2
Curr Liab To Nw (%)	4.6	11.6	40.1
Curr Liab To Inv (%)	284.7	908.1	999.9
Total Liab To Nw (%)	39.8	326.1	999.9
Fixed Assets To Nw (%)	2.6	15.7	97.7
EFFICIENCY			
Coll Period (days)	18.8	48.8	75.8
Sales To Inv (times)	70.8	47.7	10.0
Assets To Sales (%)	87.4	202.2	738.5
Sales To Nwc (times)	14.6	4.3	0.7
Acct Pay To Sales (%)	2.6	6.5	18.0
PROFITABILITY			
Return On Sales (%)	9.5	(0.5)	(31.6)
Return On Assets (%)	1.1	0.0	(85.3)
Return On Nw (%)	34.9	5.4	(2.1)

SIC 6719 HOLDING COS,NEC
(NO BREAKDOWN)
2020 (14 Establishments)

	$	%
Cash	21,365,252	14.2
Accounts Receivable	22,418,469	14.9
Notes Receivable	0	0.0
Inventory	8,726,652	5.8
Other Current	13,992,735	9.3
Total Current	**66,503,108**	**44.2**
Fixed Assets	28,135,930	18.7
Other Non-current	55,820,483	37.1
Total Assets	**150,459,521**	**100.0**
Accounts Payable	9,027,571	6.0
Bank Loans	8,726,652	5.8
Notes Payable	752,298	0.5
Other Current	36,110,285	24.0
Total Current	**54,616,806**	**36.3**
Other Long Term	58,077,375	38.6
Deferred Credits	0	0.0
Net Worth	37,765,340	25.1
Total Liab & Net Worth	**150,459,521**	**100.0**
Net Sales	174,547,008	100.0
Gross Profit	62,313,282	35.7
Net Profit After Tax	11,869,197	6.8
Working Capital	11,886,302	---

RATIOS	UQ	MED	LQ
SOLVENCY			
Quick Ratio (times)	3.7	1.5	0.7
Current Ratio (times)	4.7	2.2	1.1
Curr Liab To Nw (%)	11.1	27.4	86.5
Curr Liab To Inv (%)	220.0	463.9	999.9
Total Liab To Nw (%)	46.3	135.6	290.9
Fixed Assets To Nw (%)	13.2	44.4	110.8
EFFICIENCY			
Coll Period (days)	35.4	52.4	55.9
Sales To Inv (times)	535.4	62.2	8.9
Assets To Sales (%)	39.4	86.2	116.6
Sales To Nwc (times)	14.6	5.6	4.0
Acct Pay To Sales (%)	3.1	4.4	8.9
PROFITABILITY			
Return On Sales (%)	5.1	3.2	(1.4)
Return On Assets (%)	10.8	1.2	(2.8)
Return On Nw (%)	44.4	4.2	(2.0)

	SIC 6794 PATENT OWNERS,LESSO (NO BREAKDOWN) 2020 (10 Establishments)			SIC 6799 INVESTORS, NEC (NO BREAKDOWN) 2020 (84 Establishments)		SIC 70 HOTELS,RE LODGG PLA (NO BREAKDOWN) 2020 (47 Establishments)		SIC 7011 HOTELS AND MOTELS (NO BREAKDOWN) 2020 (37 Establishments)	
	$	%		$	%	$	%	$	%
Cash	1,354,440	14.4		4,443,540	31.0	6,023,124	13.3	24,519,894	9.2
Accounts Receivable	611,379	6.5		86,004	0.6	2,807,772	6.2	13,059,509	4.9
Notes Receivable	0	0.0		0	0.0	407,580	0.9	0	0.0
Inventory	9,406	0.1		143,340	1.0	724,586	1.6	3,464,768	1.3
Other Current	2,577,197	27.4		1,920,756	13.4	2,219,046	4.9	12,526,467	4.7
Total Current	**4,552,422**	**48.4**		**6,593,640**	**46.0**	**12,182,108**	**26.9**	**53,570,638**	**20.1**
Fixed Assets	921,771	9.8		487,356	3.4	19,518,544	43.1	130,062,046	48.8
Other Non-current	3,931,637	41.8		7,253,004	50.6	13,585,994	30.0	82,887,902	31.1
Total Assets	**9,405,830**	**100.0**		**14,334,000**	**100.0**	**45,286,646**	**100.0**	**266,520,586**	**100.0**
Accounts Payable	16,112,187	171.3		69,319,224	483.6	3,170,065	7.0	17,057,318	6.4
Bank Loans	0	0.0		0	0.0	0	0.0	0	0.0
Notes Payable	18,012,164	191.5		24,740,484	172.6	45,287	0.1	266,521	0.1
Other Current	14,701,313	156.3		37,985,100	265.0	13,268,987	29.3	94,081,766	35.3
Total Current	**48,825,664**	**519.1**		**132,044,808**	**921.2**	**16,484,339**	**36.4**	**111,405,605**	**41.8**
Other Long Term	(19,639,374)	(208.8)		31,391,460	219.0	14,582,300	32.2	106,075,193	39.8
Deferred Credits	0	0.0		0	0.0	271,720	0.6	1,865,644	0.7
Net Worth	(19,780,460)	(210.3)		(149,102,268)	(40.2)	13,948,287	30.8	47,174,144	17.7
Total Liab & Net Worth	**9,405,830**	**100.0**		**14,334,000**	**100.0**	**45,286,646**	**100.0**	**266,520,586**	**100.0**
Net Sales	2,688,148	100.0		2,698,927	100.0	24,114,295	100.0	136,817,549	100.0
Gross Profit	1,846,758	68.7		1,425,033	52.8	12,877,034	53.4	76,617,827	56.0
Net Profit After Tax	(626,338)	(23.3)		(191,624)	(7.1)	2,266,744	9.4	13,134,485	9.6
Working Capital	(44,273,242)	---		(125,451,168)	---	(4,302,231)	---	(57,834,967)	---

RATIOS	UQ	MED	LQ	UQ	MED	LQ	UQ	MED	LQ	UQ	MED	LQ
SOLVENCY												
Quick Ratio (times)	3.4	0.7	0.2	3.5	0.6	0.0	1.9	1.1	0.5	1.2	0.8	0.4
Current Ratio (times)	6.8	1.2	0.3	3.7	1.0	0.1	2.4	1.3	0.7	1.6	1.1	0.6
Curr Liab To Nw (%)	10.3	26.8	49.0	4.4	9.8	30.0	13.7	35.1	81.4	26.7	41.6	87.4
Curr Liab To Inv (%)	999.9	999.9	999.9	316.1	908.1	999.9	999.9	999.9	999.9	999.9	999.9	999.9
Total Liab To Nw (%)	21.5	43.5	66.9	120.3	999.9	999.9	25.9	93.6	404.9	35.2	167.5	439.1
Fixed Assets To Nw (%)	2.0	3.7	26.2	1.0	4.9	21.4	26.0	97.2	243.2	70.6	130.6	276.5
EFFICIENCY												
Coll Period (days)	25.0	86.1	105.5	1.9	38.0	90.0	8.1	14.2	24.9	7.7	13.9	19.4
Sales To Inv (times)	209.0	46.4	29.2	82.6	36.6	2.2	216.4	122.6	74.6	216.4	122.6	74.6
Assets To Sales (%)	253.8	349.9	616.5	107.3	531.1	966.6	47.0	187.8	267.8	48.8	194.8	267.8
Sales To Nwc (times)	7.2	5.4	0.6	89.6	2.4	0.5	16.0	9.6	6.1	16.2	9.5	4.8
Acct Pay To Sales (%)	6.9	17.3	71.2	2.9	20.9	45.8	2.3	3.8	6.0	2.1	3.6	5.9
PROFITABILITY												
Return On Sales (%)	(11.9)	(46.5)	(224.5)	(23.9)	(149.7)	(316.7)	18.1	11.2	2.3	18.1	11.8	2.3
Return On Assets (%)	(7.9)	(21.3)	(53.1)	0.7	(0.2)	(249.4)	16.1	4.9	1.4	16.1	4.6	1.4
Return On Nw (%)	(6.7)	(26.2)	(71.8)	38.6	7.3	(1.8)	73.9	19.8	5.3	73.9	19.3	5.3

Page 48

Page 49

SIC 72 PERSONAL SERVICES
(NO BREAKDOWN)
2020 (34 Establishments)

	$	%
Cash	701,178	21.4
Accounts Receivable	327,653	10.0
Notes Receivable	0	0.0
Inventory	262,123	8.0
Other Current	344,036	10.5
Total Current	**1,634,990**	**49.9**
Fixed Assets	783,092	23.9
Other Non-current	858,452	26.2
Total Assets	**3,276,534**	**100.0**
Accounts Payable	262,123	8.0
Bank Loans	0	0.0
Notes Payable	6,553	0.2
Other Current	1,094,362	33.4
Total Current	**1,363,038**	**41.6**
Other Long Term	917,429	28.0
Deferred Credits	16,383	0.5
Net Worth	979,684	29.9
Total Liab & Net Worth	**3,276,534**	**100.0**
Net Sales	3,966,748	100.0
Gross Profit	2,185,678	55.1
Net Profit After Tax	269,739	6.8
Working Capital	271,952	---

RATIOS	UQ	MED	LQ
SOLVENCY			
Quick Ratio (times)	2.0	0.9	0.4
Current Ratio (times)	2.7	1.6	0.7
Curr Liab To Nw (%)	21.0	41.0	107.6
Curr Liab To Inv (%)	187.4	596.4	999.9
Total Liab To Nw (%)	45.4	91.8	371.2
Fixed Assets To Nw (%)	7.8	35.0	94.3
EFFICIENCY			
Coll Period (days)	9.1	21.2	39.1
Sales To Inv (times)	75.5	39.2	15.2
Assets To Sales (%)	28.4	82.6	136.8
Sales To Nwc (times)	9.3	5.5	2.8
Acct Pay To Sales (%)	1.8	4.3	7.6
PROFITABILITY			
Return On Sales (%)	13.2	8.6	2.2
Return On Assets (%)	26.6	9.6	1.9
Return On Nw (%)	77.1	29.6	8.3

SIC 7299 MISC PRSNL SVCS,NEC
(NO BREAKDOWN)
2020 (13 Establishments)

	$	%
Cash	14,511,747	25.9
Accounts Receivable	4,258,273	7.6
Notes Receivable	0	0.0
Inventory	4,146,214	7.4
Other Current	2,409,287	4.3
Total Current	**25,325,521**	**45.2**
Fixed Assets	10,029,354	17.9
Other Non-current	20,675,038	36.9
Total Assets	**56,029,913**	**100.0**
Accounts Payable	4,202,243	7.5
Bank Loans	0	0.0
Notes Payable	0	0.0
Other Current	16,472,795	29.4
Total Current	**20,675,038**	**36.9**
Other Long Term	15,240,136	27.2
Deferred Credits	0	0.0
Net Worth	20,114,739	35.9
Total Liab & Net Worth	**56,029,913**	**100.0**
Net Sales	49,982,081	100.0
Gross Profit	32,738,263	65.5
Net Profit After Tax	699,749	1.4
Working Capital	4,650,483	---

RATIOS	UQ	MED	LQ
SOLVENCY			
Quick Ratio (times)	2.0	1.0	0.7
Current Ratio (times)	3.2	1.5	0.9
Curr Liab To Nw (%)	21.0	32.8	86.4
Curr Liab To Inv (%)	158.1	215.2	999.9
Total Liab To Nw (%)	39.0	54.1	145.4
Fixed Assets To Nw (%)	7.6	13.7	27.6
EFFICIENCY			
Coll Period (days)	10.8	15.3	22.3
Sales To Inv (times)	52.0	15.5	10.4
Assets To Sales (%)	34.5	112.1	186.0
Sales To Nwc (times)	13.0	4.7	3.9
Acct Pay To Sales (%)	2.0	5.1	7.0
PROFITABILITY			
Return On Sales (%)	17.4	7.7	(15.5)
Return On Assets (%)	26.6	8.6	(4.5)
Return On Nw (%)	73.9	26.1	(5.5)

SIC 73 MISC BUSINESS SVS
(NO BREAKDOWN)
2020 (1006 Establishments)

	$	%
Cash	2,085,887	25.5
Accounts Receivable	1,971,368	24.1
Notes Receivable	16,360	0.2
Inventory	188,139	2.3
Other Current	1,145,192	14.0
Total Current	**5,406,946**	**66.1**
Fixed Assets	777,095	9.5
Other Non-current	1,995,908	24.4
Total Assets	**8,179,949**	**100.0**
Accounts Payable	4,646,211	56.8
Bank Loans	8,180	0.1
Notes Payable	1,578,730	19.3
Other Current	8,384,448	102.5
Total Current	**14,617,569**	**178.7**
Other Long Term	2,159,506	26.4
Deferred Credits	49,080	0.6
Net Worth	(8,646,206)	(105.7)
Total Liab & Net Worth	**8,179,949**	**100.0**
Net Sales	13,344,126	100.0
Gross Profit	6,605,342	49.5
Net Profit After Tax	453,700	3.4
Working Capital	(9,210,623)	---

RATIOS	UQ	MED	LQ
SOLVENCY			
Quick Ratio (times)	2.4	1.2	0.6
Current Ratio (times)	3.3	1.6	1.0
Curr Liab To Nw (%)	20.8	57.9	145.7
Curr Liab To Inv (%)	223.4	851.3	999.9
Total Liab To Nw (%)	33.0	97.1	215.3
Fixed Assets To Nw (%)	3.2	10.0	25.3
EFFICIENCY			
Coll Period (days)	31.8	54.0	77.4
Sales To Inv (times)	120.3	39.4	13.3
Assets To Sales (%)	27.5	61.3	161.4
Sales To Nwc (times)	11.9	6.0	2.7
Acct Pay To Sales (%)	1.6	4.0	8.6
PROFITABILITY			
Return On Sales (%)	11.6	3.3	(5.7)
Return On Assets (%)	23.0	5.4	(6.0)
Return On Nw (%)	53.1	16.4	(3.5)

SIC 7311 ADVRTSNG AGENCIES
(NO BREAKDOWN)
2020 (30 Establishments)

	$	%
Cash	1,522,372	32.0
Accounts Receivable	1,198,868	25.2
Notes Receivable	0	0.0
Inventory	104,663	2.2
Other Current	880,120	18.5
Total Current	**3,706,023**	**77.9**
Fixed Assets	333,019	7.0
Other Non-current	718,369	15.1
Total Assets	**4,757,411**	**100.0**
Accounts Payable	2,207,439	46.4
Bank Loans	0	0.0
Notes Payable	9,515	0.2
Other Current	9,914,444	208.4
Total Current	**12,131,398**	**255.0**
Other Long Term	494,771	10.4
Deferred Credits	0	0.0
Net Worth	(7,868,758)	(165.4)
Total Liab & Net Worth	**4,757,411**	**100.0**
Net Sales	11,141,478	100.0
Gross Profit	5,047,090	45.3
Net Profit After Tax	(11,141)	(0.1)
Working Capital	(8,425,375)	---

RATIOS	UQ	MED	LQ
SOLVENCY			
Quick Ratio (times)	1.4	1.1	0.6
Current Ratio (times)	2.5	1.2	0.9
Curr Liab To Nw (%)	41.1	210.6	337.6
Curr Liab To Inv (%)	688.0	999.9	999.9
Total Liab To Nw (%)	49.8	233.8	450.5
Fixed Assets To Nw (%)	4.4	9.0	19.7
EFFICIENCY			
Coll Period (days)	31.8	49.8	107.7
Sales To Inv (times)	23.2	21.5	11.9
Assets To Sales (%)	24.5	42.7	175.4
Sales To Nwc (times)	30.2	5.6	2.6
Acct Pay To Sales (%)	10.3	16.6	70.5
PROFITABILITY			
Return On Sales (%)	10.1	1.2	(14.8)
Return On Assets (%)	10.0	2.7	(12.4)
Return On Nw (%)	88.1	22.2	(8.0)

SIC 7349 BLDNG MAINT SVC,NEC
(NO BREAKDOWN)
2020 (27 Establishments)

	$	%
Cash	391,752	27.2
Accounts Receivable	388,872	27.0
Notes Receivable	5,761	0.4
Inventory	54,730	3.8
Other Current	109,460	7.6
Total Current	**950,575**	**66.0**
Fixed Assets	362,947	25.2
Other Non-current	126,743	8.8
Total Assets	**1,440,265**	**100.0**
Accounts Payable	118,102	8.2
Bank Loans	8,642	0.6
Notes Payable	11,522	0.8
Other Current	394,632	27.4
Total Current	**532,898**	**37.0**
Other Long Term	282,292	19.6
Deferred Credits	0	0.0
Net Worth	625,075	43.4
Total Liab & Net Worth	**1,440,265**	**100.0**
Net Sales	5,394,251	100.0
Gross Profit	2,432,807	45.1
Net Profit After Tax	474,694	8.8
Working Capital	417,677	---

RATIOS	UQ	MED	LQ
SOLVENCY			
Quick Ratio (times)	2.5	1.6	1.0
Current Ratio (times)	4.6	2.4	1.4
Curr Liab To Nw (%)	17.4	40.0	149.8
Curr Liab To Inv (%)	204.9	999.9	999.9
Total Liab To Nw (%)	29.2	78.7	175.8
Fixed Assets To Nw (%)	16.7	39.2	93.1
EFFICIENCY			
Coll Period (days)	20.5	42.6	63.2
Sales To Inv (times)	458.4	89.7	13.3
Assets To Sales (%)	15.8	26.7	48.7
Sales To Nwc (times)	11.8	8.8	5.0
Acct Pay To Sales (%)	1.1	2.7	5.7
PROFITABILITY			
Return On Sales (%)	14.1	6.9	1.7
Return On Assets (%)	44.8	20.3	9.5
Return On Nw (%)	93.3	38.4	14.3

SIC 7353 HVY CONST EQPT RNTL
(NO BREAKDOWN)
2020 (12 Establishments)

	$	%
Cash	1,016,061	15.9
Accounts Receivable	1,597,581	25.0
Notes Receivable	57,513	0.9
Inventory	377,029	5.9
Other Current	370,639	5.8
Total Current	**3,418,823**	**53.5**
Fixed Assets	2,396,371	37.5
Other Non-current	575,129	9.0
Total Assets	**6,390,323**	**100.0**
Accounts Payable	460,103	7.2
Bank Loans	0	0.0
Notes Payable	345,077	5.4
Other Current	645,423	10.1
Total Current	**1,450,603**	**22.7**
Other Long Term	1,603,971	25.1
Deferred Credits	0	0.0
Net Worth	3,335,749	52.2
Total Liab & Net Worth	**6,390,323**	**100.0**
Net Sales	6,320,794	100.0
Gross Profit	2,515,676	39.8
Net Profit After Tax	309,719	4.9
Working Capital	1,968,220	---

RATIOS	UQ	MED	LQ
SOLVENCY			
Quick Ratio (times)	3.6	2.0	1.0
Current Ratio (times)	4.0	2.6	1.5
Curr Liab To Nw (%)	16.3	47.2	77.0
Curr Liab To Inv (%)	142.3	206.9	392.9
Total Liab To Nw (%)	27.4	74.1	187.6
Fixed Assets To Nw (%)	37.9	67.8	127.8
EFFICIENCY			
Coll Period (days)	46.4	59.7	90.0
Sales To Inv (times)	14.8	8.9	8.0
Assets To Sales (%)	46.7	101.1	145.8
Sales To Nwc (times)	6.3	4.4	3.9
Acct Pay To Sales (%)	3.1	5.3	7.5
PROFITABILITY			
Return On Sales (%)	15.0	6.9	(4.7)
Return On Assets (%)	13.4	8.1	(3.6)
Return On Nw (%)	22.6	18.3	(6.3)

SIC 7359 EQPT RNTL,LSING,NEC
(NO BREAKDOWN)
2020 (19 Establishments)

	$	%
Cash	7,375,510	21.4
Accounts Receivable	3,308,640	9.6
Notes Receivable	0	0.0
Inventory	2,378,085	6.9
Other Current	4,066,870	11.8
Total Current	**17,129,105**	**49.7**
Fixed Assets	11,028,800	32.0
Other Non-current	6,307,095	18.3
Total Assets	**34,465,000**	**100.0**
Accounts Payable	2,205,760	6.4
Bank Loans	0	0.0
Notes Payable	2,757,200	8.0
Other Current	5,996,910	17.4
Total Current	**10,959,870**	**31.8**
Other Long Term	9,271,085	26.9
Deferred Credits	275,720	0.8
Net Worth	13,958,325	40.5
Total Liab & Net Worth	**34,465,000**	**100.0**
Net Sales	26,737,781	100.0
Gross Profit	16,310,046	61.0
Net Profit After Tax	855,609	3.2
Working Capital	6,169,235	---

RATIOS	UQ	MED	LQ
SOLVENCY			
Quick Ratio (times)	2.6	0.8	0.3
Current Ratio (times)	3.5	1.7	1.1
Curr Liab To Nw (%)	40.4	68.5	190.8
Curr Liab To Inv (%)	174.9	354.0	999.9
Total Liab To Nw (%)	59.9	305.7	444.6
Fixed Assets To Nw (%)	15.6	38.5	321.5
EFFICIENCY			
Coll Period (days)	10.1	43.3	57.7
Sales To Inv (times)	55.4	19.3	9.3
Assets To Sales (%)	83.5	128.9	190.9
Sales To Nwc (times)	8.4	3.2	2.0
Acct Pay To Sales (%)	2.6	4.6	6.2
PROFITABILITY			
Return On Sales (%)	15.8	6.9	(0.2)
Return On Assets (%)	9.7	2.3	(0.6)
Return On Nw (%)	41.2	11.8	(1.1)

SIC 7361 EMPLOYMENT AGENCIES
(NO BREAKDOWN)
2020 (35 Establishments)

	$	%
Cash	1,564,197	12.2
Accounts Receivable	3,884,851	30.3
Notes Receivable	0	0.0
Inventory	25,643	0.2
Other Current	3,154,036	24.6
Total Current	**8,628,727**	**67.3**
Fixed Assets	551,315	4.3
Other Non-current	3,641,247	28.4
Total Assets	**12,821,289**	**100.0**
Accounts Payable	1,025,703	8.0
Bank Loans	0	0.0
Notes Payable	25,643	0.2
Other Current	4,987,481	38.9
Total Current	**6,038,827**	**47.1**
Other Long Term	4,564,379	35.6
Deferred Credits	0	0.0
Net Worth	2,218,083	17.3
Total Liab & Net Worth	**12,821,289**	**100.0**
Net Sales	43,169,323	100.0
Gross Profit	15,540,956	36.0
Net Profit After Tax	1,251,910	2.9
Working Capital	2,589,900	---

RATIOS	UQ	MED	LQ
SOLVENCY			
Quick Ratio (times)	2.7	1.4	0.9
Current Ratio (times)	3.0	2.0	1.5
Curr Liab To Nw (%)	20.0	46.0	83.4
Curr Liab To Inv (%)	215.8	215.8	215.8
Total Liab To Nw (%)	44.8	72.7	142.1
Fixed Assets To Nw (%)	2.3	8.3	15.6
EFFICIENCY			
Coll Period (days)	35.8	46.4	60.2
Sales To Inv (times)	15.2	15.2	15.2
Assets To Sales (%)	17.8	29.7	66.0
Sales To Nwc (times)	13.7	10.3	6.5
Acct Pay To Sales (%)	0.8	1.5	5.7
PROFITABILITY			
Return On Sales (%)	5.7	3.0	0.6
Return On Assets (%)	20.3	8.8	3.8
Return On Nw (%)	41.8	19.9	11.3

Page 50

	SIC 7363 HELP SUPPLY SVCS (NO BREAKDOWN) 2020 (28 Establishments)			SIC 7371 CSTM CMPTR PRGMG SV (NO BREAKDOWN) 2020 (167 Establishments)			SIC 7372 PREPACKAGED SFTWARE (NO BREAKDOWN) 2020 (171 Establishments)			SIC 7373 CPTR INTGTD SYS DGN (NO BREAKDOWN) 2020 (80 Establishments)	
	$	%		$	%		$	%		$	%
Cash	12,213,544	11.2		1,643,921	32.4		74,066,356	26.8		5,033,376	23.1
Accounts Receivable	48,636,077	44.6		1,293,827	25.5		38,415,013	13.9		6,275,377	28.8
Notes Receivable	109,050	0.1		0	0.0		0	0.0		0	0.0
Inventory	0	0.0		30,443	0.6		3,316,404	1.2		958,738	4.4
Other Current	15,594,078	14.3		750,926	14.8		45,600,555	16.5		1,852,108	8.5
Total Current	**76,552,749**	**70.2**		**3,719,117**	**73.3**		**161,398,328**	**58.4**		**14,119,599**	**64.8**
Fixed Assets	4,034,832	3.7		334,873	6.6		17,687,488	6.4		1,438,107	6.6
Other Non-current	28,461,919	26.1		1,019,840	20.1		97,281,184	35.2		6,231,799	28.6
Total Assets	**109,049,500**	**100.0**		**5,073,830**	**100.0**		**276,367,000**	**100.0**		**21,789,505**	**100.0**
Accounts Payable	10,250,653	9.4		4,678,071	92.2		159,187,392	57.6		2,287,898	10.5
Bank Loans	0	0.0		10,148	0.2		0	0.0		0	0.0
Notes Payable	109,050	0.1		3,029,077	59.7		98,939,386	35.8		87,158	0.4
Other Current	33,696,295	30.9		2,932,673	57.8		494,420,563	178.9		5,796,008	26.6
Total Current	**44,055,998**	**40.4**		**10,649,969**	**209.9**		**752,547,341**	**272.3**		**8,171,064**	**37.5**
Other Long Term	19,956,058	18.3		410,980	8.1		196,496,937	71.1		4,314,322	19.8
Deferred Credits	545,248	0.5		35,517	0.7		5,803,707	2.1		108,948	0.5
Net Worth	44,492,196	40.8		(6,022,636)	(118.7)		(678,480,985)	(245.5)		9,195,171	42.2
Total Liab & Net Worth	**109,049,500**	**100.0**		**5,073,830**	**100.0**		**276,367,000**	**100.0**		**21,789,505**	**100.0**
Net Sales	362,290,698	100.0		9,208,403	100.0		172,406,114	100.0		28,261,355	100.0
Gross Profit	88,398,930	24.4		4,733,119	51.4		108,960,664	63.2		12,604,564	44.6
Net Profit After Tax	14,491,628	4.0		488,045	5.3		(12,930,459)	(7.5)		1,469,590	5.2
Working Capital	32,496,751	---		(6,930,852)	---		(591,149,013)	---		5,948,535	---

RATIOS	UQ	MED	LQ	UQ	MED	LQ	UQ	MED	LQ	UQ	MED	LQ
SOLVENCY												
Quick Ratio (times)	3.2	1.7	1.2	2.6	1.3	0.7	1.7	1.0	0.5	2.6	1.4	0.8
Current Ratio (times)	3.4	1.8	1.3	3.6	1.6	1.0	2.6	1.4	0.8	3.7	1.6	1.2
Curr Liab To Nw (%)	43.6	82.3	187.4	19.6	65.8	159.2	31.7	58.2	119.0	24.0	56.4	152.1
Curr Liab To Inv (%)	---	---	---	176.1	999.9	999.9	802.6	999.9	999.9	253.1	877.7	999.9
Total Liab To Nw (%)	87.0	167.4	252.9	26.6	98.1	226.3	41.7	109.9	193.9	50.7	84.2	197.6
Fixed Assets To Nw (%)	3.4	8.8	11.2	2.2	7.7	21.2	4.8	10.5	20.8	1.6	5.4	12.0
EFFICIENCY												
Coll Period (days)	30.3	56.2	69.4	39.1	60.2	88.3	40.5	62.6	90.4	37.1	60.1	80.5
Sales To Inv (times)	---	---	---	472.7	100.0	16.1	150.9	49.3	13.6	120.1	47.1	12.8
Assets To Sales (%)	21.9	30.1	46.3	26.9	55.1	121.9	95.4	160.3	238.0	32.0	77.1	141.3
Sales To Nwc (times)	15.6	9.8	7.5	12.0	5.5	2.7	5.6	2.7	1.3	13.0	6.2	2.6
Acct Pay To Sales (%)	1.0	2.5	3.9	1.4	3.6	7.7	1.9	3.5	7.9	2.2	4.7	8.1
PROFITABILITY												
Return On Sales (%)	7.2	4.3	2.1	12.9	4.7	(2.0)	6.4	(8.2)	(31.3)	9.6	4.1	0.1
Return On Assets (%)	27.4	8.3	5.0	30.6	7.8	(4.3)	3.8	(6.0)	(24.1)	24.2	6.5	0.0
Return On Nw (%)	58.2	19.6	10.8	68.4	26.9	2.1	9.1	(2.6)	(37.0)	52.4	17.7	5.2

Page 51

	SIC 7374 DATA PROC.PRPRTN (NO BREAKDOWN) 2020 (49 Establishments)					SIC 7375 INFRMTN RTRVL SVCS (NO BREAKDOWN) 2020 (20 Establishments)					SIC 7379 COMP RLTD SVCS.NEC (NO BREAKDOWN) 2020 (133 Establishments)					SIC 7382 SECURITY SYS SVCS (NO BREAKDOWN) 2020 (24 Establishments)	
		$	%				$	%				$	%				$	%
Cash		11,939,040	24.0				33,180,744	24.9				812,116	28.0				556,197	22.8
Accounts Receivable		7,163,424	14.4				19,721,888	14.8				1,102,157	38.0				709,883	29.1
Notes Receivable		0	0.0				0	0.0				5,801	0.2				0	0.0
Inventory		198,984	0.4				266,512	0.2				52,207	1.8				182,959	7.5
Other Current		6,715,710	13.5				19,588,632	14.7				452,464	15.6				282,977	11.6
Total Current		**26,017,158**	**52.3**				**72,757,776**	**54.6**				**2,424,745**	**83.6**				**1,732,016**	**71.0**
Fixed Assets		4,626,378	9.3				11,460,016	8.6				121,817	4.2				275,659	11.3
Other Non-current		19,102,464	38.4				49,038,208	36.8				353,851	12.2				431,784	17.7
Total Assets		**49,746,000**	**100.0**				**133,256,000**	**100.0**				**2,900,413**	**100.0**				**2,439,459**	**100.0**
Accounts Payable		18,704,496	37.6				77,021,968	57.8				2,067,994	71.3				2,105,253	86.3
Bank Loans		0	0.0				0	0.0				11,602	0.4				0	0.0
Notes Payable		14,774,562	29.7				1,199,304	0.9				17,402	0.6				4,879	0.2
Other Current		54,770,346	110.1				343,134,200	257.5				1,157,265	39.9				13,734,154	563.0
Total Current		**88,249,404**	**177.4**				**421,355,472**	**316.2**				**3,254,263**	**112.2**				**15,844,286**	**649.5**
Other Long Term		13,083,198	26.3				25,318,640	19.0				261,037	9.0				270,780	11.1
Deferred Credits		49,746	0.1				1,332,560	1.0				5,801	0.2				4,879	0.2
Net Worth		(51,636,348)	(103.8)				(314,750,672)	(236.2)				(620,688)	(21.4)				(13,680,486)	(560.8)
Total Liab & Net Worth		**49,746,000**	**100.0**				**133,256,000**	**100.0**				**2,900,413**	**100.0**				**2,439,459**	**100.0**
Net Sales		40,943,210	100.0				93,776,214	100.0				9,149,568	100.0				5,257,455	100.0
Gross Profit		20,717,264	50.6				57,766,148	61.6				4,254,549	46.5				2,255,448	42.9
Net Profit After Tax		(614,148)	(1.5)				5,251,468	5.6				869,209	9.5				105,149	2.0
Working Capital		(62,232,246)	---				(348,597,696)	---				(829,518)	---				(14,112,270)	---
RATIOS	UQ	MED	LQ			UQ	MED	LQ			UQ	MED	LQ			UQ	MED	LQ
SOLVENCY																		
Quick Ratio (times)	2.8	1.2	0.4			2.2	1.3	0.5			3.1	1.4	1.0			3.8	1.3	0.4
Current Ratio (times)	3.0	1.4	0.8			4.2	1.7	0.8			3.8	1.9	1.2			4.4	2.0	1.1
Curr Liab To Nw (%)	11.9	40.1	74.7			12.6	39.3	107.0			23.7	72.2	162.3			18.8	47.0	140.0
Curr Liab To Inv (%)	442.0	999.9	999.9			834.0	834.0	834.0			268.3	766.9	999.9			109.5	221.8	622.2
Total Liab To Nw (%)	17.2	94.5	217.8			43.4	66.4	187.1			25.1	89.3	208.3			27.9	64.5	273.0
Fixed Assets To Nw (%)	4.5	13.8	21.3			3.2	12.2	14.7			1.4	5.5	14.2			7.5	16.2	25.2
EFFICIENCY																		
Coll Period (days)	38.2	53.3	73.6			36.1	48.9	73.7			32.0	53.1	76.0			32.0	61.0	80.7
Sales To Inv (times)	78.8	76.6	37.4			93.3	93.3	93.3			81.9	44.1	25.9			41.6	15.3	13.8
Assets To Sales (%)	65.7	121.5	239.6			80.7	142.1	169.5			19.5	31.7	56.0			26.9	46.4	128.6
Sales To Nwc (times)	6.8	4.0	2.1			9.7	3.9	2.1			14.9	8.1	3.7			15.9	4.9	3.6
Acct Pay To Sales (%)	2.5	5.8	13.7			2.1	6.9	17.0			1.5	3.1	6.9			2.2	7.1	11.2
PROFITABILITY																		
Return On Sales (%)	9.1	0.6	(42.6)			17.6	4.1	(23.1)			16.8	5.0	1.4			12.2	3.3	(8.3)
Return On Assets (%)	7.5	(2.0)	(28.9)			12.7	4.0	(46.1)			48.5	17.2	4.2			34.5	8.0	(17.3)
Return On Nw (%)	27.3	2.1	(27.9)			17.8	8.9	(35.2)			85.9	42.3	13.0			55.2	18.4	(13.3)

SIC 7389 BUS SERVICES, NEC
(NO BREAKDOWN)
2020 (150 Establishments)

	$	%
Cash	1,110,736	23.8
Accounts Receivable	802,717	17.2
Notes Receivable	28,002	0.6
Inventory	191,345	4.1
Other Current	700,044	15.0
Total Current	**2,832,844**	**60.7**
Fixed Assets	714,045	15.3
Other Non-current	1,120,070	24.0
Total Assets	**4,666,959**	**100.0**
Accounts Payable	4,181,595	89.6
Bank Loans	0	0.0
Notes Payable	448,028	9.6
Other Current	6,183,721	132.5
Total Current	**10,813,344**	**231.7**
Other Long Term	1,082,734	23.2
Deferred Credits	0	0.0
Net Worth	(7,229,119)	(154.9)
Total Liab & Net Worth	**4,666,959**	**100.0**
Net Sales	9,009,573	100.0
Gross Profit	3,847,088	42.7
Net Profit After Tax	594,632	6.6
Working Capital	(7,980,500)	—

RATIOS
	UQ	MED	LQ
SOLVENCY			
Quick Ratio (times)	2.7	1.1	0.4
Current Ratio (times)	3.4	1.6	1.0
Curr Liab To Nw (%)	18.0	55.4	142.3
Curr Liab To Inv (%)	226.0	679.2	999.9
Total Liab To Nw (%)	29.8	102.5	195.1
Fixed Assets To Nw (%)	4.8	12.7	59.3
EFFICIENCY			
Coll Period (days)	17.9	37.4	62.8
Sales To Inv (times)	89.6	44.4	11.7
Assets To Sales (%)	25.8	51.8	176.4
Sales To Nwc (times)	14.5	7.1	3.2
Acct Pay To Sales (%)	1.3	4.6	10.6
PROFITABILITY			
Return On Sales (%)	12.3	2.9	(1.5)
Return On Assets (%)	21.7	4.8	(1.7)
Return On Nw (%)	43.6	13.7	0.7

SIC 75 AUTO REPAIR,SVS,GAR
(NO BREAKDOWN)
2020 (41 Establishments)

	$	%
Cash	1,358,728	15.1
Accounts Receivable	1,043,791	11.6
Notes Receivable	17,996	0.2
Inventory	791,842	8.8
Other Current	395,922	4.4
Total Current	**3,608,279**	**40.1**
Fixed Assets	4,301,140	47.8
Other Non-current	1,088,782	12.1
Total Assets	**8,998,201**	**100.0**
Accounts Payable	746,851	8.3
Bank Loans	179,964	2.0
Notes Payable	89,982	1.0
Other Current	1,241,751	13.8
Total Current	**2,258,548**	**25.1**
Other Long Term	3,221,356	35.8
Deferred Credits	0	0.0
Net Worth	3,518,297	39.1
Total Liab & Net Worth	**8,998,201**	**100.0**
Net Sales	10,121,711	100.0
Gross Profit	4,534,527	44.8
Net Profit After Tax	1,052,658	10.4
Working Capital	1,349,731	—

RATIOS
	UQ	MED	LQ
SOLVENCY			
Quick Ratio (times)	1.8	0.9	0.5
Current Ratio (times)	2.5	1.3	1.0
Curr Liab To Nw (%)	18.2	44.1	155.0
Curr Liab To Inv (%)	77.9	156.7	990.7
Total Liab To Nw (%)	65.4	107.0	302.2
Fixed Assets To Nw (%)	57.0	111.5	245.0
EFFICIENCY			
Coll Period (days)	9.1	19.4	35.4
Sales To Inv (times)	64.5	23.4	14.9
Assets To Sales (%)	27.7	88.9	221.5
Sales To Nwc (times)	32.8	6.6	4.3
Acct Pay To Sales (%)	1.3	3.4	8.0
PROFITABILITY			
Return On Sales (%)	10.7	4.1	2.5
Return On Assets (%)	18.3	5.8	2.8
Return On Nw (%)	53.9	13.8	6.9

SIC 7538 GNRL ATMTVE RPR SHP
(NO BREAKDOWN)
2020 (11 Establishments)

	$	%
Cash	100,285	23.6
Accounts Receivable	52,692	12.4
Notes Receivable	0	0.0
Inventory	67,565	15.9
Other Current	21,248	5.0
Total Current	**241,790**	**56.9**
Fixed Assets	166,576	39.2
Other Non-current	16,572	3.9
Total Assets	**424,938**	**100.0**
Accounts Payable	21,672	5.1
Bank Loans	0	0.0
Notes Payable	0	0.0
Other Current	91,786	21.6
Total Current	**113,458**	**26.7**
Other Long Term	131,306	30.9
Deferred Credits	0	0.0
Net Worth	180,174	42.4
Total Liab & Net Worth	**424,938**	**100.0**
Net Sales	2,201,751	100.0
Gross Profit	713,367	32.4
Net Profit After Tax	85,868	3.9
Working Capital	128,332	—

RATIOS
	UQ	MED	LQ
SOLVENCY			
Quick Ratio (times)	2.8	1.2	0.5
Current Ratio (times)	3.4	1.6	1.0
Curr Liab To Nw (%)	14.7	76.1	166.6
Curr Liab To Inv (%)	0.6	41.5	123.0
Total Liab To Nw (%)	14.7	107.3	205.7
Fixed Assets To Nw (%)	10.0	60.0	84.8
EFFICIENCY			
Coll Period (days)	5.3	8.4	23.6
Sales To Inv (times)	19.6	12.1	10.0
Assets To Sales (%)	16.2	19.3	38.0
Sales To Nwc (times)	150.4	14.0	5.9
Acct Pay To Sales (%)	1.0	2.1	3.2
PROFITABILITY			
Return On Sales (%)	6.4	2.9	1.7
Return On Assets (%)	24.3	14.2	5.6
Return On Nw (%)	75.5	46.8	8.7

SIC 76 MISC REPAIR SERVICE
(NO BREAKDOWN)
2020 (62 Establishments)

	$	%
Cash	436,864	24.2
Accounts Receivable	498,242	27.6
Notes Receivable	1,805	0.1
Inventory	274,394	15.2
Other Current	137,198	7.6
Total Current	**1,348,503**	**74.7**
Fixed Assets	315,914	17.5
Other Non-current	140,808	7.8
Total Assets	**1,805,225**	**100.0**
Accounts Payable	160,665	8.9
Bank Loans	0	0.0
Notes Payable	25,273	1.4
Other Current	375,487	20.8
Total Current	**561,425**	**31.1**
Other Long Term	223,848	12.4
Deferred Credits	10,831	0.6
Net Worth	1,009,121	55.9
Total Liab & Net Worth	**1,805,225**	**100.0**
Net Sales	4,056,685	100.0
Gross Profit	1,655,127	40.8
Net Profit After Tax	235,288	5.8
Working Capital	787,078	—

RATIOS
	UQ	MED	LQ
SOLVENCY			
Quick Ratio (times)	5.3	1.7	0.9
Current Ratio (times)	6.0	3.1	1.5
Curr Liab To Nw (%)	9.6	32.2	137.2
Curr Liab To Inv (%)	77.9	178.2	677.0
Total Liab To Nw (%)	13.9	54.4	205.0
Fixed Assets To Nw (%)	8.2	20.5	59.3
EFFICIENCY			
Coll Period (days)	19.9	40.7	57.0
Sales To Inv (times)	46.7	13.5	7.1
Assets To Sales (%)	24.2	44.5	61.6
Sales To Nwc (times)	10.7	5.1	3.0
Acct Pay To Sales (%)	1.5	3.8	5.8
PROFITABILITY			
Return On Sales (%)	11.2	4.6	1.1
Return On Assets (%)	28.6	9.8	2.6
Return On Nw (%)	48.9	23.1	4.3

SIC 7629 ELECTL RPR SHPS,NEC
(NO BREAKDOWN)
2020 (14 Establishments)

	$	%
Cash	1,144,103	16.8
Accounts Receivable	1,852,358	27.2
Notes Receivable	0	0.0
Inventory	871,698	12.8
Other Current	912,558	13.4
Total Current	**4,780,717**	**70.2**
Fixed Assets	1,001,090	14.7
Other Non-current	1,028,331	15.1
Total Assets	**6,810,138**	**100.0**
Accounts Payable	905,748	13.3
Bank Loans	0	0.0
Notes Payable	0	0.0
Other Current	490,330	7.2
Total Current	**1,396,078**	**20.5**
Other Long Term	932,989	13.7
Deferred Credits	27,241	0.4
Net Worth	4,453,830	65.4
Total Liab & Net Worth	**6,810,138**	**100.0**
Net Sales	11,989,680	100.0
Gross Profit	4,544,089	37.9
Net Profit After Tax	779,329	6.5
Working Capital	3,384,639	---

RATIOS	UQ	MED	LQ
SOLVENCY			
Quick Ratio (times)	2.8	1.2	1.0
Current Ratio (times)	4.7	1.7	1.4
Curr Liab To Nw (%)	10.0	22.0	140.4
Curr Liab To Inv (%)	104.6	228.3	832.6
Total Liab To Nw (%)	10.3	54.7	152.9
Fixed Assets To Nw (%)	4.6	12.0	27.9
EFFICIENCY			
Coll Period (days)	29.6	38.4	52.8
Sales To Inv (times)	40.9	18.2	7.7
Assets To Sales (%)	23.2	56.8	75.8
Sales To Nwc (times)	13.7	6.2	3.1
Acct Pay To Sales (%)	2.6	5.0	8.8
PROFITABILITY			
Return On Sales (%)	11.2	5.9	0.7
Return On Assets (%)	70.3	12.2	1.1
Return On Nw (%)	58.3	21.0	2.9

SIC 7699 REPAIR SVCS,NEC
(NO BREAKDOWN)
2020 (34 Establishments)

	$	%
Cash	429,644	23.8
Accounts Receivable	505,463	28.0
Notes Receivable	1,805	0.1
Inventory	301,473	16.7
Other Current	128,170	7.1
Total Current	**1,366,555**	**75.7**
Fixed Assets	335,772	18.6
Other Non-current	102,898	5.7
Total Assets	**1,805,225**	**100.0**
Accounts Payable	128,171	7.1
Bank Loans	0	0.0
Notes Payable	46,936	2.6
Other Current	545,178	30.2
Total Current	**720,285**	**39.9**
Other Long Term	211,211	11.7
Deferred Credits	16,247	0.9
Net Worth	857,482	47.5
Total Liab & Net Worth	**1,805,225**	**100.0**
Net Sales	4,029,520	100.0
Gross Profit	1,789,107	44.4
Net Profit After Tax	253,860	6.3
Working Capital	646,270	---

RATIOS	UQ	MED	LQ
SOLVENCY			
Quick Ratio (times)	5.1	1.5	0.7
Current Ratio (times)	5.8	2.5	1.3
Curr Liab To Nw (%)	17.2	67.5	186.5
Curr Liab To Inv (%)	60.8	209.1	676.8
Total Liab To Nw (%)	23.3	98.2	230.7
Fixed Assets To Nw (%)	12.0	21.3	65.8
EFFICIENCY			
Coll Period (days)	15.7	45.9	74.1
Sales To Inv (times)	60.3	12.9	6.7
Assets To Sales (%)	24.2	44.8	58.3
Sales To Nwc (times)	9.8	5.6	3.0
Acct Pay To Sales (%)	1.5	3.6	5.1
PROFITABILITY			
Return On Sales (%)	11.2	4.6	1.6
Return On Assets (%)	25.6	9.8	4.0
Return On Nw (%)	50.4	28.7	10.5

SIC 78 MOTION PICTURES
(NO BREAKDOWN)
2020 (31 Establishments)

	$	%
Cash	374,756	17.8
Accounts Receivable	115,795	5.5
Notes Receivable	0	0.0
Inventory	69,477	3.3
Other Current	174,746	8.3
Total Current	**734,774**	**34.9**
Fixed Assets	745,301	35.4
Other Non-current	625,294	29.7
Total Assets	**2,105,369**	**100.0**
Accounts Payable	1,212,693	57.6
Bank Loans	0	0.0
Notes Payable	0	0.0
Other Current	2,591,709	123.1
Total Current	**3,804,402**	**180.7**
Other Long Term	423,179	20.1
Deferred Credits	16,843	0.8
Net Worth	(2,139,055)	(101.6)
Total Liab & Net Worth	**2,105,369**	**100.0**
Net Sales	1,545,792	100.0
Gross Profit	924,384	59.8
Net Profit After Tax	211,774	13.7
Working Capital	(3,069,628)	---

RATIOS	UQ	MED	LQ
SOLVENCY			
Quick Ratio (times)	3.1	0.8	0.3
Current Ratio (times)	5.5	0.9	0.5
Curr Liab To Nw (%)	7.5	33.6	91.3
Curr Liab To Inv (%)	188.3	999.9	999.9
Total Liab To Nw (%)	29.8	92.5	310.6
Fixed Assets To Nw (%)	24.5	98.4	120.8
EFFICIENCY			
Coll Period (days)	6.6	15.0	54.8
Sales To Inv (times)	151.4	124.2	59.5
Assets To Sales (%)	47.7	136.2	177.5
Sales To Nwc (times)	16.0	5.7	2.5
Acct Pay To Sales (%)	3.1	6.5	11.3
PROFITABILITY			
Return On Sales (%)	20.8	8.0	0.1
Return On Assets (%)	36.3	4.8	0.0
Return On Nw (%)	48.7	14.7	0.1

SIC 7812 MTN PCTRE,VDEO PROD
(NO BREAKDOWN)
2020 (17 Establishments)

	$	%
Cash	190,408	15.8
Accounts Receivable	93,999	7.8
Notes Receivable	0	0.0
Inventory	53,025	4.4
Other Current	139,794	11.6
Total Current	**477,226**	**39.6**
Fixed Assets	394,073	32.7
Other Non-current	333,817	27.7
Total Assets	**1,205,116**	**100.0**
Accounts Payable	1,236,449	102.6
Bank Loans	0	0.0
Notes Payable	0	0.0
Other Current	2,550,025	211.6
Total Current	**3,786,474**	**314.2**
Other Long Term	200,050	16.6
Deferred Credits	10,846	0.9
Net Worth	(2,792,254)	(231.7)
Total Liab & Net Worth	**1,205,116**	**100.0**
Net Sales	1,751,622	100.0
Gross Profit	947,628	54.1
Net Profit After Tax	325,802	18.6
Working Capital	(3,309,248)	---

RATIOS	UQ	MED	LQ
SOLVENCY			
Quick Ratio (times)	1.6	0.6	0.1
Current Ratio (times)	2.5	1.2	0.5
Curr Liab To Nw (%)	24.7	49.1	108.2
Curr Liab To Inv (%)	188.3	999.9	999.9
Total Liab To Nw (%)	33.6	89.2	357.4
Fixed Assets To Nw (%)	41.0	81.0	115.7
EFFICIENCY			
Coll Period (days)	11.1	22.3	54.8
Sales To Inv (times)	394.1	133.9	59.5
Assets To Sales (%)	26.3	68.8	164.6
Sales To Nwc (times)	19.8	6.2	5.7
Acct Pay To Sales (%)	3.1	6.6	28.4
PROFITABILITY			
Return On Sales (%)	22.6	15.8	0.1
Return On Assets (%)	45.5	16.4	0.1
Return On Nw (%)	91.4	24.7	0.1

SIC 79 AMUSE RECREATION SVCS
(NO BREAKDOWN)
2020 (145 Establishments)

	$	%
Cash	1,618,281	19.2
Accounts Receivable	370,856	4.4
Notes Receivable	42,143	0.5
Inventory	42,143	0.5
Other Current	1,095,710	13.0
Total Current	**3,169,133**	**37.6**
Fixed Assets	4,079,416	48.4
Other Non-current	1,179,997	14.0
Total Assets	**8,428,546**	**100.0**
Accounts Payable	8,731,974	103.6
Bank Loans	25,286	0.3
Notes Payable	75,857	0.9
Other Current	4,214,272	50.0
Total Current	**13,047,389**	**154.8**
Other Long Term	2,225,136	26.4
Deferred Credits	134,857	1.6
Net Worth	(6,978,836)	(82.8)
Total Liab & Net Worth	**8,428,546**	**100.0**
Net Sales	3,669,371	100.0
Gross Profit	2,267,671	61.8
Net Profit After Tax	179,799	4.9
Working Capital	(9,878,256)	---

RATIOS	UQ	MED	LQ
SOLVENCY			
Quick Ratio (times)	3.3	1.3	0.3
Current Ratio (times)	6.5	2.3	0.9
Curr Liab To Nw (%)	6.0	14.0	45.3
Curr Liab To Inv (%)	642.0	999.9	999.9
Total Liab To Nw (%)	14.8	53.8	97.7
Fixed Assets To Nw (%)	35.5	95.9	136.9
EFFICIENCY			
Coll Period (days)	5.1	17.4	81.0
Sales To Inv (times)	387.2	108.6	43.5
Assets To Sales (%)	97.9	229.7	505.7
Sales To Nwc (times)	7.0	2.0	0.9
Acct Pay To Sales (%)	1.6	3.6	7.8
PROFITABILITY			
Return On Sales (%)	13.9	1.8	(4.9)
Return On Assets (%)	5.2	0.6	(1.7)
Return On Nw (%)	12.3	2.2	(2.1)

SIC 7922 THTRCL PRDCRS.SVCS
(NO BREAKDOWN)
2020 (22 Establishments)

	$	%
Cash	238,093	26.2
Accounts Receivable	49,981	5.5
Notes Receivable	11,814	1.3
Inventory	0	0.0
Other Current	235,367	25.9
Total Current	**535,255**	**58.9**
Fixed Assets	230,823	25.4
Other Non-current	142,674	15.7
Total Assets	**908,752**	**100.0**
Accounts Payable	94,510	10.4
Bank Loans	0	0.0
Notes Payable	0	0.0
Other Current	188,112	20.7
Total Current	**282,622**	**31.1**
Other Long Term	154,488	17.0
Deferred Credits	31,806	3.5
Net Worth	439,836	48.4
Total Liab & Net Worth	**908,752**	**100.0**
Net Sales	1,283,548	100.0
Gross Profit	988,332	77.0
Net Profit After Tax	101,400	7.9
Working Capital	252,633	---

RATIOS	UQ	MED	LQ
SOLVENCY			
Quick Ratio (times)	2.8	1.3	0.3
Current Ratio (times)	7.8	2.4	1.2
Curr Liab To Nw (%)	8.2	17.0	50.3
Curr Liab To Inv (%)	999.9	999.9	999.9
Total Liab To Nw (%)	13.6	53.3	121.3
Fixed Assets To Nw (%)	6.5	39.4	89.1
EFFICIENCY			
Coll Period (days)	9.9	15.3	19.2
Sales To Inv (times)	---	---	---
Assets To Sales (%)	28.2	70.8	477.1
Sales To Nwc (times)	8.2	2.3	1.3
Acct Pay To Sales (%)	1.4	4.9	6.4
PROFITABILITY			
Return On Sales (%)	14.8	7.9	0.8
Return On Assets (%)	26.9	13.1	1.4
Return On Nw (%)	51.3	25.9	2.8

SIC 7929 ENTRS.ENTRTNMNT GRP
(NO BREAKDOWN)
2020 (13 Establishments)

	$	%
Cash	180,947	11.8
Accounts Receivable	150,278	9.8
Notes Receivable	0	0.0
Inventory	1,533	0.1
Other Current	349,628	22.8
Total Current	**682,386**	**44.5**
Fixed Assets	449,301	29.3
Other Non-current	401,765	26.2
Total Assets	**1,533,452**	**100.0**
Accounts Payable	82,806	5.4
Bank Loans	0	0.0
Notes Payable	16,868	1.1
Other Current	368,029	24.0
Total Current	**467,703**	**30.5**
Other Long Term	277,555	18.1
Deferred Credits	3,067	0.2
Net Worth	785,127	51.2
Total Liab & Net Worth	**1,533,452**	**100.0**
Net Sales	864,891	100.0
Gross Profit	204,114	23.6
Net Profit After Tax	96,868	11.2
Working Capital	214,683	---

RATIOS	UQ	MED	LQ
SOLVENCY			
Quick Ratio (times)	5.2	0.8	0.2
Current Ratio (times)	11.9	2.3	1.1
Curr Liab To Nw (%)	5.5	14.8	40.0
Curr Liab To Inv (%)	481.3	740.6	999.9
Total Liab To Nw (%)	7.6	14.8	69.9
Fixed Assets To Nw (%)	2.2	49.4	102.9
EFFICIENCY			
Coll Period (days)	0.9	5.5	100.9
Sales To Inv (times)	685.7	428.1	170.5
Assets To Sales (%)	79.4	177.3	314.3
Sales To Nwc (times)	20.1	2.2	1.0
Acct Pay To Sales (%)	1.8	2.2	2.8
PROFITABILITY			
Return On Sales (%)	34.8	3.2	(4.5)
Return On Assets (%)	47.1	1.7	(0.9)
Return On Nw (%)	50.7	13.7	0.0

SIC 7997 MBRSHP SPT.RCTN CLB
(NO BREAKDOWN)
2020 (19 Establishments)

	$	%
Cash	1,070,664	17.2
Accounts Receivable	392,162	6.3
Notes Receivable	0	0.0
Inventory	74,698	1.2
Other Current	124,495	2.0
Total Current	**1,662,019**	**26.7**
Fixed Assets	4,158,161	66.8
Other Non-current	404,612	6.5
Total Assets	**6,224,792**	**100.0**
Accounts Payable	367,263	5.9
Bank Loans	136,945	2.2
Notes Payable	0	0.0
Other Current	554,007	8.9
Total Current	**1,058,215**	**17.0**
Other Long Term	1,444,152	23.2
Deferred Credits	49,798	0.8
Net Worth	3,672,627	59.0
Total Liab & Net Worth	**6,224,792**	**100.0**
Net Sales	4,018,587	100.0
Gross Profit	2,837,122	70.6
Net Profit After Tax	88,409	2.2
Working Capital	603,804	---

RATIOS	UQ	MED	LQ
SOLVENCY			
Quick Ratio (times)	2.2	1.6	1.0
Current Ratio (times)	2.6	2.1	1.1
Curr Liab To Nw (%)	7.2	15.8	45.3
Curr Liab To Inv (%)	554.3	925.6	999.9
Total Liab To Nw (%)	17.1	76.3	97.7
Fixed Assets To Nw (%)	86.2	131.1	146.1
EFFICIENCY			
Coll Period (days)	15.5	26.7	62.4
Sales To Inv (times)	69.9	57.1	29.4
Assets To Sales (%)	109.8	154.9	171.3
Sales To Nwc (times)	14.7	7.2	4.5
Acct Pay To Sales (%)	2.4	2.7	4.6
PROFITABILITY			
Return On Sales (%)	5.6	3.5	(1.2)
Return On Assets (%)	3.1	2.3	(0.9)
Return On Nw (%)	4.3	2.7	(2.8)

Page 56

SIC 7999 AMUSEMENT,RCRTN,NEC
(NO BREAKDOWN)
2020 (51 Establishments)

	$	%
Cash	3,867,022	13.9
Accounts Receivable	973,711	3.5
Notes Receivable	0	0.0
Inventory	139,102	0.5
Other Current	3,366,255	12.1
Total Current	**8,346,090**	**30.0**
Fixed Assets	16,664,360	59.9
Other Non-current	2,809,850	10.1
Total Assets	**27,820,300**	**100.0**
Accounts Payable	1,084,992	3.9
Bank Loans	0	0.0
Notes Payable	83,461	0.3
Other Current	2,837,670	10.2
Total Current	**4,006,123**	**14.4**
Other Long Term	6,927,255	24.9
Deferred Credits	0	0.0
Net Worth	16,886,922	60.7
Total Liab & Net Worth	**27,820,300**	**100.0**
Net Sales	6,167,213	100.0
Gross Profit	3,842,174	62.3
Net Profit After Tax	178,849	2.9
Working Capital	4,339,967	---

RATIOS
	UQ	MED	LQ
SOLVENCY			
Quick Ratio (times)	4.9	1.9	0.3
Current Ratio (times)	7.9	4.1	1.8
Curr Liab To Nw (%)	4.6	8.6	35.8
Curr Liab To Inv (%)	762.3	999.9	999.9
Total Liab To Nw (%)	26.8	54.6	88.0
Fixed Assets To Nw (%)	76.5	107.7	145.4
EFFICIENCY			
Coll Period (days)	2.2	20.1	177.0
Sales To Inv (times)	907.6	221.0	112.8
Assets To Sales (%)	240.1	451.1	593.7
Sales To Nwc (times)	3.8	1.3	0.8
Acct Pay To Sales (%)	1.6	3.6	6.4
PROFITABILITY			
Return On Sales (%)	9.7	0.6	(3.9)
Return On Assets (%)	2.4	0.2	(1.3)
Return On Nw (%)	5.6	0.3	(2.4)

SIC 80 HEALTH SERVICES
(NO BREAKDOWN)
2020 (363 Establishments)

	$	%
Cash	8,715,205	14.9
Accounts Receivable	6,141,587	10.5
Notes Receivable	116,983	0.2
Inventory	643,404	1.1
Other Current	6,960,466	11.9
Total Current	**22,577,645**	**38.6**
Fixed Assets	19,711,571	33.7
Other Non-current	16,202,092	27.7
Total Assets	**58,491,308**	**100.0**
Accounts Payable	4,211,374	7.2
Bank Loans	0	0.0
Notes Payable	116,983	0.2
Other Current	6,258,570	10.7
Total Current	**10,586,927**	**18.1**
Other Long Term	19,536,097	33.4
Deferred Credits	233,965	0.4
Net Worth	28,134,319	48.1
Total Liab & Net Worth	**58,491,308**	**100.0**
Net Sales	47,826,090	100.0
Gross Profit	22,956,523	48.0
Net Profit After Tax	669,565	1.4
Working Capital	11,990,718	---

RATIOS
	UQ	MED	LQ
SOLVENCY			
Quick Ratio (times)	2.5	1.3	0.8
Current Ratio (times)	3.9	2.1	1.2
Curr Liab To Nw (%)	10.5	23.5	55.8
Curr Liab To Inv (%)	591.1	999.9	999.9
Total Liab To Nw (%)	25.2	70.7	159.5
Fixed Assets To Nw (%)	25.4	58.2	113.8
EFFICIENCY			
Coll Period (days)	26.7	38.3	50.7
Sales To Inv (times)	98.7	59.6	38.8
Assets To Sales (%)	70.0	122.3	174.0
Sales To Nwc (times)	11.7	5.4	2.7
Acct Pay To Sales (%)	2.1	4.3	7.4
PROFITABILITY			
Return On Sales (%)	8.2	2.6	(4.9)
Return On Assets (%)	7.1	2.1	(3.9)
Return On Nw (%)	15.4	6.1	(4.7)

SIC 8011 OFCS,CLNS OF MDL DR
(NO BREAKDOWN)
2020 (46 Establishments)

	$	%
Cash	3,217,037	24.8
Accounts Receivable	1,634,462	12.6
Notes Receivable	0	0.0
Inventory	103,775	0.8
Other Current	972,895	7.5
Total Current	**5,928,169**	**45.7**
Fixed Assets	4,566,117	35.2
Other Non-current	2,477,638	19.1
Total Assets	**12,971,924**	**100.0**
Accounts Payable	1,400,968	10.8
Bank Loans	0	0.0
Notes Payable	90,803	0.7
Other Current	(1,647,434)	(12.7)
Total Current	**(155,663)**	**(1.2)**
Other Long Term	3,463,504	26.7
Deferred Credits	0	0.0
Net Worth	9,664,083	74.5
Total Liab & Net Worth	**12,971,924**	**100.0**
Net Sales	13,741,445	100.0
Gross Profit	6,252,357	45.5
Net Profit After Tax	(137,414)	(1.0)
Working Capital	6,083,832	---

RATIOS
	UQ	MED	LQ
SOLVENCY			
Quick Ratio (times)	2.6	1.2	0.8
Current Ratio (times)	3.1	1.7	1.1
Curr Liab To Nw (%)	9.3	29.9	83.6
Curr Liab To Inv (%)	619.4	957.2	999.9
Total Liab To Nw (%)	22.3	56.6	157.2
Fixed Assets To Nw (%)	42.9	58.5	112.5
EFFICIENCY			
Coll Period (days)	24.5	36.1	51.5
Sales To Inv (times)	215.1	86.5	48.9
Assets To Sales (%)	25.0	94.4	131.5
Sales To Nwc (times)	19.8	8.6	3.8
Acct Pay To Sales (%)	1.6	4.7	8.4
PROFITABILITY			
Return On Sales (%)	9.2	(3.2)	(10.8)
Return On Assets (%)	16.1	(2.3)	(6.2)
Return On Nw (%)	37.6	8.2	(9.7)

SIC 8051 SKLLD NRSNG CR FCLT
(NO BREAKDOWN)
2020 (44 Establishments)

	$	%
Cash	496,920	1.0
Accounts Receivable	3,975,357	8.0
Notes Receivable	298,152	0.6
Inventory	99,384	0.2
Other Current	2,335,522	4.7
Total Current	**7,205,335**	**14.5**
Fixed Assets	28,324,422	57.0
Other Non-current	14,162,211	28.5
Total Assets	**49,691,968**	**100.0**
Accounts Payable	2,285,831	4.6
Bank Loans	0	0.0
Notes Payable	0	0.0
Other Current	8,845,170	17.8
Total Current	**11,131,001**	**22.4**
Other Long Term	25,541,672	51.4
Deferred Credits	944,147	1.9
Net Worth	12,075,148	24.3
Total Liab & Net Worth	**49,691,968**	**100.0**
Net Sales	23,264,030	100.0
Gross Profit	8,630,955	37.1
Net Profit After Tax	(1,139,937)	(4.9)
Working Capital	(3,925,666)	---

RATIOS
	UQ	MED	LQ
SOLVENCY			
Quick Ratio (times)	2.0	0.9	0.3
Current Ratio (times)	2.6	1.4	0.4
Curr Liab To Nw (%)	17.8	48.2	103.7
Curr Liab To Inv (%)	999.9	999.9	999.9
Total Liab To Nw (%)	83.0	158.9	516.1
Fixed Assets To Nw (%)	54.3	117.0	357.1
EFFICIENCY			
Coll Period (days)	21.2	33.4	50.4
Sales To Inv (times)	384.1	319.6	182.0
Assets To Sales (%)	80.4	213.6	383.5
Sales To Nwc (times)	14.1	5.7	3.3
Acct Pay To Sales (%)	2.1	4.0	7.5
PROFITABILITY			
Return On Sales (%)	5.4	(3.2)	(21.2)
Return On Assets (%)	2.3	2.3	(6.7)
Return On Nw (%)	21.5	4.5	(15.4)

Page 57

	SIC 8062 GNL MDL,SRGL HSPTLS (NO BREAKDOWN) 2020 (138 Establishments)			SIC 8071 MDCL LBRTRS (NO BREAKDOWN) 2020 (19 Establishments)			SIC 8082 HME HLTH CRE SVCS (NO BREAKDOWN) 2020 (23 Establishments)			SIC 8093 SPTY OTPNT CLNS,NEC (NO BREAKDOWN) 2020 (38 Establishments)	
	$		%	$		%	$		%	$	%
Cash	19,780,399		10.2	36,768,897		31.9	2,598,461		11.4	3,901,290	26.2
Accounts Receivable	20,168,250		10.4	12,563,667		10.9	3,487,408		15.3	1,221,015	8.2
Notes Receivable	581,776		0.3	0		0.0	0		0.0	0	0.0
Inventory	2,133,180		1.1	3,342,627		2.9	547,044		2.4	74,452	0.5
Other Current	22,301,432		11.5	22,130,496		19.2	2,780,810		12.2	2,397,358	16.1
Total Current	**64,965,037**		**33.5**	**74,805,687**		**64.9**	**9,413,723**		**41.3**	**7,594,115**	**51.0**
Fixed Assets	70,782,801		36.5	9,566,829		8.3	5,196,922		22.8	4,065,085	27.3
Other Non-current	58,177,645		30.0	30,890,484		26.8	8,182,873		35.9	3,231,221	21.7
Total Assets	**193,925,483**		**100.0**	**115,263,000**		**100.0**	**22,793,518**		**100.0**	**14,890,421**	**100.0**
Accounts Payable	10,859,827		5.6	8,529,462		7.4	2,142,591		9.4	1,161,453	7.8
Bank Loans	0		0.0	0		0.0	0		0.0	0	0.0
Notes Payable	193,925		0.1	922,104		0.8	0		0.0	14,890	0.1
Other Current	23,464,984		12.1	25,588,386		22.2	1,686,720		7.4	1,712,399	11.5
Total Current	**34,518,736**		**17.8**	**35,039,952**		**30.4**	**3,829,311**		**16.8**	**2,888,742**	**19.4**
Other Long Term	72,722,056		37.5	24,666,282		21.4	5,037,368		22.1	2,710,056	18.2
Deferred Credits	0		0.0	461,052		0.4	0		0.0	29,781	0.2
Net Worth	86,684,691		44.7	55,095,714		47.8	13,926,839		61.1	9,261,842	62.2
Total Liab & Net Worth	**193,925,483**		**100.0**	**115,263,000**		**100.0**	**22,793,518**		**100.0**	**14,890,421**	**100.0**
Net Sales	156,139,680		100.0	59,814,738		100.0	33,918,926		100.0	15,891,591	100.0
Gross Profit	89,936,456		57.6	33,974,771		56.8	11,396,759		33.6	8,025,253	50.5
Net Profit After Tax	5,621,028		3.6	(6,459,992)		(10.8)	678,379		2.0	1,271,327	8.0
Working Capital	30,446,301		---	39,765,735		---	5,584,412		---	4,705,373	---

RATIOS	UQ	MED	LQ	UQ	MED	LQ	UQ	MED	LQ	UQ	MED	LQ
SOLVENCY												
Quick Ratio (times)	2.1	1.3	0.8	6.8	1.6	0.7	3.0	1.7	1.0	3.0	1.7	1.1
Current Ratio (times)	3.8	2.1	1.3	10.4	2.9	1.7	5.8	2.3	1.7	4.0	2.3	1.7
Curr Liab To Nw (%)	12.0	21.1	44.1	7.3	27.7	38.5	11.7	21.6	48.1	11.3	19.9	45.3
Curr Liab To Inv (%)	626.3	878.2	999.9	479.1	980.2	999.9	204.5	397.9	701.0	453.2	999.9	999.9
Total Liab To Nw (%)	39.5	80.7	140.9	13.6	42.7	109.1	21.0	57.3	155.6	18.6	41.3	85.1
Fixed Assets To Nw (%)	46.8	71.4	122.4	3.4	5.0	11.1	8.5	22.5	76.0	11.8	50.6	87.7
EFFICIENCY												
Coll Period (days)	34.2	40.2	49.0	18.3	50.0	69.0	31.2	36.7	49.6	15.0	21.9	30.3
Sales To Inv (times)	78.5	59.2	44.0	47.2	20.7	17.7	69.5	40.1	19.9	399.3	97.9	49.1
Assets To Sales (%)	87.8	124.2	165.0	99.2	192.7	272.9	24.2	67.2	143.7	56.8	93.7	137.9
Sales To Nwc (times)	9.7	4.9	2.6	5.1	1.0	0.6	73.6	12.2	5.5	10.2	5.2	2.8
Acct Pay To Sales (%)	2.6	4.5	6.5	3.7	5.5	11.3	2.3	4.1	8.6	1.3	2.7	5.3
PROFITABILITY												
Return On Sales (%)	8.1	3.3	(2.6)	6.9	(10.5)	(38.5)	7.9	4.7	0.0	9.8	3.1	(1.0)
Return On Assets (%)	5.8	2.4	(2.3)	6.3	(5.8)	(21.4)	15.5	3.8	0.0	11.6	2.8	(1.6)
Return On Nw (%)	11.6	6.0	0.3	14.7	(2.9)	(22.9)	62.1	7.6	0.0	19.6	7.0	1.6

	SIC 8099 HLTH.ALLD SVCS.NEC (NO BREAKDOWN) 2020 (17 Establishments)			SIC 81 LEGAL SERVICES (NO BREAKDOWN) 2020 (18 Establishments)			SIC 8111 LEGAL SERVICES (NO BREAKDOWN) 2020 (18 Establishments)			SIC 82 EDUCATIONAL SERVICE (NO BREAKDOWN) 2020 (566 Establishments)	
	$	%		$	%		$	%		$	%
Cash	8,405,687	19.6		339,259	44.8		339,259	44.8		8,990,300	14.0
Accounts Receivable	6,304,266	14.7		83,300	11.0		83,300	11.0		1,541,194	2.4
Notes Receivable	0	0.0		0	0.0		0	0.0		64,216	0.1
Inventory	1,029,268	2.4		2,272	0.3		2,272	0.3		128,433	0.2
Other Current	9,134,752	21.3		121,164	16.0		121,164	16.0		8,797,651	13.7
Total Current	**24,873,973**	**58.0**		**545,995**	**72.1**		**545,995**	**72.1**		**19,521,794**	**30.4**
Fixed Assets	6,990,444	16.3		137,067	18.1		137,067	18.1		33,007,245	51.4
Other Non-current	11,021,743	25.7		74,212	9.8		74,212	9.8		11,687,390	18.2
Total Assets	**42,886,160**	**100.0**		**757,274**	**100.0**		**757,274**	**100.0**		**64,216,429**	**100.0**
Accounts Payable	5,274,998	12.3		67,397	8.9		67,397	8.9		1,669,627	2.6
Bank Loans	0	0.0		757	0.1		757	0.1		0	0.0
Notes Payable	171,545	0.4		0	0.0		0	0.0		128,433	0.2
Other Current	4,417,274	10.3		162,815	21.5		162,815	21.5		6,678,509	10.4
Total Current	**9,863,817**	**23.0**		**230,969**	**30.5**		**230,969**	**30.5**		**8,476,569**	**13.2**
Other Long Term	6,518,697	15.2		80,271	10.6		80,271	10.6		49,446,650	77.0
Deferred Credits	1,458,129	3.4		0	0.0		0	0.0		192,649	0.3
Net Worth	25,045,517	58.4		446,034	58.9		446,034	58.9		6,100,561	9.5
Total Liab & Net Worth	**42,886,160**	**100.0**		**757,274**	**100.0**		**757,274**	**100.0**		**64,216,429**	**100.0**
Net Sales	34,895,167	100.0		1,829,164	100.0		1,829,164	100.0		31,417,040	100.0
Gross Profit	19,785,560	56.7		1,273,098	69.6		1,273,098	69.6		19,667,067	62.6
Net Profit After Tax	2,058,815	5.9		296,325	16.2		296,325	16.2		1,570,852	5.0
Working Capital	15,010,156	---		315,026	---		315,026	---		11,045,225	---

RATIOS	UQ	MED	LQ		UQ	MED	LQ		UQ	MED	LQ		UQ	MED	LQ
SOLVENCY															
Quick Ratio (times)	5.8	2.4	0.9		5.5	3.6	1.0		5.5	3.6	1.0		3.0	1.4	0.5
Current Ratio (times)	15.3	3.5	2.2		6.0	4.8	1.0		6.0	4.8	1.0		5.1	2.9	1.6
Curr Liab To Nw (%)	5.1	12.5	44.7		11.6	22.5	65.9		11.6	22.5	65.9		10.2	26.4	66.0
Curr Liab To Inv (%)	235.3	500.6	773.8		999.9	999.9	999.9		999.9	999.9	999.9		999.9	999.9	999.9
Total Liab To Nw (%)	6.9	46.7	126.5		14.3	32.8	166.9		14.3	32.8	166.9		34.4	182.5	600.3
Fixed Assets To Nw (%)	2.4	22.4	55.5		5.7	26.5	88.0		5.7	26.5	88.0		69.9	157.1	502.2
EFFICIENCY															
Coll Period (days)	29.2	46.8	72.3		16.8	42.3	59.2		16.8	42.3	59.2		1.1	12.3	40.2
Sales To Inv (times)	43.8	35.5	29.3		80.1	75.9	71.6		80.1	75.9	71.6		999.9	938.4	330.8
Assets To Sales (%)	77.9	122.9	145.9		27.4	41.4	63.3		27.4	41.4	63.3		150.4	204.4	305.3
Sales To Nwc (times)	7.9	5.9	4.3		6.0	2.4	1.7		6.0	2.4	1.7		6.3	3.0	1.6
Acct Pay To Sales (%)	3.0	5.2	10.7		1.3	1.5	5.7		1.3	1.5	5.7		1.1	2.8	6.6
PROFITABILITY															
Return On Sales (%)	9.1	5.8	(1.7)		27.6	13.4	1.7		27.6	13.4	1.7		8.7	2.5	(2.0)
Return On Assets (%)	6.9	2.9	(2.4)		66.8	27.2	11.6		66.8	27.2	11.6		4.2	1.2	(0.8)
Return On Nw (%)	8.2	4.0	(10.2)		78.2	52.9	16.3		78.2	52.9	16.3		25.9	4.8	(0.4)

Page 59

	SIC 8211 ELMNTRY,SCNDRY SCLS (NO BREAKDOWN) 2020 (358 Establishments)			SIC 8221 COLLEGES,UNVRSTES (NO BREAKDOWN) 2020 (91 Establishments)			SIC 8222 JUNIOR COLLEGES (NO BREAKDOWN) 2020 (50 Establishments)			SIC 8231 LIBRARIES (NO BREAKDOWN) 2020 (11 Establishments)	
	$	%		$	%		$	%		$	%
Cash	7,261,453	12.7		43,084,825	11.0		13,078,276	11.7		6,838,633	18.0
Accounts Receivable	457,414	0.8		11,750,407	3.0		2,682,723	2.4		683,863	1.8
Notes Receivable	57,177	0.1		783,360	0.2		0	0.0		0	0.0
Inventory	57,177	0.1		391,680	0.1		111,780	0.1		0	0.0
Other Current	7,947,574	13.9		37,992,982	9.7		19,114,405	17.1		9,954,009	26.2
Total Current	**15,780,795**	**27.6**		**94,003,254**	**24.0**		**34,987,184**	**31.3**		**17,476,505**	**46.0**
Fixed Assets	33,562,779	58.7		180,172,904	46.0		46,388,758	41.5		14,323,136	37.7
Other Non-current	7,833,221	13.7		117,504,068	30.0		30,404,197	27.2		6,192,762	16.3
Total Assets	**57,176,795**	**100.0**		**391,680,226**	**100.0**		**111,780,139**	**100.0**		**37,992,403**	**100.0**
Accounts Payable	1,257,889	2.2		10,183,686	2.6		2,123,823	1.9		455,909	1.2
Bank Loans	0	0.0		0	0.0		0	0.0		0	0.0
Notes Payable	114,354	0.2		0	0.0		0	0.0		0	0.0
Other Current	5,031,558	8.8		35,642,900	9.1		6,818,588	6.1		5,052,989	13.3
Total Current	**6,403,801**	**11.2**		**45,826,586**	**11.7**		**8,942,411**	**8.0**		**5,508,898**	**14.5**
Other Long Term	54,203,602	94.8		202,106,997	51.6		63,379,339	56.7		10,637,873	28.0
Deferred Credits	0	0.0		0	0.0		0	0.0		0	0.0
Net Worth	(3,430,608)	(6.0)		143,746,643	36.7		39,458,389	35.3		21,845,632	57.5
Total Liab & Net Worth	**57,176,795**	**100.0**		**391,680,226**	**100.0**		**111,780,139**	**100.0**		**37,992,403**	**100.0**
Net Sales	30,823,070	100.0		116,467,507	100.0		16,127,563	100.0		9,065,236	100.0
Gross Profit	0	0.0		74,073,334	63.6		0	0.0		7,034,623	77.6
Net Profit After Tax	1,017,161	3.3		3,028,155	2.6		2,886,834	17.9		2,012,482	22.2
Working Capital	9,376,994	—		48,176,668	—		26,044,773	—		11,967,607	—

RATIOS	UQ	MED	LQ		UQ	MED	LQ		UQ	MED	LQ		UQ	MED	LQ
SOLVENCY															
Quick Ratio (times)	2.8	1.3	0.4		2.3	1.2	0.6		3.2	1.6	0.7		5.6	3.0	2.5
Current Ratio (times)	5.1	2.9	1.7		3.3	2.3	1.4		6.2	3.5	1.9		24.1	8.8	3.4
Curr Liab To Nw (%)	13.4	31.6	107.6		11.8	21.5	46.0		1.5	18.2	34.4		5.3	6.7	32.9
Curr Liab To Inv (%)	999.9	999.9	999.9		999.9	999.9	999.9		999.9	999.9	999.9		—	—	—
Total Liab To Nw (%)	48.1	365.6	999.9		50.1	114.2	229.7		3.6	126.0	314.7		5.8	93.4	291.9
Fixed Assets To Nw (%)	103.0	309.3	816.7		60.6	109.9	197.5		92.4	141.7	274.6		39.0	67.5	224.1
EFFICIENCY															
Coll Period (days)	0.4	1.1	9.1		12.6	31.0	47.9		26.0	60.2	116.7		1.5	10.2	54.4
Sales To Inv (times)	999.9	999.9	654.1		616.7	237.9	120.4		600.0	84.1	34.0		—	—	—
Assets To Sales (%)	142.7	185.5	240.7		229.8	336.3	488.1		380.3	693.1	999.9		332.9	419.1	568.0
Sales To Nwc (times)	6.6	3.3	1.9		6.9	3.2	1.6		1.9	1.0	0.4		1.5	0.7	0.6
Acct Pay To Sales (%)	0.8	1.6	4.0		3.8	6.6	10.4		4.5	12.5	23.0		3.6	4.7	6.8
PROFITABILITY															
Return On Sales (%)	5.8	1.7	(1.9)		7.7	3.2	(1.7)		48.3	11.7	(6.0)		32.0	3.6	(94.5)
Return On Assets (%)	3.4	0.9	(1.0)		3.3	1.4	(0.3)		5.7	1.5	(1.2)		13.0	0.7	(11.7)
Return On Nw (%)	34.5	4.2	(1.3)		7.9	2.9	0.1		20.2	8.3	1.8		20.3	2.7	(17.7)

SIC 8299 SCLS,EDCTL SVCS,NEC
(NO BREAKDOWN)
2020 (45 Establishments)

	$	%
Cash	1,216,729	27.7
Accounts Receivable	421,682	9.6
Notes Receivable	0	0.0
Inventory	61,495	1.4
Other Current	685,235	15.6
Total Current	**2,385,141**	**54.3**
Fixed Assets	1,049,813	23.9
Other Non-current	957,571	21.8
Total Assets	**4,392,525**	**100.0**
Accounts Payable	342,617	7.8
Bank Loans	0	0.0
Notes Payable	4,393	0.1
Other Current	1,120,093	25.5
Total Current	**1,467,103**	**33.4**
Other Long Term	1,405,609	32.0
Deferred Credits	162,523	3.7
Net Worth	1,357,290	30.9
Total Liab & Net Worth	**4,392,525**	**100.0**
Net Sales	3,971,542	100.0
Gross Profit	2,398,811	60.4
Net Profit After Tax	178,719	4.5
Working Capital	918,038	---

RATIOS	UQ	MED	LQ
SOLVENCY			
Quick Ratio (times)	7.2	1.6	0.7
Current Ratio (times)	8.4	3.0	1.3
Curr Liab To Nw (%)	4.1	16.4	44.7
Curr Liab To Inv (%)	975.4	999.9	999.9
Total Liab To Nw (%)	12.0	44.2	132.8
Fixed Assets To Nw (%)	6.9	18.7	76.7
EFFICIENCY			
Coll Period (days)	6.6	37.5	51.1
Sales To Inv (times)	972.9	612.5	30.6
Assets To Sales (%)	57.5	110.6	150.0
Sales To Nwc (times)	12.2	4.5	1.8
Acct Pay To Sales (%)	2.1	5.0	7.5
PROFITABILITY			
Return On Sales (%)	13.0	6.1	(1.6)
Return On Assets (%)	15.3	4.1	(1.4)
Return On Nw (%)	30.4	9.9	(0.5)

SIC 83 SOC SEV
(NO BREAKDOWN)
2020 (319 Establishments)

	$	%
Cash	931,171	30.8
Accounts Receivable	272,096	9.0
Notes Receivable	15,116	0.5
Inventory	18,140	0.6
Other Current	362,794	12.0
Total Current	**1,599,317**	**52.9**
Fixed Assets	952,334	31.5
Other Non-current	471,633	15.6
Total Assets	**3,023,284**	**100.0**
Accounts Payable	994,660	32.9
Bank Loans	0	0.0
Notes Payable	15,116	0.5
Other Current	166,281	5.5
Total Current	**1,176,057**	**38.9**
Other Long Term	665,123	22.0
Deferred Credits	12,093	0.4
Net Worth	1,170,011	38.7
Total Liab & Net Worth	**3,023,284**	**100.0**
Net Sales	4,118,916	100.0
Gross Profit	1,832,918	44.5
Net Profit After Tax	243,016	5.9
Working Capital	423,260	---

RATIOS	UQ	MED	LQ
SOLVENCY			
Quick Ratio (times)	6.8	2.6	1.2
Current Ratio (times)	8.6	3.8	1.7
Curr Liab To Nw (%)	4.2	13.2	37.9
Curr Liab To Inv (%)	149.2	785.7	999.9
Total Liab To Nw (%)	7.4	25.4	79.0
Fixed Assets To Nw (%)	13.3	48.9	86.5
EFFICIENCY			
Coll Period (days)	10.1	24.7	39.5
Sales To Inv (times)	443.7	152.6	27.9
Assets To Sales (%)	38.9	73.4	171.4
Sales To Nwc (times)	8.7	5.3	2.3
Acct Pay To Sales (%)	1.2	2.5	5.6
PROFITABILITY			
Return On Sales (%)	10.5	2.6	(1.4)
Return On Assets (%)	10.1	2.9	(1.1)
Return On Nw (%)	18.5	5.8	(1.6)

SIC 8322 INDVDL,FMLY SVCS
(NO BREAKDOWN)
2020 (166 Establishments)

	$	%
Cash	730,836	33.7
Accounts Receivable	186,504	8.6
Notes Receivable	4,337	0.2
Inventory	10,843	0.5
Other Current	268,914	12.4
Total Current	**1,201,434**	**55.4**
Fixed Assets	648,427	29.9
Other Non-current	318,792	14.7
Total Assets	**2,168,653**	**100.0**
Accounts Payable	1,190,590	54.9
Bank Loans	0	0.0
Notes Payable	6,506	0.3
Other Current	(457,585)	(21.1)
Total Current	**739,511**	**34.1**
Other Long Term	268,912	12.4
Deferred Credits	2,169	0.1
Net Worth	1,158,061	53.4
Total Liab & Net Worth	**2,168,653**	**100.0**
Net Sales	3,458,777	100.0
Gross Profit	1,905,786	55.1
Net Profit After Tax	311,290	9.0
Working Capital	461,923	---

RATIOS	UQ	MED	LQ
SOLVENCY			
Quick Ratio (times)	7.4	3.4	1.4
Current Ratio (times)	10.2	4.9	2.1
Curr Liab To Nw (%)	3.9	11.7	34.2
Curr Liab To Inv (%)	206.2	929.1	999.9
Total Liab To Nw (%)	6.5	21.6	57.2
Fixed Assets To Nw (%)	9.7	39.3	71.9
EFFICIENCY			
Coll Period (days)	13.9	24.7	39.8
Sales To Inv (times)	916.7	152.6	27.9
Assets To Sales (%)	37.4	62.7	147.7
Sales To Nwc (times)	6.9	4.7	2.2
Acct Pay To Sales (%)	0.8	2.1	5.1
PROFITABILITY			
Return On Sales (%)	13.3	3.1	(1.2)
Return On Assets (%)	11.9	3.1	(2.3)
Return On Nw (%)	15.7	6.8	(1.7)

SIC 8331 JOB TRNNG,RLTD SVCS
(NO BREAKDOWN)
2020 (25 Establishments)

	$	%
Cash	1,075,105	29.6
Accounts Receivable	526,656	14.5
Notes Receivable	0	0.0
Inventory	123,492	3.4
Other Current	359,578	9.9
Total Current	**2,084,831**	**57.4**
Fixed Assets	1,100,529	30.3
Other Non-current	446,750	12.3
Total Assets	**3,632,110**	**100.0**
Accounts Payable	446,750	12.3
Bank Loans	0	0.0
Notes Payable	0	0.0
Other Current	5,455,429	150.2
Total Current	**5,902,179**	**162.5**
Other Long Term	417,692	11.5
Deferred Credits	0	0.0
Net Worth	(2,687,761)	(74.0)
Total Liab & Net Worth	**3,632,110**	**100.0**
Net Sales	5,065,704	100.0
Gross Profit	1,818,588	35.9
Net Profit After Tax	349,534	6.9
Working Capital	(3,817,348)	---

RATIOS	UQ	MED	LQ
SOLVENCY			
Quick Ratio (times)	3.4	1.9	1.1
Current Ratio (times)	5.1	2.9	1.6
Curr Liab To Nw (%)	7.8	19.5	44.9
Curr Liab To Inv (%)	104.2	175.9	588.3
Total Liab To Nw (%)	8.9	35.4	87.2
Fixed Assets To Nw (%)	15.3	51.7	79.8
EFFICIENCY			
Coll Period (days)	14.2	33.2	57.7
Sales To Inv (times)	42.4	6.7	1.9
Assets To Sales (%)	66.8	71.7	85.2
Sales To Nwc (times)	9.6	4.0	3.0
Acct Pay To Sales (%)	2.3	3.1	7.5
PROFITABILITY			
Return On Sales (%)	9.0	1.1	(0.3)
Return On Assets (%)	11.4	1.6	(0.3)
Return On Nw (%)	9.0	0.5	(0.4)

	SIC 8351 CHILD DAY CARE SVCS (NO BREAKDOWN) 2020 (30 Establishments)			SIC 8361 RESIDENTIAL CARE (NO BREAKDOWN) 2020 (45 Establishments)			SIC 8399 SOCIAL SVCS.NEC (NO BREAKDOWN) 2020 (53 Establishments)			SIC 84 MUSEUM,BOT,ZOO GARD (NO BREAKDOWN) 2020 (35 Establishments)	
	$		%	$		%	$		%	$	%
Cash	700,265		32.7	1,865,125		16.1	1,731,375		33.7	502,833	24.5
Accounts Receivable	137,055		6.4	1,088,955		9.4	436,697		8.5	12,314	0.6
Notes Receivable	0		0.0	173,769		1.5	46,239		0.9	0	0.0
Inventory	0		0.0	11,585		0.1	35,963		0.7	38,995	1.9
Other Current	261,261		12.2	1,366,987		11.8	616,513		12.0	71,833	3.5
Total Current	**1,098,581**		**51.3**	**4,506,421**		**38.9**	**2,866,787**		**55.8**	**625,975**	**30.5**
Fixed Assets	715,256		33.4	5,155,160		44.5	1,294,678		25.2	804,532	39.2
Other Non-current	327,647		15.3	1,923,048		16.6	976,147		19.0	621,871	30.3
Total Assets	**2,141,484**		**100.0**	**11,584,629**		**100.0**	**5,137,612**		**100.0**	**2,052,378**	**100.0**
Accounts Payable	299,808		14.0	695,078		6.0	390,459		7.6	55,414	2.7
Bank Loans	0		0.0	0		0.0	0		0.0	0	0.0
Notes Payable	6,424		0.3	220,108		1.9	5,138		0.1	0	0.0
Other Current	359,770		16.8	973,109		8.4	580,549		11.3	67,729	3.3
Total Current	**666,002**		**31.1**	**1,888,295**		**16.3**	**976,146**		**19.0**	**123,143**	**6.0**
Other Long Term	323,364		15.1	3,197,357		27.6	2,918,164		56.8	41,047	2.0
Deferred Credits	0		0.0	243,277		2.1	15,413		0.3	0	0.0
Net Worth	1,152,118		53.8	6,255,700		54.0	1,227,889		23.9	1,888,188	92.0
Total Liab & Net Worth	**2,141,484**		**100.0**	**11,584,629**		**100.0**	**5,137,612**		**100.0**	**2,052,378**	**100.0**
Net Sales	2,913,584		100.0	7,359,993		100.0	8,562,687		100.0	1,099,292	100.0
Gross Profit	850,767		29.2	2,929,277		39.8	4,358,408		50.9	920,107	83.7
Net Profit After Tax	206,864		7.1	161,920		2.2	51,376		0.6	148,404	13.5
Working Capital	432,579		---	2,618,126		---	1,890,641		---	502,832	---
RATIOS	UQ	MED	LQ	UQ	MED	LQ	UQ	MED	LQ	UQ MED	LQ
SOLVENCY											
Quick Ratio (times)	5.4	2.5	0.7	3.5	1.4	0.6	10.5	2.8	1.3	14.6 4.0	2.0
Current Ratio (times)	5.3	2.6	1.1	4.0	1.9	1.3	13.7	4.8	1.9	15.2 4.9	2.8
Curr Liab To Nw (%)	3.9	19.5	48.9	9.3	18.2	67.5	3.1	9.1	27.4	1.0 3.0	7.7
Curr Liab To Inv (%)	999.9	999.9	999.9	999.9	999.9	999.9	69.2	240.1	999.9	132.6 573.3	999.9
Total Liab To Nw (%)	6.4	30.8	121.3	17.4	38.7	249.9	5.9	22.6	78.8	2.0 4.3	8.9
Fixed Assets To Nw (%)	44.3	66.9	115.9	48.7	84.0	183.4	9.9	37.2	80.8	13.5 36.0	87.8
EFFICIENCY											
Coll Period (days)	2.4	19.7	48.9	9.9	25.2	35.0	7.7	20.1	32.9	1.8 5.5	15.7
Sales To Inv (times)	999.9	542.7	85.4	488.1	364.0	130.1	221.3	19.5	4.9	127.6 75.8	21.4
Assets To Sales (%)	29.7	73.5	131.2	59.9	157.4	421.1	35.4	60.0	168.4	131.4 186.7	517.0
Sales To Nwc (times)	10.1	5.4	3.7	9.3	5.8	2.4	9.4	5.5	1.8	2.1 1.4	1.0
Acct Pay To Sales (%)	1.8	4.7	8.1	1.7	3.8	6.3	1.2	1.6	3.0	2.7 3.7	6.7
PROFITABILITY											
Return On Sales (%)	15.5	4.9	(0.3)	9.8	2.7	(4.7)	6.3	1.1	(1.4)	15.5 8.5	4.4
Return On Assets (%)	15.9	6.5	(0.1)	6.1	1.7	(2.0)	12.6	1.3	(1.0)	10.4 4.9	1.7
Return On Nw (%)	21.4	9.1	(3.4)	16.3	2.8	(3.7)	16.7	5.8	(0.1)	11.1 5.0	1.8

	SIC 8412 MUSEUMS, ART GALLRS (NO BREAKDOWN) 2020 (31 Establishments) $	%	SIC 86 MEMBERSHIP ORGANIZATI (NO BREAKDOWN) 2020 (277 Establishments) $	%	SIC 8611 BUSINESS ASSNS (NO BREAKDOWN) 2020 (54 Establishments) $	%	SIC 8621 PRFSSNL ORGNZTNS (NO BREAKDOWN) 2020 (32 Establishments) $	%
Cash	382,347	24.1	978,402	28.7	458,503	44.6	856,208	34.2
Accounts Receivable	9,519	0.6	88,636	2.6	42,149	4.1	110,155	4.4
Notes Receivable	0	0.0	30,682	0.9	5,140	0.5	7,511	0.3
Inventory	33,317	2.1	23,863	0.7	2,056	0.2	5,007	0.2
Other Current	50,768	3.2	327,270	9.6	80,187	7.8	270,381	10.8
Total Current	**475,951**	**30.0**	**1,448,853**	**42.5**	**588,035**	**57.2**	**1,249,262**	**49.9**
Fixed Assets	621,909	39.2	937,493	27.5	179,906	17.5	235,332	9.4
Other Non-current	488,643	30.8	1,022,720	30.0	260,092	25.3	1,018,937	40.7
Total Assets	**1,586,503**	**100.0**	**3,409,066**	**100.0**	**1,028,033**	**100.0**	**2,503,531**	**100.0**
Accounts Payable	38,076	2.4	160,226	4.7	56,542	5.5	127,680	5.1
Bank Loans	0	0.0	0	0.0	0	0.0	0	0.0
Notes Payable	0	0.0	0	0.0	0	0.0	0	0.0
Other Current	50,768	3.2	207,953	6.1	109,999	10.7	232,828	9.3
Total Current	**88,844**	**5.6**	**368,179**	**10.8**	**166,541**	**16.2**	**360,508**	**14.4**
Other Long Term	34,903	2.2	323,861	9.5	127,476	12.4	237,836	9.5
Deferred Credits	0	0.0	3,409	0.1	0	0.0	0	0.0
Net Worth	1,462,756	92.2	2,713,617	79.6	734,016	71.4	1,905,187	76.1
Total Liab & Net Worth	**1,586,503**	**100.0**	**3,409,066**	**100.0**	**1,028,033**	**100.0**	**2,503,531**	**100.0**
Net Sales	1,077,787	100.0	1,814,298	100.0	382,595	100.0	3,561,211	100.0
Gross Profit	902,108	83.7	1,110,350	61.2	215,401	56.3	2,115,359	59.4
Net Profit After Tax	133,646	12.4	235,859	13.0	8,800	2.3	338,315	9.5
Working Capital	387,107	---	1,080,674	---	421,494	---	888,754	---

RATIOS	UQ	MED	LQ	UQ	MED	LQ	UQ	MED	LQ	UQ	MED	LQ
SOLVENCY												
Quick Ratio (times)	15.4	4.3	1.8	13.3	3.2	1.3	18.6	3.0	1.3	11.4	1.8	0.9
Current Ratio (times)	16.3	5.6	2.8	17.7	5.2	2.1	22.0	4.2	1.8	11.5	2.8	1.4
Curr Liab To Nw (%)	0.9	2.3	7.2	1.4	4.8	16.7	3.2	8.8	29.0	3.1	16.8	32.2
Curr Liab To Inv (%)	125.8	251.2	999.9	232.6	548.3	999.9	619.9	999.9	999.9	699.5	999.9	999.9
Total Liab To Nw (%)	1.8	3.9	7.5	2.3	9.7	33.8	4.4	17.5	54.6	4.2	21.9	41.9
Fixed Assets To Nw (%)	23.9	36.0	87.8	4.4	25.4	70.7	2.8	14.1	38.3	2.1	6.0	15.8
EFFICIENCY												
Coll Period (days)	1.1	8.8	23.6	3.9	10.8	25.2	23.7	39.3	50.7	16.8	21.5	38.7
Sales To Inv (times)	131.1	61.9	5.3	203.7	82.1	49.8	56.0	40.7	18.9	8.5	8.5	8.5
Assets To Sales (%)	131.4	147.2	517.0	70.1	187.9	323.8	48.2	268.7	543.6	54.4	70.3	346.1
Sales To Nwc (times)	1.9	1.3	1.0	6.5	3.7	1.4	5.7	2.5	1.1	7.2	4.6	2.6
Acct Pay To Sales (%)	2.6	3.3	6.5	1.2	3.8	6.8	2.0	3.2	10.8	2.1	4.3	8.9
PROFITABILITY												
Return On Sales (%)	12.4	7.9	4.4	15.9	5.8	(1.3)	14.0	3.0	(13.2)	21.9	6.9	0.7
Return On Assets (%)	10.4	3.2	1.7	18.4	2.9	(1.1)	6.3	1.2	(5.3)	35.7	2.9	1.0
Return On Nw (%)	11.1	3.3	1.8	25.7	5.5	(1.3)	10.4	2.4	(6.1)	42.7	3.5	1.1

Page 62

SIC 8641 CIVIC,SOCL ASSNS
(NO BREAKDOWN)
2020 (105 Establishments)

	$	%
Cash	1,036,688	20.8
Accounts Receivable	79,745	1.6
Notes Receivable	74,761	1.5
Inventory	19,936	0.4
Other Current	448,568	9.0
Total Current	**1,659,698**	**33.3**
Fixed Assets	1,923,854	38.6
Other Non-current	1,400,525	28.1
Total Assets	**4,984,077**	**100.0**
Accounts Payable	169,459	3.4
Bank Loans	0	0.0
Notes Payable	0	0.0
Other Current	279,108	5.6
Total Current	**448,567**	**9.0**
Other Long Term	423,647	8.5
Deferred Credits	4,984	0.1
Net Worth	4,106,879	82.4
Total Liab & Net Worth	**4,984,077**	**100.0**
Net Sales	2,914,665	100.0
Gross Profit	947,266	32.5
Net Profit After Tax	545,042	18.7
Working Capital	1,211,131	—

RATIOS	UQ	MED	LQ
SOLVENCY			
Quick Ratio (times)	9.4	3.2	1.3
Current Ratio (times)	12.4	5.2	2.1
Curr Liab To Nw (%)	1.4	4.0	13.6
Curr Liab To Inv (%)	200.8	410.2	999.9
Total Liab To Nw (%)	2.2	10.3	26.7
Fixed Assets To Nw (%)	13.2	47.4	89.1
EFFICIENCY			
Coll Period (days)	0.7	3.9	6.6
Sales To Inv (times)	245.2	161.6	83.5
Assets To Sales (%)	85.3	171.0	269.5
Sales To Nwc (times)	6.4	2.4	0.7
Acct Pay To Sales (%)	0.6	2.0	5.2
PROFITABILITY			
Return On Sales (%)	43.0	6.2	0.0
Return On Assets (%)	18.4	4.3	0.0
Return On Nw (%)	20.0	5.5	0.0

SIC 8661 RELIGIOUS ORGNZTNS
(NO BREAKDOWN)
2020 (17 Establishments)

	$	%
Cash	692,071	17.0
Accounts Receivable	48,852	1.2
Notes Receivable	4,071	0.1
Inventory	24,426	0.6
Other Current	533,303	13.1
Total Current	**1,302,723**	**32.0**
Fixed Assets	2,279,764	56.0
Other Non-current	488,521	12.0
Total Assets	**4,071,008**	**100.0**
Accounts Payable	138,414	3.4
Bank Loans	0	0.0
Notes Payable	0	0.0
Other Current	130,273	3.2
Total Current	**268,687**	**6.6**
Other Long Term	688,000	16.9
Deferred Credits	0	0.0
Net Worth	3,114,321	76.5
Total Liab & Net Worth	**4,071,008**	**100.0**
Net Sales	1,796,561	100.0
Gross Profit	1,489,349	82.9
Net Profit After Tax	79,049	4.4
Working Capital	1,034,036	—

RATIOS	UQ	MED	LQ
SOLVENCY			
Quick Ratio (times)	13.9	5.1	0.8
Current Ratio (times)	17.2	6.8	2.9
Curr Liab To Nw (%)	0.7	1.6	5.6
Curr Liab To Inv (%)	131.9	311.2	571.3
Total Liab To Nw (%)	1.2	3.0	33.3
Fixed Assets To Nw (%)	35.0	68.8	98.5
EFFICIENCY			
Coll Period (days)	1.1	2.8	4.4
Sales To Inv (times)	13.2	13.2	13.2
Assets To Sales (%)	184.2	226.6	284.5
Sales To Nwc (times)	6.1	5.0	3.8
Acct Pay To Sales (%)	0.9	1.2	3.9
PROFITABILITY			
Return On Sales (%)	8.8	2.9	(3.0)
Return On Assets (%)	4.8	1.0	(2.6)
Return On Nw (%)	5.3	1.2	(2.6)

SIC 8699 MBRSHP ORGNZTNS.NEC
(NO BREAKDOWN)
2020 (60 Establishments)

	$	%
Cash	728,474	26.6
Accounts Receivable	46,557	1.7
Notes Receivable	24,648	0.9
Inventory	52,034	1.9
Other Current	320,418	11.7
Total Current	**1,172,131**	**42.8**
Fixed Assets	575,111	21.0
Other Non-current	991,382	36.2
Total Assets	**2,738,624**	**100.0**
Accounts Payable	183,488	6.7
Bank Loans	0	0.0
Notes Payable	0	0.0
Other Current	84,897	3.1
Total Current	**268,385**	**9.8**
Other Long Term	172,534	6.3
Deferred Credits	5,477	0.2
Net Worth	2,292,228	83.7
Total Liab & Net Worth	**2,738,624**	**100.0**
Net Sales	1,549,872	100.0
Gross Profit	1,201,151	77.5
Net Profit After Tax	213,882	13.8
Working Capital	903,746	—

RATIOS	UQ	MED	LQ
SOLVENCY			
Quick Ratio (times)	10.3	4.0	1.5
Current Ratio (times)	20.9	6.4	2.2
Curr Liab To Nw (%)	1.0	3.5	8.9
Curr Liab To Inv (%)	138.7	451.4	999.9
Total Liab To Nw (%)	1.2	6.1	19.2
Fixed Assets To Nw (%)	6.1	21.9	52.2
EFFICIENCY			
Coll Period (days)	7.3	21.0	27.4
Sales To Inv (times)	546.4	134.7	79.2
Assets To Sales (%)	68.5	176.7	395.5
Sales To Nwc (times)	7.2	4.3	1.3
Acct Pay To Sales (%)	1.8	4.9	9.3
PROFITABILITY			
Return On Sales (%)	24.1	6.0	(2.9)
Return On Assets (%)	33.3	8.5	(0.8)
Return On Nw (%)	55.4	15.7	(0.4)

SIC 87 ENGINEERING MGMT SVC
(NO BREAKDOWN)
2020 (703 Establishments)

	$	%
Cash	1,750,450	27.5
Accounts Receivable	1,610,414	25.3
Notes Receivable	25,461	0.4
Inventory	152,767	2.4
Other Current	948,424	14.9
Total Current	**4,487,516**	**70.5**
Fixed Assets	846,581	13.3
Other Non-current	1,031,174	16.2
Total Assets	**6,365,271**	**100.0**
Accounts Payable	1,483,108	23.3
Bank Loans	6,365	0.1
Notes Payable	286,437	4.5
Other Current	4,691,205	73.7
Total Current	**6,467,115**	**101.6**
Other Long Term	1,222,132	19.2
Deferred Credits	70,018	1.1
Net Worth	(1,393,994)	(21.9)
Total Liab & Net Worth	**6,365,271**	**100.0**
Net Sales	14,020,421	100.0
Gross Profit	6,126,924	43.7
Net Profit After Tax	911,327	6.5
Working Capital	(1,979,599)	—

RATIOS	UQ	MED	LQ
SOLVENCY			
Quick Ratio (times)	3.3	1.6	0.8
Current Ratio (times)	5.0	2.2	1.2
Curr Liab To Nw (%)	14.7	43.4	111.3
Curr Liab To Inv (%)	211.8	789.3	999.9
Total Liab To Nw (%)	27.7	64.1	178.1
Fixed Assets To Nw (%)	3.4	11.9	37.2
EFFICIENCY			
Coll Period (days)	32.1	54.4	80.3
Sales To Inv (times)	107.2	31.0	10.1
Assets To Sales (%)	26.6	45.4	99.1
Sales To Nwc (times)	11.4	5.8	2.6
Acct Pay To Sales (%)	1.5	4.5	11.0
PROFITABILITY			
Return On Sales (%)	10.7	4.2	(0.2)
Return On Assets (%)	25.3	6.1	(2.0)
Return On Nw (%)	58.2	16.7	(0.3)

	SIC 8711 ENGINEERING SVCS (NO BREAKDOWN) 2020 (131 Establishments)					SIC 8712 ARCHITECTURAL SVCS (NO BREAKDOWN) 2020 (26 Establishments)					SIC 8721 ACCTNG,AUDTNG,BKPNG (NO BREAKDOWN) 2020 (13 Establishments)					SIC 8731 COMMRCL PHYS RSRCH (NO BREAKDOWN) 2020 (104 Establishments)	
	$				%	$				%	$				%	$	%
Cash	1,303,726				20.7	863,355				13.7	120,546				27.5	18,464,589	37.2
Accounts Receivable	2,361,823				37.5	3,062,705				48.6	51,725				11.8	6,105,227	12.3
Notes Receivable	18,895				0.3	18,906				0.3	0				0.0	99,272	0.2
Inventory	176,349				2.8	44,113				0.7	0				0.0	992,720	2.0
Other Current	951,027				15.1	642,790				10.2	48,657				11.1	11,019,189	22.2
Total Current	**4,811,820**				**76.4**	**4,631,869**				**73.5**	**220,928**				**50.4**	**36,680,997**	**73.9**
Fixed Assets	717,994				11.4	1,027,204				16.3	93,807				21.4	4,417,603	8.9
Other Non-current	768,380				12.2	642,790				10.2	123,615				28.2	8,537,391	17.2
Total Assets	**6,298,194**				**100.0**	**6,301,863**				**100.0**	**438,350**				**100.0**	**49,635,991**	**100.0**
Accounts Payable	1,587,145				25.2	724,714				11.5	29,808				6.8	30,426,862	61.3
Bank Loans	12,596				0.2	0				0.0	0				0.0	248,180	0.5
Notes Payable	44,087				0.7	25,207				0.4	438				0.1	11,664,458	23.5
Other Current	8,685,210				137.9	4,115,117				65.3	145,094				33.1	24,222,364	48.8
Total Current	**10,329,038**				**164.0**	**4,865,038**				**77.2**	**175,340**				**40.0**	**66,561,864**	**134.1**
Other Long Term	925,834				14.7	529,357				8.4	148,162				33.8	12,756,450	25.7
Deferred Credits	18,895				0.3	25,207				0.4	0				0.0	2,928,523	5.9
Net Worth	(4,975,573)				(79.0)	882,261				14.0	114,848				26.2	(32,610,846)	(65.7)
Total Liab & Net Worth	**6,298,194**				**100.0**	**6,301,863**				**100.0**	**438,350**				**100.0**	**49,635,991**	**100.0**
Net Sales	14,379,438				100.0	16,497,024				100.0	1,019,419				100.0	25,480,488	100.0
Gross Profit	6,082,502				42.3	6,648,301				40.3	744,176				73.0	11,873,907	46.6
Net Profit After Tax	1,092,837				7.6	1,022,815				6.2	285,437				28.0	(1,528,829)	(6.0)
Working Capital	(5,517,218)				—	(233,169)				—	45,588				—	(29,880,867)	—
RATIOS	UQ	MED			LQ	UQ	MED			LQ	UQ	MED			LQ	UQ MED	LQ
SOLVENCY																	
Quick Ratio (times)	3.2	1.6			0.9	3.6	1.4			0.8	1.9	1.1			0.3	3.9 1.9	0.9
Current Ratio (times)	4.0	2.2			1.3	3.7	1.7			0.9	2.7	1.4			0.8	7.5 3.4	1.4
Curr Liab To Nw (%)	25.6	58.2			128.0	28.2	62.1			158.4	36.5	47.8			100.5	12.8 24.8	63.9
Curr Liab To Inv (%)	112.6	439.4			999.9	404.4	740.7			999.9	—	—			—	227.4 764.2	999.9
Total Liab To Nw (%)	31.8	96.4			185.3	28.2	91.8			187.2	37.4	47.8			138.5	23.0 49.7	144.4
Fixed Assets To Nw (%)	5.3	15.5			37.4	10.5	14.3			47.1	4.6	10.4			24.6	2.3 7.6	18.0
EFFICIENCY																	
Coll Period (days)	46.4	64.8			89.1	73.8	85.4			107.7	16.1	44.6			69.9	34.5 54.4	78.5
Sales To Inv (times)	95.4	38.5			15.2	578.7	91.3			19.6	—	—			—	33.6 9.9	6.3
Assets To Sales (%)	31.9	43.8			58.7	24.3	38.2			49.5	12.8	43.0			75.5	64.1 194.8	701.9
Sales To Nwc (times)	10.7	5.7			3.7	8.2	5.4			4.0	28.9	14.6			4.1	6.8 1.2	0.3
Acct Pay To Sales (%)	1.0	3.6			8.4	3.5	5.1			11.0	1.3	2.3			5.0	4.0 10.2	30.2
PROFITABILITY																	
Return On Sales (%)	9.2	5.1			2.1	6.3	4.0			2.0	50.5	(32.4)			3.6	3.1 (32.4)	(417.6)
Return On Assets (%)	28.9	10.5			2.9	31.1	8.9			4.0	171.9	44.7			6.0	(0.8))(32.3)	(96.4)
Return On Nw (%)	60.0	23.6			7.6	48.5	18.3			8.8	113.4	(38.2)			0.1	1.3 (38.2)	(99.9)

	SIC 8732 COMMRCL NPHYS RSRCH (NO BREAKDOWN) 2020 (18 Establishments)		SIC 8733 NCMRCL RSCH ORGNZTN (NO BREAKDOWN) 2020 (22 Establishments)		SIC 8734 TESTING LABRTRS (NO BREAKDOWN) 2020 (11 Establishments)		SIC 8741 MANAGEMENT SERVICES (NO BREAKDOWN) 2020 (54 Establishments)	
	$	%	$	%	$	%	$	%
Cash	894,055	18.7	3,270,548	31.1	1,833,950	21.5	5,176,066	20.7
Accounts Receivable	1,434,313	30.0	1,472,272	14.0	1,279,500	15.0	5,001,030	20.0
Notes Receivable	38,248	0.8	42,065	0.4	0	0.0	225,046	0.9
Inventory	9,562	0.2	10,516	0.1	119,420	1.4	875,180	3.5
Other Current	659,784	13.8	1,356,594	12.9	588,570	6.9	4,450,919	17.8
Total Current	**3,035,962**	**63.5**	**6,151,995**	**58.5**	**3,821,440**	**44.8**	**15,728,241**	**62.9**
Fixed Assets	358,578	7.5	767,685	7.3	1,552,460	18.2	4,650,958	18.6
Other Non-current	1,386,503	29.0	3,596,550	34.2	3,156,099	37.0	4,625,953	18.5
Total Assets	**4,781,043**	**100.0**	**10,516,230**	**100.0**	**8,529,999**	**100.0**	**25,005,152**	**100.0**
Accounts Payable	1,166,574	24.4	925,428	8.8	187,660	2.2	4,525,933	18.1
Bank Loans	0	0.0	0	0.0	0	0.0	0	0.0
Notes Payable	119,526	2.5	0	0.0	0	0.0	175,036	0.7
Other Current	4,274,253	89.4	862,331	8.2	1,612,170	18.9	5,676,169	22.7
Total Current	**5,560,353**	**116.3**	**1,787,759**	**17.0**	**1,799,830**	**21.1**	**10,377,138**	**41.5**
Other Long Term	812,777	17.0	1,020,075	9.7	1,339,210	15.7	4,800,989	19.2
Deferred Credits	0	0.0	241,873	2.3	0	0.0	100,021	0.4
Net Worth	(1,592,087)	(33.3)	7,466,523	71.0	5,390,959	63.2	9,727,004	38.9
Total Liab & Net Worth	**4,781,043**	**100.0**	**10,516,230**	**100.0**	**8,529,999**	**100.0**	**25,005,152**	**100.0**
Net Sales	13,621,205	100.0	5,497,245	100.0	10,543,880	100.0	47,994,534	100.0
Gross Profit	7,042,163	51.7	1,038,979	18.9	4,902,904	46.5	13,246,491	27.6
Net Profit After Tax	585,712	4.3	(142,928)	(2.6)	421,755	4.0	143,984	0.3
Working Capital	(2,524,391)	---	4,364,236	---	2,021,610	---	5,351,103	---

RATIOS	UQ	MED	LQ	UQ	MED	LQ	UQ	MED	LQ	UQ	MED	LQ
SOLVENCY
Quick Ratio (times)	1.6	0.9	0.5	6.5	2.3	1.3	4.4	2.2	0.6	1.8	1.0	0.5
Current Ratio (times)	1.8	1.3	0.7	9.8	3.2	1.5	5.1	4.5	0.9	3.3	1.7	1.0
Curr Liab To Nw (%)	56.3	109.8	201.3	6.5	12.9	58.3	13.7	28.9	33.8	33.1	60.0	170.1
Curr Liab To Inv (%)	999.9	999.9	999.9	987.5	999.9	999.9	442.0	443.6	999.9	409.7	999.9	999.9
Total Liab To Nw (%)	99.7	128.8	294.5	7.5	19.1	110.2	26.8	47.8	84.8	50.8	120.3	275.7
Fixed Assets To Nw (%)	1.2	18.2	31.6	0.4	3.2	14.7	3.8	9.9	38.7	6.4	24.6	78.1
EFFICIENCY
Coll Period (days)	21.9	61.0	109.0	47.9	94.2	570.1	54.6	66.8	86.6	13.7	38.4	57.0
Sales To Inv (times)	81.9	81.9	81.9	145.3	105.1	2.1	28.4	17.0	16.3	222.4	48.9	17.0
Assets To Sales (%)	21.2	35.1	75.8	56.9	191.3	615.9	41.3	80.9	179.0	23.8	52.1	90.2
Sales To Nwc (times)	26.4	13.8	6.7	14.7	7.6	0.4	5.4	2.6	1.5	17.1	7.5	3.7
Acct Pay To Sales (%)	0.9	4.4	14.4	5.1	11.1	19.3	1.3	4.3	4.8	2.1	6.5	13.1
PROFITABILITY
Return On Sales (%)	7.5	3.9	0.7	3.2	1.4	(21.2)	4.1	2.0	(3.3)	7.1	1.6	(1.4)
Return On Assets (%)	33.5	5.7	4.2	4.2	2.5	(6.9)	5.6	5.0	(22.3)	16.3	1.5	(2.1)
Return On Nw (%)	78.1	39.4	10.6	9.0	5.0	(7.4)	15.5	7.5	(27.5)	42.1	14.9	(0.4)

SIC 8742 MNGMNT CNSLTNG SVCS
(NO BREAKDOWN)
2020 (150 Establishments)

	$	%
Cash	893,155	29.7
Accounts Receivable	748,807	24.9
Notes Receivable	3,007	0.1
Inventory	102,247	3.4
Other Current	354,857	11.8
Total Current	**2,102,073**	**69.9**
Fixed Assets	405,980	13.5
Other Non-current	499,204	16.6
Total Assets	**3,007,257**	**100.0**
Accounts Payable	568,372	18.9
Bank Loans	0	0.0
Notes Payable	87,210	2.9
Other Current	3,094,467	102.9
Total Current	**3,750,049**	**124.7**
Other Long Term	556,343	18.5
Deferred Credits	12,029	0.4
Net Worth	(1,311,164)	(43.6)
Total Liab & Net Worth	**3,007,257**	**100.0**
Net Sales	7,811,057	100.0
Gross Profit	3,249,400	41.6
Net Profit After Tax	617,074	7.9
Working Capital	(1,647,976)	---

RATIOS	UQ	MED	LQ
SOLVENCY			
Quick Ratio (times)	3.4	1.6	0.8
Current Ratio (times)	4.4	2.1	1.2
Curr Liab To Nw (%)	14.8	39.7	96.5
Curr Liab To Inv (%)	155.5	813.9	999.9
Total Liab To Nw (%)	24.2	59.5	144.8
Fixed Assets To Nw (%)	3.1	11.9	37.1
EFFICIENCY			
Coll Period (days)	24.8	48.2	67.5
Sales To Inv (times)	80.0	26.4	10.5
Assets To Sales (%)	23.7	38.5	75.9
Sales To Nwc (times)	13.1	6.3	3.2
Acct Pay To Sales (%)	1.2	4.4	9.7
PROFITABILITY			
Return On Sales (%)	15.7	4.7	0.4
Return On Assets (%)	29.7	7.8	0.0
Return On Nw (%)	67.0	20.8	4.0

SIC 8744 FCLTS SPPRT SVCS
(NO BREAKDOWN)
2020 (14 Establishments)

	$	%
Cash	791,883	21.5
Accounts Receivable	1,436,439	39.0
Notes Receivable	0	0.0
Inventory	3,683	0.1
Other Current	552,478	15.0
Total Current	**2,784,483**	**75.6**
Fixed Assets	357,268	9.7
Other Non-current	541,427	14.7
Total Assets	**3,683,178**	**100.0**
Accounts Payable	813,982	22.1
Bank Loans	0	0.0
Notes Payable	0	0.0
Other Current	6,007,264	163.1
Total Current	**6,821,246**	**185.2**
Other Long Term	453,031	12.3
Deferred Credits	0	0.0
Net Worth	(3,591,099)	(97.5)
Total Liab & Net Worth	**3,683,178**	**100.0**
Net Sales	9,616,653	100.0
Gross Profit	2,048,347	21.3
Net Profit After Tax	86,550	0.9
Working Capital	(4,036,763)	---

RATIOS	UQ	MED	LQ
SOLVENCY			
Quick Ratio (times)	2.0	1.3	0.4
Current Ratio (times)	2.0	1.7	1.1
Curr Liab To Nw (%)	50.8	92.7	109.1
Curr Liab To Inv (%)	999.9	999.9	999.9
Total Liab To Nw (%)	101.9	143.5	178.9
Fixed Assets To Nw (%)	2.1	7.5	37.0
EFFICIENCY			
Coll Period (days)	42.4	60.4	94.2
Sales To Inv (times)	691.6	529.2	366.7
Assets To Sales (%)	33.4	38.3	56.1
Sales To Nwc (times)	11.9	7.3	6.2
Acct Pay To Sales (%)	2.6	7.9	11.8
PROFITABILITY			
Return On Sales (%)	9.9	2.4	(5.1)
Return On Assets (%)	29.6	5.8	(3.8)
Return On Nw (%)	65.2	21.3	2.6

SIC 8748 BUS CNSLTNG.NEC
(NO BREAKDOWN)
2020 (151 Establishments)

	$	%
Cash	1,282,344	31.2
Accounts Receivable	932,987	22.7
Notes Receivable	28,771	0.7
Inventory	94,532	2.3
Other Current	575,410	14.0
Total Current	**2,914,044**	**70.9**
Fixed Assets	682,273	16.6
Other Non-current	513,759	12.5
Total Assets	**4,110,076**	**100.0**
Accounts Payable	402,787	9.8
Bank Loans	0	0.0
Notes Payable	20,550	0.5
Other Current	1,471,408	35.8
Total Current	**1,894,745**	**46.1**
Other Long Term	953,538	23.2
Deferred Credits	0	0.0
Net Worth	1,261,793	30.7
Total Liab & Net Worth	**4,110,076**	**100.0**
Net Sales	10,511,703	100.0
Gross Profit	5,276,875	50.2
Net Profit After Tax	1,103,729	10.5
Working Capital	1,019,299	---

RATIOS	UQ	MED	LQ
SOLVENCY			
Quick Ratio (times)	3.7	1.6	0.9
Current Ratio (times)	5.3	2.5	1.3
Curr Liab To Nw (%)	11.6	32.9	98.8
Curr Liab To Inv (%)	254.1	824.4	999.9
Total Liab To Nw (%)	20.4	52.6	232.8
Fixed Assets To Nw (%)	3.5	12.4	56.6
EFFICIENCY			
Coll Period (days)	17.4	44.2	73.0
Sales To Inv (times)	235.3	66.1	31.5
Assets To Sales (%)	21.5	39.1	112.6
Sales To Nwc (times)	11.4	6.0	2.3
Acct Pay To Sales (%)	1.2	3.0	6.9
PROFITABILITY			
Return On Sales (%)	16.6	7.3	2.2
Return On Assets (%)	42.9	12.7	2.8
Return On Nw (%)	70.5	27.9	7.0

SIC 89 MISC SERVICES
(NO BREAKDOWN)
2020 (13 Establishments)

	$	%
Cash	357,062	44.4
Accounts Receivable	240,454	29.9
Notes Receivable	0	0.0
Inventory	44,231	5.5
Other Current	(36,189)	(4.5)
Total Current	**605,558**	**75.3**
Fixed Assets	28,951	3.6
Other Non-current	169,685	21.1
Total Assets	**804,194**	**100.0**
Accounts Payable	101,328	12.6
Bank Loans	0	0.0
Notes Payable	0	0.0
Other Current	201,853	25.1
Total Current	**303,181**	**37.7**
Other Long Term	19,301	2.4
Deferred Credits	0	0.0
Net Worth	481,712	59.9
Total Liab & Net Worth	**804,194**	**100.0**
Net Sales	3,378,966	100.0
Gross Profit	1,267,112	37.5
Net Profit After Tax	361,549	10.7
Working Capital	302,377	---

RATIOS	UQ	MED	LQ
SOLVENCY			
Quick Ratio (times)	4.4	1.9	1.7
Current Ratio (times)	4.5	2.5	1.6
Curr Liab To Nw (%)	18.0	35.9	83.1
Curr Liab To Inv (%)	70.5	493.2	935.9
Total Liab To Nw (%)	23.0	35.9	83.2
Fixed Assets To Nw (%)	3.7	8.0	13.4
EFFICIENCY			
Coll Period (days)	17.2	49.3	98.6
Sales To Inv (times)	1.5	1.5	1.5
Assets To Sales (%)	14.8	23.8	44.3
Sales To Nwc (times)	16.2	9.3	5.3
Acct Pay To Sales (%)	4.6	7.3	8.4
PROFITABILITY			
Return On Sales (%)	11.8	10.7	1.8
Return On Assets (%)	61.2	41.5	10.0
Return On Nw (%)	119.0	86.4	49.6

APPENDEX – SIC NUMBERS APPERING IN THIS DIRECTORY

01	**AGRICULTURL CROPS**	**p 1**
07	**AGRICULTURAL SERVICES**	**p 1**
0782	LAWN GARDEN SVCS	p 1
10	**METAL MINING**	**p 1**
1041	GOLD ORES	p 2
13	**OIL,GAS EXTRACTION**	**p 2**
1381	DRILL OIL,GAS WELLS	p 2
1382	OIL GAS EXPLOR SVCS	p 2
1389	OIL GAS FLD SVC,NEC	p 3
14	**NONMETALLIC MINERALS**	**p 3**
15	**GEN'L BLDG CONTRS**	**p 3**
1521	SNGL-FAM HSNG CNSTR	p 3
1522	RSDNTL CNSTR, NEC	p 4
1541	INDL BLDNGS,WRHSES	p 4
1542	NONRESID CONSTR,NEC	p 4
16	**HEAVY CONSTR CONTRS**	**p 4**
1611	HIGHWAY,ST CONSTR	p 5
1622	BRDGE,TNNEL,ELV HGY	p 5
1623	WTER,SWER,UTIL LNES	p 5
1629	HEAVY CONSTR,NEC	p 5
17	**SPECIAL TRADE CONTRS**	**p 6**
1711	PLBNG,HTNG,AIR-COND	p 6
1721	PNTNG,PAPER HANGING	p 6
1731	ELECTRICAL WORK	p 6
1741	MSNRY,OTHER STNWRK	p 7
1742	PLSTRNG,DWALL,INSUL	p 7
1751	CARPENTRY WORK	p 7
1752	FLR LAYING WORK,NEC	p 7
1761	RRNF,SDNG,SHT MTLWK	p 8
1771	CONCRETE WORK	p 8
1791	STRUCT STEEL ERCTN	p 8
1793	GLASS,GLAZING WORK	p 8
1794	EXCAVATION WORK	p 9
1799	SPCL TRD CNTRS,NEC	p 9
20	**FOOD,KINDRED PRODUCT**	**p 9**
2086	BOTL,CND SFT DRNKS	p 9
2099	FOOD PRPRTNS,NEC	p 10
22	**TEXTILE MILL PDTS**	**p 10**
23	**APPAREL,RELATED PDTS**	**p 10**
24	**LUMBER,WOOD PRODUCTS**	**p 10**
25	**FURNITURE,FIXTURES**	**p 11**
26	**PAPER,ALLIED PDTS**	**p 11**
27	**PRINTING,PUBLISHING**	**p 11**
2752	COMMRCL PRTNG,LITH	p 11
28	**CHEMICALS,ALLIED PDT**	**p 12**
2819	IND INORG CHEM,NEC	p 12
2833	MEDCNLS,BOTANICALS	p 12
2834	PHRMCTCL PREPRTNS	p 12
2835	DGNOSTIC SUBSTANCES	p 13
2836	BIOL PRD,EXC DGNSTC	p 13
2842	POLISHES,SANT GOODS	p 13
2844	TOILET PREPARATIONS	p 13
2869	IND ORG CHEM, NEC	p 14
30	**RUBBER & PLASTICS**	**p 14**
3089	PLSTCS PRODUCTS,NEC	p 14
32	**STONE CLAY,GLASS PDT**	**p 14**
33	**PRIMARY METAL INDS**	**p 15**
34	**FABRICATED METAL PDT**	**p 15**
3441	FBRCTED STRCTRL MTL	p 15
3443	FBRCT PLT WK BLR SH	p 15
3444	SHEET METALWORK	p 16
3469	METAL STAMPINGS,NEC	p 16
35	**MACHINERY EX ELECTRL**	**p 16**
3559	SPEC IND MCHNRY,NEC	p 16
3577	CMPTR PRPRL EQP,NEC	p 17
3589	SVC IND MCHNRY,NEC	p 17
3599	IND MACHINERY,NEC	p 17
36	**ELECTRICAL EQUIPMENT**	**p 17**
3621	MOTORS,GENERATORS	p 18
3651	HSHLD AUDIO,VDEO EQ	p 18
3661	TLPHNE,TLGPH APPTUS	p 18
3663	RDIO,TV CMMNCTNS EQ	p 18
3669	CMMNCTNS EQPMNT,NEC	p 19
3674	SMCNDCTRS,RLTD DVCS	p 19
3679	ELEC COMPONENTS,NEC	p 19
3699	ELEC EQPT,SPPLS,NEC	p 19
37	**TRANSPORTATION EQPT**	**p 20**
3711	MTR VHCL,CAR BODIES	p 20
3714	MTR VHCLE PRTS,ACCS	p 20
3728	AIRCRFT PRT,EQP,NEC	p 20
38	**INSTRUMENTS RLTD PDTS**	**p 21**
3812	SEARCH,NVGTN EQPMNT	p 21
3823	PROC CNTL INSTRMNTS	p 21
3825	INSTRMNTS MEAS ELEC	p 21
3829	MEAS,CTLNG DVCS,NEC	p 22
3841	SRGL,MDCL INSTRMNTS	p 22
3842	SRGCL APPL,SUPPLS	p 22
3845	ELECTROMDCL EQPT	p 22
3861	PHTGRPH EQPT,SUPPLS	p 23
39	**MISC MANUFACTURING**	**p 23**
3993	SIGNS,ADVT SPCLTIES	p 23
3999	MFG INDUSTRIES, NEC	p 23
41	**LOCAL PASSENGER TRAN**	**p 24**
4111	LCL SUBURNAN TRANS	p 24
4119	LCL PASS TRANS NEC	p 24
42	**TRUCKING & WAREHSNG**	**p 24**
4212	LCL TRCKG W/O STRGE	p 25
4213	TRCKG, EXCEPT LOCAL	p 25
4214	LCL TRCKG WTH STRGE	p 25
4225	GNRL WRHSG, STRGE	p 25
4581	ARPTS,FLY FLDS,SVCS	p 26
47	**TRANSPORTATION SVS**	**p 26**
4724	TRAVEL AGENCIES	p 26
4731	FRGT TRANS ARNGMNT	p 26
48	**COMMUNICATION**	**p 27**
4812	RDIO TELPHON COMM	p 27
4813	TEL COMM,EXC RDIO	p 27
4833	TEL BRDCSTG STNS	p 27
4899	COMMNCTN SVCS,NEC	p 28
49	**ELEC,GAS,SANITARY SV**	**p 28**
4911	ELECTRIC SERVICES	p 28
4941	WATER SUPPLY	p 28
4952	SEWERAGE SYSTEMS	p 29
4953	REFUSE SYSTEMS	p 29
4959	SANITARY SVCS,NEC	p 29
50	**WHOLESALE TRADE**	**p 29**
5013	MTR VHCL SPLS, PRTS	p 30
5021	FURNITURE	p 30
5023	HOMEFURNISHINGS	p 30
5031	LBR,PLYWD,MILLWRK	p 30
5045	CMPTRS,PERIPH SFTWR	p 31
5046	CMMRCL EQUIP, NEC	p 31
5047	MEDICAL HOSP EQUIP	p 31
5051	METLS SVC CNTRS,OFF	p 31
5063	ELEC APPRATUS,EQUIP	p 32
5065	ELEC PARTS, EQUIP	p 32
5072	HARDWARE	p 32
5074	PLMBG HDRNC,HTG SUP	p 32
5075	WRM AIR HTG,AC	p 33
5082	CONSTR, MINNG MACH	p 33
5083	FARM,GRDN MACH	p 33
5084	INDL MCHNRY,EQPT	p 33
5085	INDUSTRIAL SUPPLIES	p 34
5088	TRNSPRTN EQPT,SUPPL	p 34
5099	DURABLE GOODS, NEC	p 34
51	**WHLE TRD NONDURBL GDS**	**p 34**
5122	DRGS,PRPRTRS,SNDRS	p 35
5137	WMNS,CLDRNS CLTHNG	p 35
5141	GROCERIES,GNRL LNE	p 35
5147	MEATS,MEAT PRDTS	p 35
5148	FRSH FRTS,VGTBLES	p 36
5149	GRCRS,RLTD PRDS,NEC	p 36
5153	GRAIN,FIELD BEANS	p 36
5169	CHEM,ALLD PRDTS, NEC	p 36
5171	PETRO BLK STNS,TMNL	p 37
5172	PETRO PRDTS,NEC	p 37
5191	FARM SUPPLIES	p 37
5199	NNDRBL GDS,NEC	p 37
52	**BLD MTLS HDW GDN SUP**	**p 38**
5211	LMBR,BLDNG MTRLS	p 38
5251	HARDWARE STORES	p 38
53	**GEN MERCHANDISE**	**p 38**
5311	DEPARTMENT STORES	p 39
54	**FOOD STORES**	**p 39**
5411	GROCERY STORES	p 39
55	**AUTO DEALER SVC STATN**	**p 39**
5511	NEW,USED CAR DLRS	p 40
5531	AUTO,HOME SPPL STRS	p 40
5541	GASLNE SVC STATIONS	p 40
56	**APPAREL ACCES STORES**	**p 40**
5611	MNS,BYS CLTHNG STRS	p 41
5621	WOMENS CLTHNG STRS	p 41
5651	FMLY CLTHNG STRS	p 41
5661	SHOE STORES	p 41
57	**FURN,HOME FURNISHGS**	**p 42**
5712	FURNITURE STORES	p 42
5713	FLR CVRNG STRS	p 42
5731	RDO,TV,ELECTRNC STR	p 42
5734	COMPTR,SOFTWRE STRS	p 43
58	**EATING,DRINKG PLACES**	**p 43**
5812	EATING PLACES	p 43
59	**MISC RETAIL STORES**	**p 43**
5912	DRG STRS,PRPRTRY ST	p 44
5941	SPTG GDS,BCYLE SHPS	p 44
5942	BOOK STORES	p 44
5944	JEWELRY STORES	p 44
5961	CTLG,ML-ORDER HSES	p 45
5983	FUEL OIL DEALERS	p 45
5999	MISC RTL STRS,NEC	p 45
61	**CREDIT AGENC EX BANK**	**p 45**
62	**SEC,COM BROKERS,SVS**	**p 46**
65	**REAL ESTATE**	**p 46**
6512	NRSDNTL BLDG OPTRS	p 46
6513	APMNT BLDG OPRTRS	p 46
6531	RL ESTE AGNTS,MGRS	p 47
6552	SBDVDRS,DVLPRS,NEC	p 47
67	**HOLDG,RE INVESTM COS**	**p 47**
6719	HOLDING COS,NEC	p 47
6794	PATENT OWNERS,LESSO	p 48
6799	INVESTORS, NEC	p 48
70	**HOTELS,RE LODGG PLA**	**p 48**
7011	HOTELS AND MOTELS	p 48
72	**PERSONAL SERVICES**	**p 49**
7299	MISC PRSNL SVCS,NEC	p 49
73	**MISC BUSINESS SVS**	**p 49**
7311	ADVRTSNG AGENCIES	p 49
7349	BLDNG MAINT SVC,NEC	p 50
7353	HVY CONST EQPT RNTL	p 50
7359	EQPT RNTL,LSING,NEC	p 50
7361	EMPLOYMENT AGENCIES	p 50
7363	HELP SUPPLY SVCS	p 51
7371	CSTM CMPTR PRGMG SV	p 51
7372	PREPACKAGED SFTWARE	p 51
7373	CPTR INTGTD SYS DGN	p 51
7374	DATA PROC,PRPRTN	p 52
7375	INFRMTN RTRVL SVCS	p 52
7379	COMP RLTD SVCS,NEC	p 52
7382	SECURITY SYS SVCS	p 52
7389	BUS SERVICES, NEC	p 53
75	**AUTO REPAIR,SVS,GAR**	**p 53**
7538	GNRL ATMTVE RPR SHP	p 53
76	**MISC REPAIR SERVICE**	**p 53**
7629	ELECTL RPR SHPS,NEC	p 54
7699	REPAIR SVCS,NEC	p 54
78	**MOTION PICTURES**	**p 54**
7812	MTN PCTRE,VDEO PROD	p 54
79	**AMUSE RECREATION SVCS**	**p 55**
7922	THTRCL PRDCRS,SVCS	p 55
7929	ENTRS,ENTRTNMNT GRP	p 55
7997	MBRSHP SPT,RCTN CLB	p 55
7999	AMUSEMENT,RCRTN,NEC	p 56
80	**HEALTH SERVICES**	**p 56**
8011	OFCS,CLNS OF MDL DR	p 56
8051	SKLLD NRSNG CR FCLT	p 56
8062	GNL MDL,SRGL HSPTLS	p 57
8071	MDCL LBRTRS	p 57
8082	HME HLTH CRE SVCS	p 57
8093	SPTY OTPNT CLNS,NEC	p 57
8099	HLTH,ALLD SVCS,NEC	p 58
81	**LEGAL SERVICES**	**p 58**
8111	LEGAL SERVICES	p 58
82	**EDUCATIONAL SERVICE**	**p 58**
8211	ELMNTRY,SCNDRY SCLS	p 59
8221	COLLEGES,UNVRSTES	p 59
8222	JUNIOR COLLEGES	p 59
8231	LIBRARIES	p 59
8299	SCLS,EDCTL SVCS,NEC	p 60
83	**SOC SEV**	**p 60**
8322	INDVDL,FMLY SVCS	p 60
8331	JOB TRNNG,RLTD SVCS	p 60
8351	CHILD DAY CARE SVCS	p 61
8361	RESIDENTIAL CARE	p 61
8399	SOCIAL SVCS,NEC	p 61
84	**MUSEUM,BOT,ZOO GARD**	**p 61**
8412	MUSEUMS,ART GALLRS	p 61
86	**MEMBERSHIP ORGANIZATI**	**p 62**
8611	BUSINESS ASSNS	p 62
8621	PRFSSNL ORGNZTNS	p 62
8641	CIVIC,SOCL ASSNS	p 63
8661	RELIGIOUS ORGNZTNS	p 63
8699	MBRSHP ORGNZTNS,NEC	p 63
87	**ENGINEERING MGMT SVC**	**p 63**
8711	ENGINEERING SVCS	p 64
8712	ARCHITECTURAL SVCS	p 64
8721	ACCTNG,AUDTNG,BKPNG	p 64
8731	COMMRCL PHYS RSRCH	p 64
8732	COMMRCL NPHYS RSRCH	p 65
8733	NCMRCL RSCH ORGNZTN	p 65
8734	TESTING LABRTRS	p 65
8741	MANAGEMENT SERVICES	p 65
8742	MNGMNT CNSLTNG SVCS	p 66
8744	FCLTS SPPRT SVCS	p 66
8748	BUS CNSLTNG,NEC	p 66
89	**MISC SERVICES**	**p 66**

This Page left intentionally blank

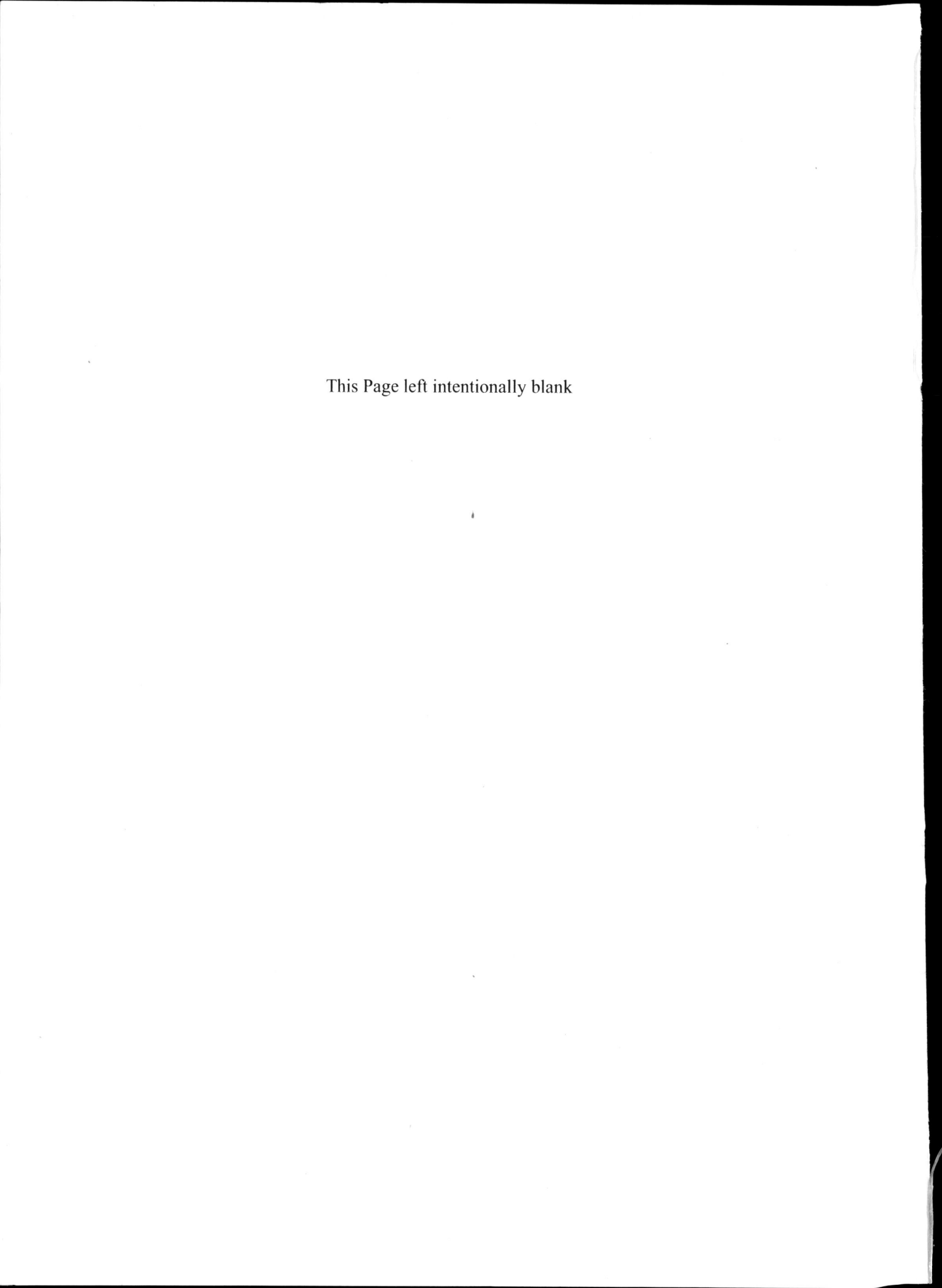